SECOND EDITION

TEACHING READING IN THE MIDDLE GRADES

D0916412

Richard J. Smith
Thomas C. Barrett
University of Wisconsin

SECOND EDITION
TEACHING READING IN THE MIDDLE GRADES

Addison-Wesley
Publishing Company

Reading, Massachusetts
Menlo Park, California
London
Amsterdam
Don Mills, Ontario
Sydney

This book is in the
Addison-Wesley Series in Education

PREFACE

The second edition of *Teaching Reading in the Middle Grades* is largely an expanded version of the first edition; that is, the original philosophy and contents of the book have been retained, and new material has been added. Specifically, the references have been updated; more practical, how-to-teach suggestions have been added; discussions of certain topics in the original chapters have been expanded; and two new chapters have been added: "The Reading Class for the Upper Middle Grades" and "Teaching Reading-Study Skills in the Middle Grades."

The content for the first edition of the book was determined by a survey of middle grades teachers and administrators from six states in different parts of the country. The 369 teachers and the 43 principals of grades four through eight who responded to the survey indicated the topics they would like information about in regard to teaching reading in the middle grades. The chapters for the first edition of *Teaching Reading in the Middle Grades* were decided upon and written to respond to the stated needs and preferences of those surveyed.

Before the second edition of *Teaching Reading in the Middle Grades* was planned and written the authors and the publishers, formally and informally, surveyed users of the book to discover desired changes. Essentially, users of the book said that the original content was well chosen and still relevant to middle grades reading instruction. They did, however, specify needed additions and revisions for the book. Their specifications were relied upon heavily when the second edition was planned and written. The authors are grateful to the teachers, administrators, professors of reading methods classes, and their students who assisted in determining the content, writing style, and format for the second edition of *Teaching Reading in the Middle Grades.*

Madison, Wisconsin   R. J. S.
October 1978   T. C. B.

CONTENTS

3

WORD IDENTIFICATION AND READING VOCABULARY 35

4

A TAXONOMY OF READING COMPREHENSION AND RELATED TEACHING STRATEGIES 61

5

6

7

8

9

10

**THE POOR READER
IN THE MIDDLE GRADES 179**

11

**EVALUATING READING GROWTH
IN THE MIDDLE GRADES 199**

1

ORGANIZING THE MIDDLE GRADES FOR READING INSTRUCTION: AN OVERVIEW

Individualizing Instruction

Children vary greatly in their reading aptitudes, preferences, and growth. The highly individual nature of reading development is probably the most consistent finding of reading specialists who diagnose and teach students with reading problems. And informal observation of reading instruction in the classroom provides conclusive evidence that no two children are quite alike in what they bring to and what they take away from the same reading selection. Consequently, considerable emphasis in reading curriculum development has been given to "individualizing" reading instruction at all academic levels.

The need for individualization of reading instruction is apparent in the primary as well as later grades. However, the range of reading achievement within a group of students increases as the students receive instruction. When formal reading instruction is initiated, the environmental, personal, and instructional forces that influence reading development are not as evident in a child's performance as they later become. In effect, students who have much going for them move farther and farther away from those students with fewer advantages. In a typical sixth-grade population, for example, it would not be unusual to find the general level of reading achievement ranging from what we would expect of third graders to what we would expect of eighth or ninth graders. Jones (1977), provides the following table and explanation to emphasize the need for individualized instruction:

If you have pupils at this grade level	You can expect a chronological age span of	And you can expect a mental age span of
K	4-5-6	3-4-5-6-7
1	5-6-7	3-4-5-6-7-8
2	6-7-8	4-5-6-7-8-9-10
3	7-8-9	5-6-7-8-9-10-11
4	8-9-10	6-7-8-9-10-11-12-13
5	9-10-11	6-7-8-9-10-11-12-13-14
6	10-11-12	7-8-9-10-11-12-13-14-15

[The table] indicates not only the levels of ability to expect but also the spread within a group at any given grade level. One significant item to note is that the higher the grade level the wider the spread. This says something for the importance of varying goals and individualizing the instructional program to incorporate goals that are both possible and challenging for the pupils. This suggests that each year you may expect a chronological age span of about two years, sometimes expanding to three or more years depending on the school's policies about retention and/or double promotions.

At the same time you will have children in all these age groups who vary in ability. . . . With these variations you will find mental ages spreading over a wider span than chronological ages and over an increasingly wider span as the years progress. . . . By sixth grade it is not at all uncommon to find some children with mental ages as low as seven and others as high as fifteen, representing an eight-year span. [1]

In addition to differences in general level of achievement, the differences in the degree of mastery of specific skills which contribute to the overall reading process, the differences in interests, the differences in motivation to learn to read, and differences in other factors which influence reading growth cause the need for individualized instruction to be a pressing concern for teachers in the middle grades.

Although the middle grades provide pressing concerns for individualizing reading instruction, in some ways they also provide more opportunities for "teaching to differences" than lower and higher academic levels provide. One advantage that middle grade teachers have is that by fourth grade many students have well-developed basic skills and can be turned loose "to learn to read by reading" with a minimum of direct instruction. Another advantage is the prevailing philosophy that the middle grades should be essentially exploratory for students in regard to developing knowledge and interests in specific content areas. Most school districts acknowledge that developing and fostering interests and

1. Daisy M. Jones, *Curriculum Targets in the Elementary School*, © 1977, pp. 317, 318. Reprinted by permission of Prentice-Hall, Inc., Englewood Cliffs, New Jersey.

study skills are more important objectives for the middle grades curriculum than accumulating stores of knowledge in science, social studies, literature, and other academic disciplines. This philosophy is supportive of the teacher who emphasizes the development of reading skills rather than content mastery. A final advantage resides in the personal characteristics of most middle graders. Different though they may be as individuals, most teachers who have taught at higher and/or lower grade levels as well as in the middle grades agree that collectively students in grades four through eight present special challenges and offer unique opportunities for developing their growth in and through reading. The curiosity, enthusiasm, mood changes, interests, self-concepts, and other personal characteristics that they share as a group can be capitalized upon for the benefit of their reading programs. The challenge is to use the attributes of middle graders as a group to meet their reading needs as individuals within that group. Hass, Wiles, and Bondi (1970) have stated the situation well:

The similarities among students are important in planning the curriculum because they are, to a large extent, instructed in groups. Understanding the likenesses among them aids in the formation of those aspects of the curriculum that may be considered suitable for many students at a particular age or grade level. For planning the curriculum and for teaching, an understanding of each learner's uniqueness is also a necessary guide line, since learning success often is determined largely by differences.[2]

Some approaches to individualizing reading instruction have seemed to ignore the benefits to be derived from group interactions relative to reading experiences. In practice these approaches appear designed to move students farther apart from each other physically as well as intellectually. Materials rather than personal interactions are often found in the center of these approaches, and the teachers are found on the periphery of the instructional setting scoring exercises, hearing reports, and charting progress through programmed books, "uni-pacs," or self-correcting vocabulary and comprehension tests. Unfortunately, what begins as a sincere effort to meet individual reading needs for a group of students sometimes becomes a mechanical, impersonal operation that ignores or at least de-emphasizes the nature of reading as a communication process. Approaches which function in this fashion are depriving students of the many opportunities to develop positive attitudes toward reading and use reading skills for communication purposes that occur as a part of group work with other students.

Some teachers have reportedly been able to individualize instruction so that in effect each student is working within a program designed just for him or her and is learning to read for communication purposes through personal interactions relative to a variety of reading experiences. Generally, however, many if

---

2. Glen Hass, Kimball Wiles, and Joseph Bondi, *Readings in Curriculum,* 2d ed., Boston: Allyn and Bacon, 1970, p. 136. Reprinted by permission.

not most teachers have been overwhelmed by the planning, one-to-one conferencing, and record keeping involved in completely individualized approaches. Therefore, most school districts have resorted to some kind of organizational arrangement to facilitate as much individualization as possible for students who are grouped for reading instruction. Hence, our discussion in the present chapter will not advocate or describe a completely individualized approach to reading instruction for middle grades students. Instead, we will discuss what we believe are the strengths and weaknesses of five major organizational plans for teaching reading to groups of students in terms of how well each provides for some degree of individualization as well as worthwhile group activities. We feel that a good reading program in the middle grades must provide for both dimensions if students are to become mature readers. Moffett (1968) points out that language is a symbol system and, "Symbol systems are not primarily about themselves; they are about other subjects. When a student 'learns' one of these systems, he learns how to operate it. The main point is to think and talk about other things by means of this system." (p. 6) While certain aspects of reading may be learned best by individual activity, the "system" does not become fully operational until we test and retest with others the ideas and feelings gained from reading. The five organizational plans we discuss are (1) departmentalization, (2) team teaching, (3) the Joplin Plan, (4) nongraded and unitized schools, and (5) self-contained classrooms.

Departmentalization

In a departmentalized curriculum teachers teach their subject matter specialty to groups of students who are with them for varying time periods on varying days of the week. In departmentalized schools there are, for example, science teachers, math teachers, social studies teachers, language arts teachers, reading teachers, and teachers for other curriculum areas. Often the reading classes are "tracked" so that students of similar reading achievement are grouped together for instruction. The basic assumption made by schools favoring a departmentalized organization is that no teacher can be proficient in all areas of the curriculum, and teachers do a better job when they are teaching their specialties.

Children's reading instruction in departmentalized schools may profit in two ways:

1   By having a special reading class they are safeguarded against having their time for reading instruction skipped or shortened because their teacher prefers or feels it is more important to teach science or some other subject. We discuss reading classes for the upper middle grades in Chapter 2.

2   Their teacher may indeed be or may try to become better informed about teaching reading than a teacher who is responsible for teaching all subjects.

These are very real concerns in the middle grades where formal reading instruction is sometimes considered unnecessary and where teachers have indicated more self-perceived deficiencies to teach reading than their primary grades counterparts.

The negative aspects of departmentalization in regard to reading instruction are:

1 Reading may come to be thought of and taught as another content area when in fact reading should be thought of and taught as a process, not a subject in itself.

2 Teachers in the content areas may become so engrossed with transmitting their subject that they neglect to teach the reading study skills necessary for students to read the material they assign or they may feel that it is unnecessary for them to incorporate the teaching of reading into their subject matter teaching at all because someone else is the reading teacher.

These negative aspects are extremely detrimental to the reading growth of middle grades students and could outweigh the positive aspects of departmentalization mentioned in the preceding paragraph. Therefore, teachers and administrators in departmentalized schools should be aware of the dangers inherent in them. Specifically, teachers who teach reading must never lose sight of the fact that reading is a communication *process* and teach it accordingly, and content area teachers must become skillful at and committed to incorporating the teaching of reading into their content area teaching.

Team teaching

How teams of teachers are formed and how they function varies considerably from school to school. In some schools what is called team teaching amounts to little more than departmentalization with some time allocated for teachers at the different grade levels to meet and tell one another what they are doing. In other schools teams of teachers are attempting interdisciplinary instruction on a nongraded basis. Generally, it seems safe to say that team teaching has not made the positive impact on children's learning that was once anticipated. In addition, some administrators have found team teaching to be rather expensive and not merely a matter of allocating financial resources differently. Consequently, some schools have not been able to procure special services and materials which may be more beneficial to students' reading development than the effects of team teaching.

For reading instruction, team teaching at its best has permitted teachers to arrange flexible groupings for students and arrive at more individualized instruction. At its worst it has meant assigning the poor readers to one team member, the average readers to another team member, and the good readers to yet another team member. As the number of teachers in the team grows, so does the number of ability groups. One school we observed had students divided into as many as seven different ability groups with a different teacher for each group. Unfortunately, each group was taught as a unit; and individualization within each group was considered unnecessary because of the "homogeneous" grouping practices. In most schools we have observed that team teaching has not had much of an impact on the reading instruction given to middle graders. As a matter of fact, reading instruction has in some schools been ignored in favor of the development of highly sophisticated science or social studies teams which stress content mastery rather than study skills development. Some exceptions have been noted in schools which employ a reading consultant to ensure that the teaching teams integrate reading study skills instruction with content instruction.

The Joplin Plan

Like team teaching, the Joplin Plan has apparently not resulted in substantially better reading instruction for students in the middle grades, although some schools strongly favor it. The basic assumption underlying the Joplin Plan is that grouping students for reading instruction on the basis of achievement regardless of grade placement permits teachers to meet individual needs better because they deal with decreased ranges of reading ability. In practice, the Joplin Plan has students assigned to ability groups that cross grade lines for reading instruction. Teachers are assigned to different ability groups and supposedly can be more effective because regardless of the different chronological ages of the children there is a sameness in their reading achievement.

Five criticisms of the Joplin Plan seem valid to us and in combination are reasons not to recommend it for reading instruction in the middle grades:

1   The reading teacher is different from the content area teachers; hence, many opportunities for coordinating instruction in the reading curriculum with instruction in the content areas are lost.

2   Teachers often assume that because they are teaching students who have been grouped according to ability they can teach them all alike.

3   Poor readers can learn much about reading from good readers, and segregating them as definitively as the Joplin Plan does reduces possibilities for productive interaction between good and poor readers.

4   Moving a student from one group to another when progress is noted is difficult because the student must change teachers *and* rooms *as well as* classmates and materials.

5   The teacher of the "low" group is given the unreasonable task of providing corrective instruction usually to fifteen or more retarded readers who differ greatly in the nature and cause of their problem. Providing good instruction for fifteen poor readers is much more difficult than providing good instruction for five poor readers and twenty better readers who do

not require as much individual attention. In addition, lowering the pupil-teacher ratio in the low group means raising it for the top group thereby making individualization within the top group extremely difficult.

All in all, the Joplin Plan appears to be more convenient for teachers and administrators who want to feel they are individualizing instruction than it is beneficial to the students who are supposed to benefit from it. In fact, the Joplin Plan seems much less popular than it was some years ago.

Many schools have modified the Joplin Plan by grouping students according to ability within each grade instead of across grades. The same disadvantages cited for the Joplin Plan also apply to this modification of the plan. Therefore, we feel the Joplin Plan and modifications of it are generally more harmful than helpful to the reading growth of students in the middle grades. Students in the middle grades represent too wide a variety of skills development and interests to group them as definitively as the Joplin Plan attempts to group them. In addition, middle grades students profit from learning to read in small groups composed of students with mixed reading abilities. Group projects such as creative dramatics or panel discussions relative to reading experiences are excellent activities for middle graders. These projects, if properly guided, permit good and poor readers to share reading experiences to good advantage for the poor readers without appreciably slowing down the growth of the good readers.

Nongraded and unitized schools

Most educators have recognized the artificiality of assigning students to a fixed curriculum according to their chronological age or the number of years they have spent in school. Nongraded and unitized school organizations are attempts to do away with the stifling effects of having students proceed through a prescribed curriculum on a grade-by-grade basis. Flexibility is the goal of nongraded schools and multiage instructional units. In a "unitized" school, for example, the traditional six- or eight-grade organizational structure may be replaced by two or more units with teams of teachers and teacher aides within each unit. These teams work with students of various chronological ages, grouped and regrouped for different kinds of instructional activities. No child "fails" in the traditional sense of the term—he or she just spends more time learning certain things than other children in his or her age group spend. The same concept prevails in the nongraded school that may not have clearly defined instructional units but operates on a multiage grouping for reading instruction, as follows:

In facilitating the learning of reading, the teacher not only assists in bringing together the learner, a task, and appropriate materials, he also brings together groups of individual learners who can profit from working together. A group of youngsters who have a common need might be brought together for some identified learning purposes. A youngster would then leave the groups as his need is fulfilled. Or the entire group may be dispensed after a period of time.

Another purpose for bringing youngsters together in a group situation is to provide a learning opportunity that has many facets and, consequently, may meet differing needs. Thus, the learning opportunity that is offered has a wide range of outcomes, and each child in the group is there because some need of his can be met. The teacher is an organizer of groups and thus must be aware of specific similarities of learners as well as individual differences. [3]

Any organizational plan that facilitates a departure from teaching reading to all students at a particular grade level alike should be encouraged, especially in the middle grades where individual ability differences are wide and before students have established definite interests and aspirations. However, one must question whether or not the same objectives cannot be met within traditional heterogeneously grouped "classes" with less expenditure of financial and personal resources than by implementing totally new structures. Perhaps the best position to take at the present time regarding nongraded and unitized schools is a wait-and-see attitude with plenty of encouragement for more experimentation. We share the observation made by Ramsey (1967):

Personnel of school systems jumping into nongradedness without making sure the total situation is ripe for it often live to regret their move. In recent communications with officials of over 130 nongraded schools in the nation, the writer found over 20 that had abandoned the plan in the last three years. This percentage does not necessarily indicate innate weaknesses in the nongraded philosophy, but it does very probably indicate difficulties in implementing it. (p.127)

The self-contained classroom

At the risk of being unfashionable many school districts have retained heterogeneous classrooms at least through grade six with a teacher-pupil ratio of 1 : 30 or thereabouts. Often these classrooms are not completely self-contained but make use of special teachers in areas such as art, music, and physical education. What might be termed the "basic" curriculums (reading, language arts, science, social studies, and mathematics) are, however, taught to the same students by the same teacher. Although for some curriculum areas heterogeneous self-contained classrooms may be undesirable because of the lack of resources for specialization, they provide excellent opportunities for developing reading ability.

The self-contained classroom has received some unfavorable and many times undeserved criticism. Probably no other organizational structures facilitate the integration of reading skill development, reading in the content areas, and recrea-

---

3. Jimmie E. Nations, "Caring for Individual Differences in Reading through Nongrading," in *Organizing for Individual Differences,* edited by Wallace F. Ramsey. Newark, Delaware: International Reading Association, 1967, p. 91. Reprinted with permission of Jimmie E. Nations and the International Reading Association.

tional reading so well as the self-contained classroom. If we accept that students' growth in reading is influenced by their total school experiences and their unique personal development, then the watchful eye and guiding hand of a teacher who sees them in most of their school-sponsored activities is desirable. Some would argue that this kind of observation and guidance is unnecessary and in fact detrimental in the middle grades. The fact is, however, that in many aspects of their academic and personal development many if not most middle graders are a long way from being able to cope with the decisions, personal interactions, and pressures to organize their school lives some organizational patterns force upon them.

Certainly, students in the middle grades should be moving toward taking on more responsibility for their schooling. But their development in reading needs to be nurtured carefully during these years as a basic part of their total personal development. We are in agreement with the description offered by Tillman (1970): "A self-contained classroom offers the pupil opportunities for (a) the development of strong human relationships, (b) a teacher who knows him well, (c) integration of subject matter areas, (d) individualized instruction, (e) growth in self-understanding and self-respect, and (f) choices in the use of his time." (p. 490) Since these characteristics are vital to the kind of reading program we advocate, we recommend that until other organizational plans are more satisfactorily developed than they are at the present time, some degree of self-containment be the prevailing organizational structure developed for students in the middle grades, especially grades four and five. In grades six, seven, and eight the self-contained classroom is usually replaced by some departmentalization. In these grades reading classes should be available to help students continue their growth in reading. We discuss reading classes for grades six, seven, and eight thoroughly in Chapter 2.

A Suborganization for Most Plans

The likelihood of an increasing variety of organizational plans among schools serving middle grade students seems apparent. School districts are engaging in more curriculum experimentation, innovative programs are receiving much publicity, and the "search for the best" is still a major motivational force in the life style of American education. Consequently, any recommendation for organizing an instructional reading program for students in the middle grades must: (1) take the special academic and personal needs of middle graders as individuals and as a group into consideration, and (2) be designed to function within the context of a variety of school organizational plans.

In the primary grades the emphasis in the instructional reading program must be upon the development of the basic reading skills. Utilization of these skills for getting information and for recreation must also be taught and encouraged, but the emphasis is clearly on the "how" of reading. After grade three, however, this emphasis should shift; and students should receive less instruction in how to read with materials and exercises designed primarily to teach reading skills and more help with reading materials designed primarily to transmit information or provide leisure time activity. In addition, students in the middle grades generally need less actual time under the direct observation of the teacher. Many are quite independent in their reading ability and can profit more from directed reading and free reading experiences than from developmental reading exercises. Johnson and Kress (1969) have observed that, "Two oft neglected common-sense ideas in the field of reading are these: (1) A reader is one who reads. (2) One learns to read by reading. Each individually and the two in combination have profound implications for reading instruction . . ." (p.706) The instructional reading program in the middle grades, then, must give students greater opportunities "to learn to read by reading" than are usually afforded in the primary grades where the basic skills are being developed and in the secondary school where the transmission of specific content is of greater importance.

Smith, Otto, and Hansen (1978) have conceptualized the school reading program as consisting of three distinct phases: developmental (developing reading skills with materials designed for that purpose), functional (getting information for a specific assignment), and recreational (enjoying reading experiences with self-selected materials). In a reading program that is functioning well these three phases are interdependent and mutually reinforcing. In other words, the skills learned and practiced in the developmental phase are transferred to the functional and recreational phases where they are further practiced and refined. Students' performance in the functional and recreational phases can provide teachers with diagnostic information that can be used to determine what skills need to be taught or retaught in the developmental phase. Furthermore, keeping the three phases closely related helps keep the concept of reading for meaning and for life enrichment clearly in evidence in the instructional program. A sure sign of a poorly functioning reading program is the perception on the part of the students that reading is a matter of completing exercises or progressing through some sequentially arranged materials. A well-rounded reading program in the middle grades, then, provides opportunities for as much instruction as each student needs with developmental materials and ample opportunities for applying his or her skills with functional and recreational materials.

The developmental phase

The developmental phase of the instructional reading program continues to be important throughout the middle grades and the secondary school as well for that matter. The assumption that most children do not need formal reading skills instruction beyond grade three is false. Children beyond the primary grades still need direct instruction in vocabulary enrichment, word attack skills, and comprehension skills with increasingly sophisticated material. This instruction can usually be given efficiently and effectively by an ongoing diagnosis of students' skills needs (see Chapter 11) and by grouping students who have similar needs together. In the developmental phase of the reading program the groups often remain relatively unchanged. It is not unusual, however, for good and poor readers to be placed in the same group for instruction in a particular skill in which both are weak. The key to the grouping and regrouping process lies in the skillfulness of the teacher in diagnosing strengths and weaknesses.

Principals and teachers are often doubtful about using a basal series in the middle grades. Indeed, some basal programs are designed to be used only through the first three grades, thereby giving the impression that a basal approach is undesirable after that. In addition, the content of basal series and the basal series approach itself have been frequent targets of critics who have often chosen to stress the worst features of using a basal series and ignore the advantages. If used properly, a good basal series can be of much help in the middle grades to continue the development of reading skills.

Perhaps the major fault with using basal readers is that teachers have expected too much of them. Teachers have tried to make them entertaining as well as instructive and have often felt obliged to push, pull, or drag their students through all of the selections so that nothing in the sequence would remain untaught. Students often received the impression that the basal series was to be treasured for something more than a collection of materials to help them learn how to read other more relevant materials.

Students and teachers should acknowledge the basal series as a tool to aid students in the development of reading skills. Obviously, enjoyment of the learning process is highly desirable and should be sought. But the job of the basal series is to provide materials at different ability levels that are written or selected to teach specific skills. Familiarity with the selections in a basal series permits teachers to choose for individuals or for groups of students materials at an appropriate level of difficulty for instructional purposes and also to facilitate the teaching of needed skills. Although a basal series is usually a comprehensive "package," most students will need developmental materials to supplement it. Therefore, "supplementary" developmental materials should be used in conjunction with a basal series. A basal series is also useful to familiarize teachers with a scope and sequence of reading skills and give them some helpful suggestions for teaching the various skills. Most experienced teachers would recognize the truth in the following anecdote by Ramsey: "An intimate knowledge of how reading skills are taught is most helpful in individualizing reading. One excellent supervisor whose teachers were signally successful in individualized reading gave the writer an eight-word description of the best kind of skills preparation for such teaching: 'Five years' experience in teaching basal readers.' "(p. 123)

Which basal series is best for middle grade students is largely a matter of teacher preference. Obviously, only those series which include materials for middle grade students can be considered. The most important characteristic of basal readers for middle graders is the similarity between the selections with which the reading skills are to be learned and the content area and recreational reading materials with which they will be utilized. Transfer from developmental to functional and recreational materials is greatly facilitated when the developmental materials contain selections that are expository as well as narrative, maps to read, newspaper articles, and other kinds of writing that students will encounter in their school and out-of-school reading.

In summary, then, teachers and administrators need not shun basal readers for developing reading skills in the middle grades. They serve an important function if they are used properly. The key to their usefulness lies in knowing (1) which selections are at the instructional level of difficulty for which students, (2) which selections at the various difficulty levels best lend themselves to the teaching of specific skills, and (3) proportionately, how much time the students need with developmental materials in comparison to the time they spend applying their skills with functional and recreational materials.

The functional phase

As students progress through school—and for their postschooling pursuits—the need to get information from printed material to complete assignments and for personal satisfaction becomes increasingly important. Although other media are available for getting information, printed material remains far more effective in providing answers to questions than radio, television, audio tapes, and other media on the market. Most students are surprised to find that there are relatively few questions they can ask that haven't been answered or discussed some place within the array of printed material in a medium-sized public library. Guidance in finding the right references to answer specific questions or satisfy certain needs is usually available upon request. Digging out the information itself, however, rests with the individual student and is dependent upon his or her information-getting reading skills.

Students in the middle grades are especially receptive to learning situations that plunge them into printed material in search of information to satisfy their interests. For the most part they enjoy the sense of learning independence they gain from putting their reading skills to use to satisfy personal needs. They also have many questions about their rapidly expanding and often personally confusing world. And finally, the questions they ask are usually broad enough that they are able to find a wide variety of pertinent materials at different levels of reading difficulty to answer them.

The functional reading phase of the middle grade reading program should be an integral part of the block of time allotted to reading instruction and should not be relegated to a "once in a while" happening. Students should be queried regarding their interests and put to work on projects relative to their interests that require information-type reading for completion. In most cases preliminary whole-class discussion to bring out topics of interest within the class will disclose topics that are of interest to more than one student. Class perusal and discussion of the daily newspaper are usually sufficient to trigger a host of interesting topics. When topics are identified, interest groups of various sizes can readily be formed. Students who have interests that are not shared by other students are rare, but they certainly should not be discouraged from pursuing their interests and completing a project on an individual basis. It is likely that on the next occasion they will pursue an interest shared by other students. It is the emphasis on interest that differentiates the functional phase of the reading program from teaching reading in the content area curriculums. The kind of reading done and the kind of instruction provided may be essentially the same. However, the content area curriculums have a definite body of information to be learned at successive stages or grades in school. Therefore, in the content areas the subject to be read about is prescribed and not self-chosen. For example, students with a keen interest in horses or snowmobiling may never have an opportunity to read widely about these particular interests within the context of their content area curriculums.

The projects should be such that upon completion they can be presented to the whole class. Projects of this kind provide students with opportunities to develop their listening skills, speaking skills, writing skills, artistic talents, and creative abilities as well as their reading skills. In most classes projects will include artistic models and illustrations, radio dramas, creative dramatics, panel discussions, mini newspapers or magazines, and creative-writing products. As a rule teachers need to have a repertoire of project frameworks at their fingertips to aid groups or individuals who are unable after a reasonable period of time to think of or agree upon a suitable project. In Chapter 9 we offer a number of suggestions for projects to be used in conjunction with functional reading.

Unlike the skills groups that are formed for the developmental phase of the reading program, in the functional groups good and poor readers work together as a rule rather than an exception. We agree with Moffett that

The composition of groups—and hence of classes—should be as varied as possible. Individuals would be in one group formed for one purpose and in another formed for another purpose. But for the sake of rich multiplicity of dialects, vocabulary, styles, ideas, and points of view, the class should be heterogeneously sectioned from a diverse student population. It should constitute the most powerful multilingual assembly that can be brought together. This means mixing levels of ability and achievement, mixing sexes, mixing races, and mixing socioeconomic classes. At times even ages should be temporarily mixed, and outside adults should come in and join discussions.[4]

Obviously, we prefer school organizational plans that facilitate rather than inhibit heterogeneous grouping so that students can learn language skills from one another. Students who read, write, speak, and listen well will profit from

---

4. James Moffett, *Teaching the Universe of Discourse,* Boston: Houghton Mifflin, 1968, p. 93. Reprinted by permission.

communicating with students who are less able with language skills. And poor readers often learn much about certain reading selections and how to deal with ideas in print by matching interpretations with better readers.

The teacher has several responsibilities in the functional phase of the reading program. After helping students to verbalize their interests and getting interest groups together in some kind of physical environment (we recommend tables or desks in circular arrangements, with some parts of the room reserved for getting a student away from the group temporarily for some undistracted study), the teacher's major responsibility is getting relevant materials at appropriate difficulty levels to the students. Students are asked to complete a definite project assignment; therefore the materials assigned for reading should be at levels the students can readily comprehend with the limited help the teacher can give while the various groups are assembled. Since the teacher's time must obviously be shared by the different groups, good readers can be asked to help poorer readers in their groups with words the latter can't analyze or passages they can't interpret. As a rule this kind of help from better readers is welcomed by poorer readers because the group project is being served and because getting meaning from print is all important to a good project presentation. Filmstrips, audio tapes, picture books, movies, and other nonreading media should be available for students who read so poorly that printed materials pertinent to the project and at a level they can master simply do not exist. Teachers report that locating the wide variety of materials needed for the functional reading phase becomes less difficult each year because of the collections they build up from year to year on topics that tend to be perennial favorites of particular age groups. School and community libraries and teacher aides are valuable resources for getting materials to students. We recommend that school librarians work closely with classroom teachers to make the needed materials available to students. Some teachers have found it helpful to have the librarian or the director of the instructional materials center move into the classroom to confer with student groups and guide them to materials. Other teachers and librarians have found it more efficient to have the functional phase of the reading curriculum operate right in the library or instructional materials center. Parents and community groups have also been found to be helpful in adding reading materials on various topics to classroom or school library collections.

As students read, discuss, and plan their presentations the teacher's task is to be a resource person, moving from group to group and working for brief periods with the whole group or individuals. Students typically need help with defining the parameters of their projects, making decisions about who will do what during the presentation, allocating the different reading tasks and distributing the available reading materials, understanding technical vocabulary, and interpreting difficult passages. Teachers are often able to teach many reading skills effectively during this time because the students are motivated to get meaning from their reading.

Teachers also need to keep the groups moving productively and to schedule presentations. Some groups and individuals will be ready before others, and it is best to let students show their work as soon as it is completed. During the presentations teachers join in the discussions, evaluate with the class the presentations, and assess the growing ability of individual students to get information from print. Specific skill development needs can be diagnosed and transformed into objectives for the developmental phase of the reading program.

The recreational phase

Like the developmental and functional phases of the reading program, the recreational phase needs a definite place within the middle grades reading curriculum. Television, community clubs, sports, and other nonreading activities strongly compete for the students' out-of-school time. Hence most students need school time to help them develop the reading habit and gain the benefits that accrue from recreational reading. Vocabulary is increased, skills are refined, positive attitudes toward reading are formed, and good leisure-time habits are established through self-selected reading experiences that are directed only at personal enjoyment. Some overzealous administrators and teachers have tried to make every minute of the school day "pay off" by chasing students from one assignment to another. Many teachers feel guilty if their students are quietly enjoying reading, and yet enjoyment of reading is and should be a major curriculum objective. Suffice it to say here that recreational reading should be an important consideration in the organization of school reading programs. Specific considerations include: a variety of materials from which students select their preferences regardless of difficulty level; time and place to read without distraction; and opportunities for students to converse with, not report to, fellow students and their teacher about their reading experiences. The groups themselves may be formed because a number of students are reading the same book, or a number are reading materials relevant to a particular theme or topic, or merely because a group of students would appear to profit from a discussion of books. The judgment of the teacher is heavily relied upon for the actual composition of the groups.

Implementing the Suborganization

Too many school reading programs have relied upon materials rather than teachers to teach students how to read. Although this is unfortunate at all academic levels, it is especially unfortunate in the middle grades, where most students need the sensitivity, spontaneity, and creativity of a teacher more than they need a specially controlled vocabulary, systematically arranged phonemic elements, or college or vocationally preparatory content. No instructional materials exist that will do more than assist the middle grade teacher of reading. The job of teaching reading, if the ultimate objective of having students use reading to enrich their lives is to be realized, rests squarely upon the teacher. And how well the teacher can respond to this challenge depends to a large extent upon the teacher's skill in implementing the three phases of the reading program we have described so that they are carefully integrated and mutually reinforcing.

The first task of teachers is to learn as much as possible at the beginning of the school year about the reading abilities, interests, and habits of the students assigned to them for reading instruction. Because these three aspects of a student's reading may change considerably over the summer months and from teacher to teacher, we advise teachers to rely less heavily upon a student's past test performance and reports from previous teachers than upon current formal and informal diagnostic assessments (see Chapter 11). The first several weeks of a new year, then, might be spent discussing past reading experiences, selecting materials for a classroom library or reading corner, silent reading of self-selected materials, private conferences between the teacher and individual students, diagnostic testing with standardized tests, informal assessments using the basal series or other materials that indicate the level of general competence with developmental materials at different levels of difficulty as well as specific skills strengths and weaknesses, small group discussions, and other activities that help teachers get a picture of the class as a group and of students as individuals within that group.

Since the recreational phase of the reading program can be initiated with less diagnostic information and planning than either the developmental or functional phase and because it can be relied upon to give students worthwhile reading activity while the teacher is attending to other responsibilities, it should be initiated first. As a matter of fact, some teachers have recommended getting the recreational phase started the first day of school by having a supply of materials ready for students to select from and the furniture arranged for silent reading followed by small group conversation.

Functional reading groups can be started soon after recreational reading groups get underway so that by the third or fourth week of school students may be reading and conversing two or three days in their recreational groups and the remaining days reading, planning, and preparing projects in their functional reading groups. By the fourth or fifth week of school the teacher should have enough information about the skills needs of the members of the class to form skills groups. Most teachers are able to keep four or five skills groups meeting for instruction in the basal readers and supplementary materials most of the time. Although movement of students from one skills group to another is desirable, in actual practice the poorer readers tend to stay together and to get more direct instruction from the teachers; and the better readers tend to stay together and spend more time reading their functional and recreational materials. At times no skills groups may meet for several weeks if the teacher feels all the time available for reading is needed for the functional and/or the recreational reading groups.

Some weeks certain skills groups may meet every day while others meet only one or two days. The key to the whole approach is flexibility based upon teacher observation and judgment. For some classes functional reading groups may be operative only two or three times during the school year and for no more than a week or two each time. For other classes they may be a major emphasis of the reading curriculum. It is unlikely that any two teachers would follow the same schedule with the same class because the personality of each class is so strongly influenced by the teacher's personality. At the same time, it is unlikely that the same teacher would follow the same schedule with two different classes because of the unique characteristics of each class.

The following schedule (Table 1.1) for a hypothetical heterogeneous class of 30 fourth graders illustrates how the three different phases might be coordinated throughout a three-week period. The schedule assumes a 50-minute time block for reading instruction five days a week and represents a period of time during which four different skills groups are meeting regularly for developmental instruction—at times combined and at other times broken up. In Chapter 2 we present an illustrative schedule for a reading class in the upper middle grades.

In the illustrative schedule of Table 1.1, students received specific skills instruction in flexible groups, worked independently and in small groups on interesting reading-related projects, read and discussed material of their own choosing, and formally presented some projects to their classmates. At the conclusion of this particular three-week period the class appears ready to wrap up the unit. The next several class periods would probably be spent on completing unfinished group work and having the remaining functional reading group project presentations. Students who were finished with their group responsibilities might do some additional free reading, work in supplementary materials, or under the direction of the teacher, tutor some students needing special help. The teacher would probably be busy prodding the procrastinators so that the unit could be completed before enthusiasm waned. After all groups had completed their project presentations and their recreational group conversations, several days would be spent setting up new functional and recreational groups and doing some whole-class activities such as listening to a recorded story or discussing interesting characters the students had met in their reading.

The schedule we have discussed is only a model and as such has limited usefulness. The model suggests how a teacher and a class might operate during the beginning of a school year. Teachers and students need time to learn about each other and to learn how to conduct themselves within any organizational plan. Certainly the plan we recommend is not easy to implement. Many demands are made upon the teacher, the students, and other resources of the school and community. Providing students in the middle grades with a good reading program is hard work that challenges a teacher's creativity, sense of organization, enthusiasm, and knowledge of the reading process. That's why the essential ingredient in a good reading program is a creative, organized, enthusiastic, knowledgeable

Table 1.1

A FIRST WEEK

MONDAY

	Developmental	Functional	Recreational
9:00–9:15	10 students[1]		20 students
9:15–9:40	5 students[2]		25 students
9:40–9:50			30 students

TUESDAY

	Developmental	Functional	Recreational
9:00–9:20	8 students[3]		22 students
9:20–9:30			30 students
9:30–9:50		30 students	

WEDNESDAY

	Developmental	Functional	Recreational
9:00–9:10	7 students[4]	6 students[5]	17 students
9:10–9:20	5 students	6 students	19 students
9:20–9:50		30 students	

THURSDAY

	Developmental	Functional	Recreational
9:00–9:15	10 students	4 students[6]	16 students
9:15–9:30	5 students	10 students[7]	15 students
9:30–9:50			30 students[8]

FRIDAY

	Developmental	Functional	Recreational
9:00–9:10	8 students	22 students	
9:10–9:50		30 students[9]	

A SECOND WEEK

MONDAY

	Developmental	Functional	Recreational
9:00–9:30	15 students[10]		15 students
9:30–9:50			30 students

1. Middle ability group.
2. Low ability group.
3. Another middle ability group.
4. High ability group.
5. A functional group that defined a project well enough the previous day to get started on it.
6. The same functional group that worked on Wednesday with two students removed for developmental instruction.
7. Students representing several functional groups working independently on their parts of the group projects.
8. Ten minutes of conversation in recreational groups.
9. All functional groups meeting with teacher available for consultation.
10. One middle and low ability groups combined.

Table 1.1 *cont.*

TUESDAY

	Developmental	Functional	Recreational
9:00–9:20	5 students	17 students	8 students
9:20–9:50	15 students[11]		15 students

WEDNESDAY

	Developmental	Functional	Recreational
9:00–9:50	30 students[12]		

THURSDAY

	Developmental	Functional	Recreational
9:00–9:15	30 students[13]		
9:15–9:50			30 students

FRIDAY

	Developmental	Functional	Recreational
9:00–9:50		30 students	

A THIRD WEEK

MONDAY

	Developmental	Functional	Recreational
9:00–9:15	2 students[14]	28 students	
9:15–9:30	10 students	20 students	
9:30–9:50	5 students	25 students	

TUESDAY

	Developmental	Functional	Recreational
9:00–9:15	2 students[15]		28 students
9:15–9:30	7 students		23 students
9:30–9:50	8 students		22 students

WEDNESDAY

	Developmental	Functional	Recreational
9:00–9:50			30 students[16]

THURSDAY

	Developmental	Functional	Recreational
9:00–9:50		30 students[17]	

FRIDAY

	Developmental	Functional	Recreational
9:00–9:10	2 students[18]	20 students	8 students
9:10–9:50	15 students[19]	7 students	8 students

11. Two middle groups combined.
12. Whole class instruction in some skill.
13. Whole class review of skill taught Wednesday.

---

14. Intensive work with two students having trouble with a particular skill.
15. Same two students who received special help on Monday.
16. Recreational groups completing this round of reading and conversing together.
17. Two functional reading group project presentations.
18. Teacher conference with students who need help finding additional reading material to read before new recreational groups are formed.
19. Two middle groups working together on a troublesome skill.

teacher. We agree with Herrick (Macdonald *et al.*, 1965) that "the most important educational experience happening to a student is his teacher."(p. 65) We do know from our work with good teachers that implementing the three-phase plan we have described is much more difficult and frustrating the first year it is tried than it is in following years. We ask only that teachers try the plan for at least two years before they judge their satisfaction with it and the benefits their students receive from it.

Something to Think and Talk About

My staff and I are extremely pleased with our team-teaching arrangement for reading instruction. The three teachers at each grade level decide who works with each ability group best. Then, on the basis of reading achievement test scores and teacher judgment, students are assigned to teacher A, B, or C for reading instruction.

This approach substantially reduces the range of ability within each class and gives each teacher the opportunity to work with the kind of readers he or she does the best job with. The teacher who chooses the group that reads the poorest is given fewer students than the teachers of the other two groups. The teacher of the best readers is assigned the most students. This team-teaching approach also includes 45 minutes a day for planning so that the teachers can coordinate their teaching and share insights regarding the progress of individual students.

The teachers have found team teaching for reading so satisfactory that we are working on a plan to use a similar approach for science, math, and social studies. What we are considering is letting our middle grades teachers teach the subjects they are best prepared to teach. Kids are a lot smarter now than they used to be and need the best teaching they can get in the content areas. As a matter of fact, Mr. Davis now teaches all of the sixth-grade science, and Mrs. Johnson teaches his language arts. The kids are getting the best both have to offer. We think we can move even further in this direction.

(See Appendix 1 at the end of the book for Authors' Response to "Something to Think and Talk About.")

References

Hass, Glen, Kimball Wiles, and Joseph Bondi (1970). *Readings in Curriculum,* 2d ed. Boston: Allyn and Bacon.

Johnson, Marjorie Seddon, and Roy Kress (1969). "Readers and Reading," *The Reading Teacher* 22 (7): 594.

Jones, Daisy Marvel (1977). *Curriculum Targets in the Elementary School.* Englewood Cliffs, New Jersey: Prentice-Hall.

Macdonald, James B., Dan W. Anderson, and Frank B. May (1965). *Strategies of Curriculum Development—Selected Writings of the Late Virgil E. Harrick*. Columbus, Ohio: Charles E. Merrill.

Moffett, James (1968). *Teaching the Universe of Discourse*. Boston: Houghton Mifflin.

Nations, Jimmie E. (1967). "Caring for Individual Differences in Reading through Nongrading." In *Organizing for Individual Differences*, edited by Wallace Ramsey. Newark, Delaware: International Reading Association, pp. 79–96.

Ramsey, Wallace (1967). "A Conclusive Look at the Caring for Individual Differences in Reading." In *Organizing for Individual Differences*. Newark, Delaware: International Reading Association, pp. 115–133.

Smith, Richard J., Wayne Otto, and Lee Hansen (1978). *The School Reading Program: A Handbook for Teachers, Supervisors and Specialists*. Boston: Houghton Mifflin.

Tillman, Rodney (1970). "Self-Contained Classroom: Where Do We Stand?" *Readings in Curriculum,* 2d ed. Boston: Allyn and Bacon, pp. 487–490.

2

THE READING CLASS
FOR THE UPPER MIDDLE
GRADES

The purpose of this chapter is to offer some suggestions for developing curriculum for classes designed to improve the reading ability of students in grades six, seven, and eight, whether the students are good readers, average readers, or poor readers. Nearly all students can profit from some specific reading instruction in the upper middle grades, and reading classes can be designed and conducted to meet the wide range of reading needs among the student body in those grades. Heilman (1977) says, "In order to assure that children continue to develop skills that are commensurate with the reading tasks they are asked to perform in the intermediate grades, systematic instruction must be continued." (p. 513)

Reading classes are prevalent in middle schools throughout the country; and, therefore, middle school teachers should know something about them, whether they do or do not teach a reading class. Reading classes should be an integral part of the entire middle grades curriculum. As such they are most effective if all middle grades teachers understand the role they play and how they play that role so that all teachers can build upon what is done in the reading class in other classes. A continuing problem with reading classes has been the lack of follow-up from what students learn in their reading classes to how that learning is reinforced, applied, and continued in their other classes.

Furthermore, middle grades content area teachers may be called upon to teach a reading class whether they have had much training in the teaching of reading or not. In the Aurora, Colorado, Public Schools, for example, nearly every middle school (grades six, seven, and eight) teacher teaches a reading class with the assistance of the reading specialist(s) assigned to the school. This stipulation of employment is not unique to Aurora. Other districts as well are assuming that middle grades teachers can teach reading and are assigning them to teach classes with increasing frequency as the trend toward formalized reading instruction beyond the primary grades continues to grow.

Certainly it is true that curriculum plans or learning environments other than the class structure are used to teach reading in the middle grades. Some schools have reading laboratories, units of study in language arts classes, tutoring programs, and other vehicles for continuing students' reading growth. However, the reading class has remained popular in many middle schools, perhaps because it is well suited to helping students improve their reading and helping them make the transition from the more individualized reading programs in the elementary school to the more departmentalized structure of most senior high schools. Perhaps it is also popular because it is an economical and efficient plan for making reading instruction available to all students within the departmentalized or semi-departmentalized structure of most middle schools.

Reading classes for middle grades students may be good or bad, depending, as all learning environments do, upon the curriculum designed for the classes and the skillfulness of the teachers who teach them. Scheduling classes and assigning students to them does not guarantee reading improvement.

When reading classes are created for middle grades students, several questions need to be asked. We shall pose the questions and then answer them according to our evaluation of what conditions are needed for good reading instruction to occur in reading classes and according to the ideas and preferences expressed to us by middle school reading teachers, middle school teachers in other curriculum areas, and middle school principals whom we have informally surveyed.

The questions are as follows:

1 Should reading classes be available to students in grades six through eight?
2 Should all students be required to take a reading class in every grade a reading class is offered?
3 Should classes be homogeneous according to reading ability?
4 Should classes cross grade lines (for example, sixth, seventh, and eighth graders assigned to the same class)?
5 What materials are needed for reading classes?
6 What might a typical week in a reading class look like?

Should Reading Classes Be Available to Students in Grades Six Through Eight?

We think classes should be available to students in grades six through eight. The highly individual nature of reading development is well known. Some students are just beginning to achieve some reading strength by grade six. Other students have learned most or all of the basic skills, but still need a good deal of practice and instruction to master those skills and put them to work with more challenging material than they are exposed to in earlier grades. Still other students need reading classes to help them maintain the basic skills they have mastered and to help them sample the wide variety of reading experiences available to them. In fact, given what is known about the importance of practicing basic skills to master them and reading widely for different purposes to learn to value reading, reading instruction through all the middle grades for most students seems to be a critical responsibility of schools. And since "most" students have these needs, reading classes may be the most efficient and effective vehicle to meet them.

Should All Students Be Required to Take a Reading Class in Every Grade a Reading Class Is Offered?

Most students do need and do profit from well-designed and skillfully taught reading classes in grades six through eight. We would suggest that three types of students probably are not helped much by their enrollment in reading classes: (1) severely disabled readers (that is, students who have little or no independence in reading and need the assistance of a teacher for any kind of productive reading experience), (2) unmotivated students whose lack of motivation is expressed in disruptive behavior and refusal to do assigned tasks, and (3) accelerated students who are self-motivated to read and who may be bored by the pace of a class or frustrated by the constraints a class structure imposes.

Students who are severely disabled need individual or small-group remedial instruction in an out-of-the-classroom setting to be substantially helped. Unmotivated, disruptive students are likely to profit more from assignment to other classes or projects and assignment to a trained counselor who may be able to help them understand the importance of learning to read in our society or at least reduce their hostility toward reading. Until students make a commitment to learn to read and are able to attend to instruction, even the most skillful of teachers will be unable to improve their reading skills. The third type of students who probably don't belong in reading classes, accelerated readers, are likely to have their reading development served best by giving them "free-reading" periods which provide them with time to improve their reading by reading materials of their choosing. One or more of these accelerated students' content area teachers could be given the responsibility of suggesting good reading to these students and arranging to discuss their reading with them on a regular basis (for example, every Monday during a preparation period). Students who don't fall into these three classifications, the vast majority of the student population in most middle schools, should be able to benefit from the kind of reading instruction that can be given in a class of fifteen to twenty-five middle grades students.

Should Classes Be Homogeneous According to Reading Ability?

In Chapter 1 we stated our position that probably more is lost than is gained by not letting students of various abilities learn to read together. We think this is especially true for sixth-, seventh-, and eighth-grade reading classes. Homogeneous ability grouping in these grades may on the surface appear to be the only way to develop classroom curriculums for the wide range of reading achievement differences among students in those grades. However, when students are grouped according to reading ability, the groups in reality possess other homogeneous characteristics. The students in the low reading ability class, for example, tend also to be less motivated, more disruptive, and to have poorer experiential backgrounds for reading than their classmates who are better readers. As a group, the lower reading achievers respond better to instruction when they have more able students after whom to model their behavior, and they learn much about valuing reading and how to read from their classroom associations with good readers.

One argument against heterogeneous ability grouping for middle grades reading classes that is often given by teachers and administrators is that the progress of good readers is impeded by their slower-learning, lesser-motivated classmates. A second argument is that teachers cannot realistically be expected to plan and teach classes to students whose ability range in reading may be four or five years. These are not invalid arguments. In truth, when classes are comprised of fast learners and slow learners, some impositions on both are bound to occur. For example, questions asked of the entire class may cause the fast learners to be impatient if slow learners are called upon to answer, and slow learners to be frustrated if fast learners are called upon. But the impositions need not be so serious that the learning of either fast or slow learners is significantly affected. A good classroom management plan and a curriculum that provides for individual and small-group learning experiences as well as for whole-class learning experiences can minimize the disadvantages of heterogeneity and maximize the advantages. We present such a plan and curriculum when we discuss materials for reading classes and describe a typical week in a reading class later in this chapter.

Should Reading Classes Cross Grade Lines?

There are several advantages and few, if any, disadvantages to scheduling middle grade students to classes that enroll students at two or more grade levels. We have watched with interest the development of an innovative plan in a middle school in Madison, Wisconsin, wherein sixth, seventh, and eighth graders are assigned to teams of teachers who teach them in all curriculum areas, often in groups that cross grade lines. It is not unusual, for example, to watch sixth, seventh, and eighth graders discussing the same short story, conducting a science experiment, or working together in small groups on a math assignment. After a year of this cross-grade instruction, students become much less conscious of what grade they are in and seem to feel quite comfortable learning with older and younger schoolmates. The students in this school stay together with the same team of teachers for three years. Teachers get to know the students well, students have access to all of the teachers in the team for three years, the group changes each year as sixth graders enter and eighth graders leave, and the wide variety of abilities and interests among students can be utilized to good advantage for a number of learning activities.

We described the school plan above because it appears to be working well as an entire school organization plan and because it seems to suggest the plausibility and even the advisability of forming middle grades reading classes comprised of older and younger students with a range of abilities and interests. Developing reading ability is such an amorphous process, especially after the primary grades, and is so dependent upon personal attributes that trying to administer separate, sequential curriculums for each of the middle grades is approaching the teaching of reading in a way that is contrary to what is known about the nature of the reading process and how individuals mature in their ability to use that process. Therefore, we would encourage administrators and teachers in the middle grades to experiment with cross-grade grouping for reading classes if they are not already doing so. However, we would advise against scheduling all of the high-ability sixth graders to the same class as the low-ability eighth graders or some other arrangement based only upon achieving homogeneity in skills development. The cross-grade scheduling plan we see as having most potential for student reading growth is one that has both high and low achievers at the two or more grade levels being combined scheduled in classes together. The highest achievers and the lowest achievers should be spread throughout the number of reading classes in the total schedule. In this way, the variety of groups that can be formed for skill development, functional reading, and recreational reading purposes is increased and older and younger students can profit socially and academically from sharing reading experiences with each other.

In short, grade lines need not be crossed to form good reading classes for middle grades students. However, we see no good reason why they should not be, and we believe the mixture of ages between eleven and fourteen for the purpose of development in reading may result in some excellent learning experiences if the curriculum is carefully planned.

What Materials Are Needed for Reading Classes?

In keeping with our emphasis upon creating balanced reading programs for middle grades students (that is, skill development, functional reading, and recreational reading), we recommend that reading classes be well-equipped with materials for these three phases or that students in reading classes have ready access to these materials in a central library or instructional materials center.

Because of the rapidly changing market in instructional reading materials it may be more misleading than helpful to specify titles and publishing companies here. By the time textbooks like this one are published the instructional materials market is likely to have changed enough to make what we would specify obsolete. However, the different types of materials are quite stable, so we shall tell our preferences in regard to the most popular types of materials for middle grades reading classes according to whether they would be used primarily for the skill development, functional reading, or recreational reading phase.

For skill development

The following six types of instructional materials should be considered by teachers of reading classes. All types are designed primarily for the purpose of helping students develop specific reading skills.

1 *Basal series (readers and workbooks).* For skill development we have yet to find better materials than those produced explicitly for the purpose of teaching skills. If basal readers and workbooks are presented to students as materials to help them master specific basic skills, and if teachers use them primarily and explicitly for that purpose, there is no need for students to be offended by them or for teachers to feel they are being condescending to students by using them. Basal materials designed for poor readers are especially helpful in teaching basic skills to students with poor skill development. Every reading class that enrolls poor readers should be equipped with a basal series designed especially for use with students with poor basic skills development. The manual accompanying the series will offer many good teaching suggestions and can be an invaluable resource for the teacher with minimal training in the teaching of reading.

2 *Supplementary skill development workbooks.* Several companies publish workbooks that are not coordinated with a series of readers, but are designed to give students practice in basic skills development. The workbooks usually are available at several difficulty levels. One or two sets (for variety) are valuable to help students improve word identification skills, vocabulary, and reading comprehension. Teachers should not expect the workbooks to teach the skills themselves. Assignments in the workbooks should be accompanied by careful explanation and guided completion of one or two exercises before students are allowed to proceed on their own. The key to the effectiveness of workbooks in building reading skills is in students' knowing what to do in them and doing it without error. There is little, if any, value to students in doing exercises incorrectly, even if they are required to go back and correct their errors. The deadliness of self-correction may more than negate any inherent good in the exercise.

3 *Kits.* Kits with short selections and accompanying exercises on cards, pamphlets, and other formats, often with self-scoring answer sheets, are plentiful on the market. The kits usually contain exercises for improving vocabulary, comprehension, and reading rate with material at several levels of reading difficulty. These kits are very helpful if teachers use them to teach specific skills and help students to master increasingly difficult material. The kits are also helpful in reading classes for giving students the practice they need to master skills they have already been taught. Teachers should be cautioned against expecting the mate-

rials in the kits to be self-teaching, although they sometimes give that impression. Several different kinds of kits should be available to students in reading classes so that they have material to use to practice skills with a minimum of teacher assistance and to give them a variety of formats to use for skill building.

4 *Reading machines.* Machines for teaching reading can be classified into three different types: (1) film projection devices, (2) tachistoscopic devices, and (3) pacers or accelerators. These machines are probably used best to get poorly motivated students interested in their gimmicry. However, in our experience the motivation is usually short-lived. While students sometimes improve their performance on the machines themselves and the coordinated exercises, the improvement does not always transfer to materials that are not used with the machines. If reading machines are used at all in middle grades reading classes, they should be used sparingly. For reading, the learner should be in control. When machines are used, they are in control. Poor readers cannot keep up with the machines and good readers observe that they don't read that way (that is, with a preset, mechanical pace). Reading machines are also expensive.

5 *Teaching films.* Educational films addressed to reading improvement may be helpful in reading classes to get students more interested in improving their reading and to teach some general concepts about reading and reading improvement. We would not advise their purchase for reading classes; but if they can be rented without putting too big a dent in the budget, we would recommend their occasional use. The big question is what materials will not be bought if films are purchased. We see them as a luxury item.

6 *Teaching games.* Games to teach reading skills, especially word identification skills, are also plentiful in the marketplace. All in all, we think the reading skills of middle grades are improved very little from these games unless their play is carefully supervised by a teacher and the playing of each game is followed by some reading assignments designed to put the skills used with the game to work with an actual reading selection. In classes reading games are probably used best to give students some fun with a reading-related activity and to provide them with some diversion that doesn't lead them too far from the purpose of the class. A variety of games would be useful in reading classes to be used for instructional "breaks" or to add variety and fun to the class.

For functional reading

1 *Reference materials* are needed to satisfy the informational interests of a class of middle grades students. The number and kind are obviously too great to be housed in a classroom. Therefore, the bulk of materials for the functional phase of the reading class curriculum must be housed in a central library or instructional materials center.

The materials needed run the gamut from encyclopedias, to newspapers, to magazines, to film strips, to atlases, to how-to-do-it books, to pamphlets, to catalogs, to *The Old Farmer's Almanac,* to you name it. Generally, short stories, poems, novels, and personal essays are not used. The need and the problem is to collect materials with the content desired at various difficulty levels. Materials designed for skills development are helpful in this regard. For example, kits, workbooks, and other materials for improving reading comprehension often contain selections with content keyed to students' interests at a variety of difficulty levels. These selections, without the skill-building questions and exercises, are excellent for students to use in their functional reading groups.

2   *Content area textbooks* are another source of material for use in the functional reading groups. They include those used in earlier grades, later grades, or those the students are currently using in their content area classes. Students intent upon finding information about a topic of their expressed interest are often more willing to use textbooks as resource material, even if they are the same books they were assigned in earlier grades, than they are to use them to complete an assigned course of study. We have known a few content area teachers who object to students using the textbooks from their classes in reading classes because the chapters are read out of sequence and because they fear students may resent re-reading them for their assignments. We think these arguments, if they are valid, are countered by the great value students receive from learning to value textbooks as a ready and life-long source of information to satisfy personal interests and needs, not to mention the reading-study skills they learn and practice with the actual materials for which they are learning the skills.

3   *Audiovisual materials* help meet the needs of those students whose reading ability is too poor to extract enough information from print to allow good participation in functional group activities. For these students picture books, films, filmstrips, phonograph records, and audio tapes can often provide the information they need. We recommend that teachers of reading classes (and of other classes for that matter) create a library of audio tapes for storage in the classroom, the central library, or the instructional materials center for poor readers to use instead of printed material. Good readers from senior high school English classes, drama groups, and forensic teams are excellent candidates for recording information on tape, as are teachers, parents, senior citizens, and other community members who are good oral readers.

For recreational reading

Very little needs to be said about materials for students to use for recreational reading in reading classes. We recommend that any reading material not offensive to community standards be permitted. We would include comic books, movie and television magazines, newspapers, popular novels, regardless of literary merit, and anything else students choose to read. However, some teachers limit students' recreational reading in class to books. We have no quarrel with this. However, the objectives of providing reading class time for recreational reading are somewhat different when materials restrictions are imposed.

Obviously, many kinds of materials at different difficulty levels need to be available to students, probably too many to be housed in the classroom. However, a small classroom library of recreational-type reading materials is good for students who don't like using the library or who need the daily stimulation of attractive covers and titles to get interested in a book or a magazine. In a school where one of these authors taught a reading class for low-ability ninth graders the librarian brought a cart of books, magazines, and newspapers into the classroom for students to use for a week. At the end of each week a new cartload was brought in, students were allowed to check out (in the classroom) any of the materials brought in the previous week, the materials not checked out were returned to the library, and the new cartload was left in the classroom for a week.

In that same school the librarian and the reading teacher started a paperback book store in a conference room at the entrance to the library. A local paperback book distributor furnished racks for the books and arranged to stock the shelves with whatever books were wanted and to change the selection on a periodic basis. A committee of parents, students, and teachers was formed to select the books, and the store opened for business. The end of the story is a happy one. Business flourished. Good and poor readers alike became regular customers, and the books the students purchased were used often during recreational reading time in reading classes. Davis (1975) describes the organization and implementation of book clubs in the middle grades. Book clubs can be very effective in the promotion of recreational reading and in getting recreational reading materials into the hands of middle graders.

What Might a Week in a Typical Reading Class Look Like?

Through our own experiences teaching middle school reading classes and from discussions with reading teachers in middle schools, we have come to the conclusion that students and teachers alike prefer some kind of pattern or system in the conduct of reading classes. The pattern should not be so rigid that the class becomes mechanical, and the patterns should include a variety of activities; however, a reading class with some routine is desirable. Perhaps the best characteristic of our preference for a middle school reading class is one that has a routine which can be interrupted when students and/or teachers tire of the routine and when students' learning is enhanced by interrupting the routine; for example, eliminating all skill development activities for a week or two in favor of some functional or recreational reading group activities.

With the understanding that teachers and classes differ and that classroom programs should differ accordingly, we suggest the following description of what a week in a sixth-, seventh-, or eighth-grade reading class might look like.

Monday

9:00–9:15   Silent reading of self-selected materials in recreational reading groups. Teacher reads a novel at teacher's desk or with one of the groups.

9:15–9:25   Conversation in small groups to share what was read in the preceding fifteen minutes. Teacher moves from group to group or participates with one group.

9:25–9:45   Students work independently with skill development exercises to strengthen skills weaknesses determined by diagnostic testing near the beginning of the school year. A program has been planned with each student so that he or she knows which materials to use, how to use them, and what kind of records to keep. The teacher either moves from student to student giving individual assistance or calls a group of students together in a corner of the room to teach some skill or to test progress with the development of one or more skills. In the twenty minutes given to skill development the teacher might work with two groups of students on skill development activities.

9:45–9:55   Teacher reads to students from novel, short story, newspaper, or magazine article.

   Note: Some teachers prefer to read to the students at the beginning of class and have the recreational reading groups at the end of class. Reading to students first is a good procedure for a class that has trouble settling down.

Tuesday

9:00–9:25   Repeat Monday's schedule.

9:25–9:45   Repeat Monday's schedule with the teacher working with different individuals and/or groups.

9:45–9:55   Repeat Monday's schedule.

Wednesday

9:00–9:10   Whole class discussion of procedural matters (for example, "I need a library pass." "Your groups are getting too noisy.") regarding functional reading groups.

9:10–9:45   Functional reading groups at work. Some students in the library or instructional materials center, some students in the classroom, one group in a conference room rehearsing their presentation. Teacher assists students in classroom. Librarians or instructional materials center staff members assist and/or supervise students in their area. Students in conference room are unsupervised.

9:45–9:55   One member from each group reports on group progress to date. Teacher reacts with praise and/or suggestions.

Thursday

9:00–9:25   Repeat Monday's schedule.

9:25–9:55   Functional reading groups at work.

Friday

9:00–9:15   Teacher reads to students.

9:14–9:35   Students work independently with skill development exercises. Teacher holds individual conferences with students regarding their skill development programs.

9:25–9:55   Students may (1) continue work with skill development exercises, (2) read whatever they are reading in their recreational reading groups or (3) work independently on their functional reading group projects. Teacher continues individual conferences.

The activities and schedule described above might be the basic curriculum for a middle grades reading class. The class would probably also include selected activities of the kind we describe in Chapters 4 and 7. In all likelihood, the class would also provide for frequent informal testing and formal testing at the beginning, end, and perhaps the middle of the class (see Chapter 11).

Vacca and Vacca (1974) describe a "stations approach" to middle school reading instruction which may also be of interest to teachers looking for an organizational plan for reading classes in the middle grades.

Something to Think and Talk About

I'm an English teacher, so reading classes are really none of my business. But I'm confused. Why are *all* students required to take a reading class in the upper middle grades? Reading classes are okay for poor readers, but why the good readers? Good readers should be spending their school time learning science, social studies, how to study good literature, mathematics, and how to do things they don't already know how to do.

Besides, I hear students talking about what a snap reading class is. One of my poorer seventh graders is reading a book in his reading class that looks more like a book for a third grader. I know I'm not in a popularity contest, but he got a "D" from me and a "B" in reading class. Why should I be a villain just because the reading teacher is a soft touch?

(See Appendix 2 at the end of the book for Authors' Response to "Something to Think and Talk About.")

References

Davis, Dorothy Voight (1975). "Book Clubs in the Middle Grades," *Journal of Reading* **19** (2): 150–153.

Heilman, Arthur W. (1977). *Principles and Practices of Teaching Reading*, 4th ed. Columbus, Ohio: Charles E. Merrill.

Vacca, Richard T., and Joanne L. Vacca. (1974). "Consider a Stations Approach to Middle School Reading Instruction," *The Reading Teacher* **28** (1): 18–21.

WORD IDENTIFICATION AND READING VOCABULARY

The emphasis given to word identification skills and reading vocabulary in the middle grades often depends on teachers' relative acceptance of two assumptions. The first of these is the supposition that middle graders, with some few exceptions, master word identification skills in the primary grades and that their reading vocabularies will develop almost automatically as a result. The second and somewhat related assumption revolves around the idea that word identification and reading vocabulary activities are necessarily either too boring, "babyish," or stifling for middle grade students to endure.

Our position on this matter is that both assumptions are unfounded and should be rejected out of hand. In other words, we believe, based on our own experiences and discussions with knowledgeable middle grade teachers, that attention must be given to the ongoing development of word identification skills and reading vocabularies during the middle grade years, with the proviso that the degree and type of instruction provided should be in an outgrowth of the individual needs exhibited by students as they deal with word identification and vocabulary in their daily reading activities.

Word Identification

Although such terms as word analysis, word attack, word recognition, and word identification are used interchangeably throughout the professional literature to denote the collection of skills employed by readers to process words in print, only the term word identification will be used for our purposes here. Our choice of this term was influenced by Smith (1971) who defines word identification as the ability to assign meaning, through a variety of devices, to printed words not previously encountered or learned. We agree with the three points Smith includes in his definition and will take a moment to expand on them. First, word identification is not complete until a reasonable meaning has been attached to the word in question. It is more than simply being able to pronounce a word. Second, Smith's variety of devices, to our way of thinking, refer to three sets of skills, context, structure, and phonics, and the understandings, attitudes, and strategies required to implement the skills. Third, word identification skills are most significant when the reader is called upon to process printed words not previously encountered or learned. To put it another way, the more familiar a given word becomes the fewer word identification skills the reader needs to process it until eventually the word becomes a part of the sight vocabulary, which means the reader can process it instantly in or out of context with minimal cues.

Word identification skills and teaching strategies in perspective

The skills of word identification, context, structure, and phonics are rarely employed in isolation and, if at all possible, should not be taught in isolation. Perhaps the combination of skills most often used by a reader attempting to identify an unfamiliar word is context and phonics. For example, in the sentence, "It is exciting to look at the *catalogue* and order toys for Christmas," the sixth grader may stumble on the word *catalogue*. Applying phonics ability that child may pronounce "kat-a-l . . . " but may not be able to finish the word. By reading the remainder of the sentence and combining contextual information with a partial pronunciation, it is likely that the student may think, "Oh! *catalogue*—I know that." Though in this section the subskills of word identification are generally discussed as separate entities, the reader is urged to remember that middle school students will often use them in combination—and they should be encouraged to do so.

Word identification ability is most effectively enhanced in the middle grades when instruction is based on assessment. Although it may be satisfactory to have all children complete identical exercises in first grade, this will rarely be necessary with older children. Not only can it be a waste of time, but drill activity in word identification can be a severe detriment to reading enjoyment when children are required to work on skills already mastered. Group-administered assessment devices can be easily constructed by the teacher, and many are commercially available. It is sound educational practice to pretest children before embarking on a new venture, and exempting those who do not need the experience. If the teacher intends to present a unit on prefixes and suffixes, it should develop from an assessed need. Perhaps a half dozen or even a majority of the pupils may demonstrate competence with structural analysis. These children could be allowed to read independently while the others are receiving instruction in structural analysis. Suggestions for diagnostic activity are included in some of the subsections which follow.

Context analysis

Context analysis is probably the most important word identification skill to be considered here since it is fundamental to the efficient use of the other word identification skills. Context analysis requires the reader to search for semantic and/or syntactic cues surrounding an unknown word as a means of reducing the possibilities as to what the word is. In other words, context analysis should be the first step in the strategy used by readers to identify an unfamiliar word. It involves simultaneously "figuring out" the way in which the word is used in a sentence or paragraph and asking the question, what word fits or makes sense here? Therefore, teachers should not just admonish children to "look it up in the dictionary" if they meet a word they do not know. Rather, they might better say, "Read before and after the word and make an educated guess: then confirm your prediction with a dictionary if necessary."

Context analysis also involves more than a procedure. It requires a mind set, an attitude, or a predisposition to act in certain ways. Consider, for example, the characteristics of the poorer readers in the middle grades. They are often called word-by-word readers. They seem to be able to process individual words but they do so haltingly and without any apparent anticipation of what is coming next. In contrast, the better readers seem to put words together into meaningful groupings. This type of reading can be attributed in part to their set to predict what will follow in a passage. It is this attitude of anticipation or expectancy about what is being read that is part and parcel of context analysis. Middle grade readers must be helped to realize that the serial occurrence of certain words will facilitate them in semantically anticipating words and phrases which will follow and in turn will help them in identifying unknown words.

To illustrate these points further, before turning to techniques for assessing and teaching context analysis, consider some of the types of context cues that readers should be aware of and searching for in written discourse.

1 *Direct definitions.* Many sentences or paragraphs directly define a word in context. Key words to direct definition are *is* and *means.* For example: A morpheme is the smallest unit of meaning in a language. To export products means to ship them out of the country.

2 *Restatements.* Some sentences or passages use different words to say the same thing. Key words to restatements are *in other words, that is,* and *or.* For example: A cockroach has two feelers, or antennae, on its head. He felt despondent. In other words, he was very sad.

3 *Description.* Sometimes words are defined through a description of the qualities or characteristics of the object. A key word in description is *is.* A Nupe is an African tribesman who lives in the middle belt of Nigeria. A tangerine is a round, orange, easily peeled citrus fruit.

4 *Comparison or Contrast.* Words may liken or contrast unfamiliar words with something known. Key words to comparison are *like, as* or *similar to,* and to contrast are *unlike, in contrast, but,* or *conversely.* For example: A machete, like a sword, can be very dangerous. Jim's fearlessness was in contrast to Gordon's timidity.

5 *Synonyms and Antonyms.* Synonyms do not necessarily have identical meanings and antonyms may not be exact opposites. Nonetheless, some sentences contain synonyms or antonyms of unfamiliar words which repeat the unfamiliar word. For example: I was elated when my father came home. Never before had I been so happy. Mr. Spratt was quite thin while his wife was certainly obese.

6 *Summary.* Various ideas may be summarized to provide clues to unfamiliar words. Several sentences may be necessary before the meaning emerges. For example: The umbilical cord was not tied properly. This resulted in an enlarged navel which looked like a small balloon tied a half-inch below the tip.

7 *Reflection of a Mood.* Sometimes a mood or tone is established which is reflected by the unfamiliar word. For example: The night was dark and still with no moon and no breeze. In the distance a howling sound began. Goose bumps formed on my neck. When I heard a footstep outside the bedroom window, I became utterly terrified.

These seven context cues have one thing in common; they aid the reader in applying meaning to the unknown word. In so doing, they may provide the reader with a flash of recognition that the word he or she has heard before; that is, the word is in the reader's listening vocabulary. This in turn may aid the reader to reassess pronunciation of the word and to adjust it accordingly if need be. However, even if a given word is neither pronounced accurately nor a part of one's listening vocabulary, the types of context cues suggested here permit the reader to attach meaning to the unknown word, which is the ultimate goal of word identification. Of course, it is hoped the reader will make note of such words so that accurate pronunciation as well as meaning will be applied to them in the future.

As a way of summarizing the types of context cues that do appear in written materials, consider the following sentences and determine which of the seven context cues is being employed by the writer.

1   The visitor was being *facetious* again, but her wit was always fun to have around during a cold winter's night.
2   The pointed-beaked, yellow-feathered, slope-winged *tanager* was beautiful.
3   My uncle was an *itinerant* preacher who traveled from town to town "saving souls" for money.
4   The *Ohio Cobbler*, a potato with a smooth skin and deep eyes, is better boiled than baked.

Assessing context analysis.   Some adolescent children have highly developed contextual analytic ability; others have practically none. To avoid unnecessary teaching and to determine which children may be exempted from lessons in context usage, it is desirable to administer context clues pretests. Two methods of assessing pupils' ability to use context clues are simple to construct, administer, and score.

The first is the *cloze procedure*. To construct a cloze test, select a passage of 100 to 200 words. Leave the first sentence intact; then delete every fifth word and leave a blank space. The modified passage can be duplicated and given to each member of the class whose task is to read it and fill in the blank spaces. Exact replacements and reasonable synonyms should be considered correct. Children scoring 75 percent or better are obviously skilled at using context clues.

A second diagnostic method calls for *interpretation of nonsense words* within context. For example, in the sentence, "For my twelfth *Schnorsle* I had a pizza slumber party and received a new bicycle," students are asked to define *Schnorsle* from among the following choices: (a) summer, (b) holiday, (c) birthday, (d) friendship. Any teacher can quickly construct ten or twenty similar items to determine which children are effectively using context.

Teaching context analysis. As stated earlier, one of the primary jobs for the teacher in this area is to help students develop a mind set to search the semantic and syntactic cues surrounding an unknown word as the first step in attempting to identify such a word. The importance of instilling a reader with the predisposition to act in this way cannot be overemphasized. It must be promoted by doing such things as asking students to predict where a given selection is going and the words the author might use to get there, or encouraging students to read around an unknown word and to make an educated guess as to what word would make sense in the given context.

There are a number of learning strategy activities which will help develop the procedures involved in the use of context and, to a degree, the mental set we have emphasized. Two of the activities we suggest are similar to the two methods of assessment just described; namely, the completion of cloze passages or the interpretation of nonsense words in sentences. We will not expand on what has been said about these activities other than to say they can be instructionally useful.

On the other hand, there are sentence completion activities using variations of the cloze procedure. Three of these include partial deletion of letters from the target word while the fourth provides prompts for the number of letters in the target word. Examples of the four presented from least to most difficult according to Emans (1971) are:

1 She had the pretty, red k__rch__f on her head.
2 She had the pretty, red k_____f on her head.
3 She had the pretty, red k_____ on her head.
4 She had the pretty, red k_ _ _ _ _ _ _ on her head.
   (Number of letters is indicated by the number of prompts.) (p. 186)

Some middle grades teachers develop teaching cycles parallel to these four sentence completion activities. On Monday, for example, the group is asked to complete five or ten sentences with the vowels deleted from the target word. The procedure continues through all four steps (one step a day) and is then followed on the fifth day by a reinforcement lesson which includes all four deletion types.

Two other types of sentence completion activities that can be used rely to varying degrees on prediction within certain constraints. Examples of these are:

1   After his twelfth pancake, Rex leaned back . . .

2   Like her mother, Betty enjoyed sewing, knitting, and . . .

3   On the way to his first day at the new school, John felt . . . (nervous, placid, amused)

4   The slumber party was really a . . . (blame, blast, block)

Sentence 1 is completely open-ended, and many words or phrases would fit. The choices to sentence 2 are somewhat more restricted (crocheting, needlepoint, or perhaps cooking). Sentence 3 requires a choice from among three possible moods, while sentence 4 combines phonics with semantics.

Seven other learning strategy activities are also worth considering here, since they can provide some variation to the instructional program.

Deciphering scrambled sentences:	The cheerleaders of the voices were loud.
	Flop Mr. Olson's was experiment a science.
Predicting author's words:	Students can read the title and one or two pages of a selection and then predict the words the author will use to present his or her thoughts in the remainder of the selection. The predictions can be recorded on the chalkboard and the students can determine the accuracy of their predictions.
Oral cloze:	One student is asked to read several sentences and then stop in mid-sentence. The listener's task is to supply either the next word or the remainder of the sentence.
Mystery messages:	Who took my prompbrush?
	My premp nee brushing.
Homographs:	Please wind my watch for me.
	The wind was very strong.
Mutilated messages:	You're brighter by far on a star.
	The drink that is excellence p_____.
	So hop in your c_____.
	Don't travel too _____.
	To load up the trunk with bright _____.

Secret codes: What season is this?_____
                                          1 2 3 4 5
                                    What kind of musician is he?

                            _____

                                    6 5 2 3 3 4 5

Again, the ability to use context to identify words is fundamental. As mature readers, it is probably the word identification skill we use most frequently. While students will have received some instruction in context analysis in the primary grades, middle grade teachers must give careful attention to the further development of this skill.

Structural analysis

Where context analysis concerns a search of *surrounding* context to aid in identifying a word, structural analysis refers to the examination of elements *within* the unidentified word itself. Structural analysis is sometimes called morphemic analysis. A "morpheme" is a linguistic term denoting the smallest meaningful unit of language. For example, the word *book* is one morpheme when it refers to a bound set of printed pages. It is a different morpheme when indicating a function of an arresting police officer. The word *books* has two morphemes, *book* plus *s*, which means plural. There are two classes of morphemes—"free" and "bound." Free morphemes are those which can stand alone (for example, *book* and *happy*). Bound morphemes cannot stand alone, but must be affixed to a free morpheme (*s* and *un* are examples of bound morphemes). The word *happy* can be expanded from one morpheme to two, as in *happiness*; or three, as in *unhappiness*. Structural analysis is the procedure of examining meaningful elements within a derived word. Sixth-grade students may be familiar with the word *happy* and the prefix *un* (usually meaning negative), but may not have previously encountered *unhappiness*. By analyzing the structure of the longer word and recognizing meaningful parts (morphemes), they may be able to identify the unfamiliar word.

Instruction pertinent to the most common prefixes, suffixes, and inflected endings, together with development of the habit and ability to examine words for known roots and affixes, can add greatly to a student's strategies for identifying unfamiliar words. Literally thousands of English words are formed from combinations of free and bound morphemes or from combinations of free morphemes. The latter, called compound words (for example, *stoplight, bookcase, sidewalk),* are very common in our language. Many children in the middle grades tend to "panic" when they run into long words and may often skip over them. Armed with ability in structural analysis, these long words no longer appear so terrifying.

In some books, syllabication is treated as a subskill of structural analysis. Syllabication, however, is intended to aid with the pronunciation of unfamiliar words, while structural analysis is concerned with morphemic identification.

Therefore, syllabication pronunciation strategies will be discussed in the section on phonics.

Teachers have sometimes inadvertently caused confusion in structural analysis by asking children to "look for little words within big words." With either a morphemic (structural analysis) or pronunciation (syllabication) objective, this guideline can be dangerous. Apply the guideline to such words as *father, tone, Asia, came,* and *potato,* and the problem will become evident.

To reiterate, structural analysis refers to the ability to identify words which are compound, roots with affixes or roots with variant endings. The remainder of this section will deal with the content and instruction of structural analysis.

While there are hundreds of prefixes, suffixes, and inflected endings, some of the most common are:

Prefixes

1) Negative
   - un - unable
   - in - inactive
   - im - impossible
   - il - illegal
   - ir - irresponsible
   - a - amoral
   - non - nonsense

2) Numbers
   - mono - (one) - monorail
   - uni - (one) - unicycle
   - bi - (two) - bifocal
   - di - (two) - digraph
   - tri - (three) -triangle

3) Out
   - ex - export

4) Before
   - ante - antedote

5) Against
   - anti - antisocial

6) Under
   - sub - submarine

7) Above
   - super -supernatural

8) Extra
   - over - overslept

9) Beneath
   - under - underline

Suffixes

1) Without
   - less - fearless

2) Having a quality
   - ness - kindness
   - ous - dangerous

3) The state of
   - ment - enjoyment
   - tion - education

4) Somewhat like
   - ish - childish
   - tive - destructive

5) The study of
    logy - zoology

6) Diseases
    itis - tonsillitis

7) To cause
    fy - beautify

8) Worthy of
    able - lovable
    ible - contemptible

Inflected Endings

1) Plural
    s - boys
    es - matches

2) Possessive
    's - John's
    s' - girls'

3) Tense
    ed - walked
    ing - walking

4) Comparison
    er - bigger
    est - biggest

Children will probably profit more from word building and word dissection activities than they will from memorizing long lists of prefixes, suffixes, and inflected endings. Word building activities may be of the following types.

Two columns of words can be given to children with the instruction to combine them to form compound words and write those down in column 3.

1	2	3
side	walk	_____
after	noon	_____
mail	box	_____
then		
sail	day	_____
rain	boat	_____
birth	coat	_____
and		
walk	est	_____
sweet	ing	_____
small	er	_____
and		
un	marine	_____
ex	happy	_____
sub	port	_____

In their book *Teaching Reading Vocabulary*, Johnson and Pearson (1978) have identified six types of compound words:

1   B is of A. A riverbank is the bank of a river. A fishbone is the bone of a fish.

daybreak, sunburn, coattail

2   B is from A. Cowhide is the hide from a cow. Moonlight is the light from the moon.

sawdust, hayfever, deerskin

3   B is for A. A bathroom is a room for a bath. Wallpaper is paper for a wall.

dishpan, briefcase, tearoom

4   B is like A. A boxcar is a car like a box. A catfish is a fish like a cat.

frogman, gulldog, cottontail

5   B is A. A bluebird is a bird that is blue. Ice cream is cream that is ice.

blueprint, blackbird, pipeline

6   B does A. A scrubwoman is a woman who does scrub. A racehorse is a horse that races.

towtruck, crybaby, flying fish

Based on this identification of the types of compound words, several activities can be constructed. Students can be asked questions like "What would you call the break of day?" "What would you call the dust from a saw? A pan for dishes? A fish like a dog?" etc.

After doing this with various real compound words it would be fun to have children create nonsense compound words—"What is the hose for a nose?" Certainly with primary grade children it is enough to expect them to learn important compound words. But with middle grade students, it would not be expecting too much to have them understand the *notion* of compounding to understand the relationships that create compound words.

Another activity asks children to define compound or other derived words.

1   pigtail   _____

2   riverbank   _____

3   toothache   _____

4   evergreen   _____

Root words which require the addition of other morphemes can be inserted in the context of a paragraph. For example: "I was____happy____than the whole class because I lost the race. We were play ____ football and I made six point ____. Then I start ____ feel ____ better."

Prefix, suffix, and inflectional meanings can be developed by asking the group to examine lists of known words and induce a definition.

unhappy	boys
unusual	girls
un-American	books
uncertain	papers
What does *un* mean?	What does *s* mean?

When children have developed facility in structural analysis and habitually apply it, thousands of previously unfamiliar words may become identifiable. Just as with context use, it is important to pretest the groups' ability to apply structural analysis. Some children do well with compound words but fall down on words which contain prefixes, suffixes, or inflected endings. Perhaps the best way to assess structural analytic ability is through the use of nonsense (synthetic) words. If real words are used, the teacher can never really be sure if the children possess the ability or if they just happen to know the words on the test. Compound nonsense words can be combined words consisting of real root words which do not "fit together": *broomfeather, dinnerplayer, basketmeet.* Nonsense words testing the ability to analyze words containing prefixes and suffixes would consist of a real root word and a real prefix or suffix which again "don't fit": *unball, prehead, applement, booktion, heartness.* Children who do very well on diagnostic pretests of structural analytic ability may be allowed to read freely while others are being instructed in these skills.

Phonics analysis

The sole purpose of phonics instruction (sometimes mistakenly called phonetics) is to help children *pronounce* unfamiliar words. It is known that the oral/aural vocabularies of children, particularly in elementary school, are larger than their reading vocabularies. Phonics instruction, then, is based on the assumption that if children can be helped to pronounce a word, there is a reasonable chance they will recognize it from their oral/aural vocabulary. For example, nearly all five-year-old children would know the word naming that room which contains the refrigerator, stove, and sink, and in which they eat two or three meals a day, but few would recognize the printed word *kitchen*. By applying phonics generalizations, the children might be helped to pronounce *kitchen*, thereby identifying the printed word. Phonics fails to work when children correctly pronounce a word but it is not within their oral/aural vocabulary.

Phonics is probably one area of word identification most often overlooked by teachers in the middle grades. This does not imply that middle grade teachers ignore phonics, but rather that they assume most phonics skills have been learned in the primary grades. The assumption may be valid for a sizable number of preadolescent and adolescent children, but research has shown that many of the poorer readers owe their reading deficiency to inadequate phonic (decoding) instruction (Chall, 1967).

The content of phonics. The body of "content" in phonics is the relationship which exists between letters and sounds. The English language utilizes a mere 42 to 47 (depending on dialect) phonemes, distinctive sound units. In most dialects there occur from 14 to 20 vowel and vowel/diphthong phonemes, and 26 consonant phonemes. To represent these 40-odd phonemes our alphabet uses 26 letters (graphemes) singularly and in combination. In all, there are several hundred letter-sound relationships in English. For example, the *f* sound can be spelled *f* as in *fun, ph* as in *telephone, ff* as in *cuff,* or *gh* as in *enough*. On the other hand, the letter *f* can represent the *f* sound as in *foot* or the *v* sound heard in *of*. Some letter-sound correspondences are extremely consistent and easy to learn (for example, *m* always represents the phoneme heard in *mom*). Other letters and clusters have variant correspondences which are predictable (*c* is either *cat, cot, cut* or *cell, city, cyst*), while still others have variant but unpredictable correspondences (the *s* in *sea, sugar, isle,* and *has*).

Because of the complexities of letter-sound relationships, some teachers abandon phonics instruction, considering it either hopeless or useless. It is neither. In his computer-assisted analysis of the structure of English orthography, Venezky (1970) demonstrated that letter-sound relationships are far more regular and systematic than previously believed, especially when elements larger than single letters are considered. Likewise, Berdiansky *et al.* (1969) argue that "regularities between the spelling and sound patterns found in English words far outweigh the irregularities . . . " (p. 2) An excellent resource book with a thorough listing and discussion of the letter-sound relationships of English is Mazurkiewicz's *Teaching About Phonics* (1976).

To reiterate the purpose of phonics instruction, the word will be recognized from the child's oral/aural vocabulary. Since the oral/aural vocabularies of children are much larger than their reading vocabularies, phonics is a highly useful skill of word identification.

To this end, six "categories" of letter-sound correspondences will be described in this section: single consonants (c), consonant clusters (cc), single vowels (v), vowel clusters (vv), "patterned irregularities," and syllables. In addition, procedures for teaching and assessing the use of phonics generalizations will also be mentioned.

Johnson (1973) has suggested sequences for four categories of letter-sound relationships *based on their frequency* of occurrence in printed English *and* the *predictability* of their major phonemic correspondences. The four categories are single consonants, consonant clusters, single vowels, and vowel clusters. His suggested sequences are:

1 *Single Consonants*

Set 1 (these five would be introduced first but in any sequence): *d - dog, n - now, l - lamp, m - me, b - boy.*

Set 2: *p - put, f - fat, v - vine, r - rob, h - hope, k - kiss, y - you, s - sat,* then *has, c - cat,* then *city, t - top,* then *nation.*

Set 3: *j - jump, w - water, z - zoo, x - tax,* then *exam, q(u) - quit, g - get,* then *gym.*

2 *Consonant Clusters*

Digraphs: *sh - shoe, th - this,* then *thin, ch - chin,* then *chorus, ng - sang, ph - photo.*

Double Consonants: *ss - pass, ll - hello, rr - narrow, tt - better, mm - summer, nn - manner, ff - coffee, pp - happy, cc - buccaneer,* then *success, dd - ladder, gg - egg,* then *suggest, bb - rubber, zz - puzzle.*

Consonant Blends: Consonant *+ l - black, climb,* consonant *+ r - grow, drop,* and consonant *+ s - stop, smile, string.*

3 *Single Vowels*

i - if, then *mild,* then *police, a - act,* then *about,* then *ape (*also *want* and *call), o - hot,* then *of,* then *note (*also *off), u -ugly,* then *puny,* then *tube (*also *bull), e - bed,* then *jacket,* then *blaze (*also *item* and *he).*

4 *Vowel Clusters* (Including vowel diphthongs)

Set 1 (these six would be introduced first but in any sequence): *io - action, ea - meat,* then *bread, ou - ounce, ee - bleed, ai - maid, au - because.*

Set 2: *oo - soon,* then *good, ow - own,* then *now, oi - coin, ay - day.*

Set 3: *ia - alias, oa - boat, ie - movie, ue - blue, iou - delicious, ua - actual, ui - ambiguity.*

The preceding sequences apply more to beginning instruction in phonics but can be drawn from in helping those middle grades children who need work with phonics. In addition to these sets of letter-sound correspondences, there are two others which must be included:

1 *Patterned irregularities*

knee, knife, knew and bomb, comb, lamb, wrap, wring, wreck.

2 *Syllabication*

Syllables are word segments containing vowel sounds. Unlike morphemes, which are units of meaning, syllables are units of sound with rather imprecise boundaries. A number of syllabication generalizations have been postulated as strategies for helping children pronounce unfamiliar words. In general, consonant arrangements reveal clues as to the pronunciation of preceding vowels. For example, a single consonant followed by a vowel usually signals the reader that the preceding vowel is long: *take, baby, David.* Any vowel followed by a consonant cluster is usually short: *dinner, candy, napkin.* Some teachers instruct pupils in rules for dividing words into syllables. Three rules commonly taught are given below.

In VCV words, divide before the consonant: *ba/by*

In VCCV words, divide between the consonants: *nap/kin*

In VCle words, divide before the consonant: *a/ble*

Too often, however, the emphasis has been on "line drawing" rather than on pronunciation where it belongs.

Since most phonics generalizations have been learned by the time children enter the middle grades, it is essential that diagnostic pretests be given. Many children will pass the test and need not undergo intensive phonics instruction, while it will be apparent that others need considerable practice with this skill. Phonics tests using nonsense (synthetic) words should be used to avoid confusion between knowledge of the skill and knowledge of the word. If the teacher is planning a lesson on hard and soft *c* and *g*, a simple test can be quickly constructed. Synthetic words such as *ced, cack, cobe, cide* would provide better evidence about a child's mastery of the generalization than if parallel real words were used: *cent, cap, cone, city.* If a child pronounces the latter four correctly it may just indicate they are part of the sight vocabulary. If the four synthetic words are pronounced correctly it indicates that the rule governing hard and soft *c* has been learned.

Approaches to teaching phonics. Many phonics programs, workbooks, and games are commercially available. Most basic reading programs include direct or supplementary phonics exercises. The wide array of specific strategies can be grouped into four general areas. Some programs (and teachers) follow only one of the procedures, while others use combinations of approaches. The four most common methods are:

1 *Synthetic approach.* Pupils are taught specific letter-sound correspondences and rules and are then guided to synthesize them into words. For example, *c* + /k/, *a*→/ae/ and *t*→/t/ are learned as separate correspondences. They are then blended to form /k ae t/ - *cat*. This approach requires considerable memorization of rules. In one program, for example, children are required to memorize more than 60 rules in the first grade alone.

2 *Analytic approach.* This method structures the inductive learning of letter-sound correspondences by analyzing patterns in words the children already know. Children who know the words *bat, box, baby, Bob,* and *boy* are helped to discover that they all begin with the same letter and sound. In teaching the role of the final silent *e* as a signal that the previous vowel is long, the analytic approach would not teach the rule but would organize a lesson which builds upon previously learned words. For example, if children know:

rat		*rate*
not	Final *e* is added to	*note*
cut	each word to transform	*cute*
met	it to:	*mete*
bit		*bite*

3 *Functional approach.* Two or more correspondences per week are taught by asking the pupils to bring objects or pictures from home which contain the correspondences being studied. Thus real objects, pictures of real objects, and perhaps children's names or other common names (teachers, streets, towns, buildings) become reinforcement terms. While learning the *t* sound, there may be children in the class named Tom, Tina, Toby. Children may bring from home such "*t*" objects as *toys, train, tops, twigs,* a *tent, tomato soup,* a *towel,* etc. Each item is discussed with the class emphasizing the common sound and spelling. Later, work can be done utilizing some of the objects and including labels or captions.

4 *Games approach.* Hundreds of phonics games have been developed and are commercially available. Most teachers, however, construct their own phonics games—often with the help of their pupils. The teacher-made games may be more relevant because they can be made to pertain specifically to the needs, interests, and backgrounds of the children in the class. Two books, one by Ekwall (1970), the other by Durkin (1972), contain excellent suggestions for constructing phonics games. A few of the many possible game creations are: consonant digraph dominoes (played the same as dominoes but with picturable digraph words instead of dots), vowel bingo (identical to bingo, but *a e i o u* substituted for *bingo;* words containing vowels are read by the caller and the children cover them if they are on their card), and blends race (a board game in which children shake dice, move a few spaces, and must read a word containing a blend).

Whatever method or combination of methods a middle grade teacher selects, it will be important to the increasingly mature and sophisticated interests of the early adolescent child. Many children at this age will need help with phonics but will resist it if the activity seems "babyish." The books by Mazurkiewicz (mentioned earlier), and Durkin's *Strategies for Identifying Words* (1976) and *Phonics, Linguistics and Reading* (1972) offer comprehensive discussions of phonics instruction.

Reading Vocabulary

By the end of first grade, a grade typically characterized by the intensive reading instruction provided, most children can read only a few hundred words. In contrast, the reading vocabularies of adults range from 100,000 to 200,000 words (Smith, 1971). Thus, between six years of age and adulthood most individuals exhibit a phenomenal growth in reading vocabulary development, and middle grade teachers can play an important role in determining the nature and extent of this growth.

From our perspective, middle grade teachers can influence their students' reading vocabulary development in three ways. First, they can provide instruction for the ongoing development of the word identification skills and the use of these skills by students to assign meaning to new words rather than simply to pronounce them. In so doing they enable their students to learn new words independently. Second, middle grade teachers can provide direct instruction in this area. The importance of such instruction becomes evident when one thinks of the many words—words that are general and are used in all aspects of communication and words that are specialized and are peculiar to a certain content area, profession, or endeavor—middle graders meet in their everyday reading. Third, teachers can involve their students in the use of vocabulary reference materials, particularly the dictionary and the thesaurus. Both works have valuable potential for reading vocabulary development, although the dictionary is often misused and the thesaurus is often overlooked.

Since the word identification skills were discussed earlier, only an occasional comment will be made about them in this section; however, their significance to vocabulary development, particularly when accompanied by wide reading, cannot be overemphasized. The focus of the remainder of this section, then, will be on teaching techniques and strategies designed to facilitate students' reading vocabulary development through direct instruction and the use of references, with emphasis on the former.

Techniques and strategies for teaching reading vocabulary

There are times when teachers must introduce certain words and help their students identify them. In the middle grades, such words are often dealt with in this way because (a) they are potentially troublesome words which may hamper comprehension of required reading in the content areas, or (b) they do not lend themselves to identification through the independent application of the word identification skills on the part of the reader. When words of this nature are located, the PDAR strategy—*p*resentation-*d*iscussion-*a*ctivity-*r*einforcement— has proved to be useful to middle grade teachers.

1 *Presentation.* The words may be written on the chalkboard or individual pages may be duplicated for each child. It is preferable to present the word in the context (oral or written) of a phrase or a sentence, rather than in isolation.

For example, a reading assignment in a middle school home economics course may contain the words *nutritious, vitamin,* and *organic.* Instead of simply writing the words on the board in isolation, the teacher could introduce them as follows:

Nutritious foods give us better health.

A *vitamin* pill each morning . . .

Organic foods such as wheat germ . . .

Some teachers have their students keep a dictionary of new words for each subject or alphabetized across subjects.

2 *Discussion.* Discussions of unfamiliar words often begin by inquiring whether any children recognize any of the words. It is sometimes more desirable to ask, "Can anyone use *vitamin* in a sentence?" than to ask for a definition of the word. It is easier to use a word in context than to define it, yet its use demonstrates whether or not the word is known. Discussions may develop from children's experiences with the words or previous exposures to the words in other reading. The teacher is the best judge of how much or how little time to spend on vocabulary discussion. Discussions of new vocabulary can lead to other important words and can become very profitable learning experiences as a result.

3 *Activity.* There may be times when the number of new words being introduced is sufficiently large to warrant a vocabulary building activity following the discussion. This activity could take the form of duplicated activity pages (that is, matching words to definitions or pictures, or completing sentences from among the new sight words) or a game [for example, anagrams—"The pirate drew his *words.*" (sword)]. (Spache, 1976)

4 *Reinforcement.* Few sight words are learned from one exposure. After the reading assignment containing the new sight words has been completed, teachers may wish to provide reinforcement activities. The reinforcement activity may be simply a vocabulary check test or it may be an exercise page or game. Middle grade children tend to enjoy—and learn best from—active involvement: Creative artwork portraying the new words; construction of graphs, tables, or models; and writing sales advertisements, poems, or short stories which utilize the new words are but a few of the many reinforcement activities which are possible.

While it would be terribly inefficient, and even detrimental, to attempt to teach 200,000 words through the procedures cited above, most middle grades teachers will experience the need to teach some sight words nearly every day. In addition to using worksheets and teacher-made or commercially prepared word games, it is imperative that students do a good deal of wide reading so that reinforcement of the newly learned words occurs.

It seems important to note, at this point, that vocabulary is an inseparable component of reading comprehension. One must know and understand words in order to read meaningfully. Certainly, comprehension of print involves a good deal *more* than knowing words, but *without* word knowledge there would be no comprehension. In essence, comprehension involves building bridges from the new to the known—from associating and linking what we read with what is already in our experimental, conceptual, and linguistic storehouse.

For this reason, Pearson and Johnson (1978) have identified three classifications of reading vocabulary: words with simple associations, words with complex associations, and ambiguous words. The four types of simple association words include *synonyms* (big-large, tiny-small), which are words with similar meanings; *antonyms* (help-hinder, large-small), which are words with opposite meanings; *association* (blue-sky, green-grass), which are words which often co-occur in the language; and *classes* (cheek, jaw, nose, eyes), which are words which belong to the same category (for example, parts of a face). The two types of complex associations are *analogies* (fish is to lake as cow is to pasture), which show how two pairs of words can be related in similar ways and *connotative/denotative* words (sweet-cloying, hungry-ravenous), which are two words that are synonymous at one level of meaning (denotative), but are different at a connotative level. The three types of ambiguous words are *multi-meaning words* (draw, to sketch; draw, to tie), which are simply words with more than one meaning; *homographs* (CONduct-conDUCT), which are words that are spelled alike but have different pronunciations and meanings; and, finally, *homophones* (fair, fare), which are words that are pronounced the same but have different spellings and meanings. Of these, the associative categories of vocabulary development (synonyms, antonyms, associations, classes, analogies, and connotative/denotative words) are vitally important. They hold potential to help us relate new words to known words. The remaining three categories, ambiguous words, homographs, and homophones, are perhaps less powerful but are particularly troublesome.

In our judgment, the types of words Pearson and Johnson identify as important, together with content area words and a process called semantic mapping (described later), can form the bulk of direct vocabulary instruction in the middle grades. The remainder of this section presents some suggestions for teaching these nine categories of vocabulary and concludes with a description of semantic mapping.

1 *Synonyms.* Any matching activity such as the following provides good practice with identifying synonyms.

a) Find the word with a similar meaning to the keyword:

walk - stroll, swim, run

b) Find the word that means about the same thing as the underlined word in the sentence:

Marian sent me a greeting card.

rang   mailed   hopped

c) Rank these synonyms on their degree of intensity:

love	breeze	surprise
like	gale	amaze
adore	wind	flabbergast

2 *Antonyms*

   a) Change the underlined word so the sentence has an opposite meaning.

   Jack <u>likes</u> to have a Manhattan.

   Deanne <u>destroyed</u> Ed's ego.

   Jenny bet on an <u>ugly</u> horse.

   b) Matching activities like a and under synonyms can be used:

   sit - stand, open, hope

   c) Add words along the continuum between these antonyms:

   beautiful _____ ugly

   hot_____cold

   love _____ hate

3 *Associations*

   a) Match the words in these two columns:

dark	lark
happy	sky
tall	lamb
gentle	building
blue	night

   b) Fill in the blanks (with or without multiple choices):

   The sky is _____.

   Wayne _____ the race yesterday.

   Kenny is _____ as a lamb.

   c) The following activity deals with synonyms, antonyms, and associations simultaneously:

Word Pair	Synonyms	Antonyms	Associations	Unrelated
shade-tooth				X
happy-glad	X			
solid-liquid		X		
purr-kitten			X	

4 *Classifications*

   a) Have the students sort words from a list into proper categories:

happy	dressing	car
truck	sad	source
topping	bus	angry
cart	delighted	wagon
envious	oil	gravy
(Feelings)	(Wheeled Vehicles)	(Food Toppings)

b) The following activity adds an additional constraint by having students classify by category and initial letter:

	Games	Jobs	Places	Household Items
S	Soccer	Steno	San Francisco	Stool
M	Monopoly			
I				
L	Lotto			
E				

c) A third activity requires students to delete a word that does not belong with others in a group:

toe	ankle		carrots	onions
foot	head		raisins	potatoes

5   Analogies

a) Prepare lists of analogous words. After giving a few examples, have the students complete the list and add more if they can:

Animal	-	Group	Animal	-	Home
chickens	-	flock	robin	-	nest
bees	-	swarm	lion	-	den
lions	-		snake	-	
fish	-		bear	-	
wolves	-		bees	-	

b) Now reverse the process by having students provide the first word in the analogous pair.

Animal	-	Sound	Animal	-	Offspring
cat	-	meow	lion	-	cub
dog	-	bark	goat	-	kid
	-	roar		-	calf
	-	chirp		-	kitten
	-	whinny		-	puppy

6   Denotative/Connotative Words

a) Create sentences with a word deleted. Give several synonymous words that fit in the deletion and discuss with the class the different meanings. (A thesaurus is a good source for synonyms):

1. It is true that I _____ her sister.

   (tolerate, love, admire, adore, like)

2. Last night Dick felt _____ when he went down into the basement to fix the fuse.

   (nervous, afraid, panicky, frightened, scared, terrified)

b) Have students write sentences that best show the meaning of such pairs of words as the following:

ignorant - uninformed	lean	- skinny
sweet - cloying	ate	- gorged
cute - gorgeous	sneaked - strode

7   Ambiguous Words

a) Provide the class with lists of multi-meaning words. For each word have them see how many different sentences they can generate—each of which must clearly show a different meaning for the word.

fun	plant	frame
check	back	skip
order	draw	swing

b) Write multi-meaning words in several contexts and ask the students to latter match sentences or definitions as shown below.

I like to *watch* football.	Your *watch* is nice.
Mom gave me a new *watch*.	Did you *watch* the parade?
We fished off the *bank*.	financial institution
The *bank* is where I save.	side of river

8   Homographs

Prepare a list of homographs for the students. Using a dictionary if need be, have them create two sentences for each homograph showing the different meanings.

live	close	tear
minute	conduct	wound
perfect	clove	hinder

9   Homophones

Activities similar to the homograph activity work equally well with homophones. Provide homophones that are to be used in meaning designaling sentences:

fair	fare	sun	son	grate	great
threw	through	steel	steal	plain	plane
two	to	meet	meat	blue	blew

Other activities that are useful in helping expand a reading vocabulary include the preparation of semantic maps and doing semantic feature analyses.

Semantic maps

To construct semantic maps the teacher begins by writing a word on the center of the chalkboard. Class members are then asked to suggest words that are associated with the word on the board. As they call out words the teacher writes them on the board in clusters according to semantic category. In the illustration below, the teacher has written the word *tree*. As the students offered words related to tree the teacher wrote them on the board in clusters which were kinds of trees, uses of trees, parts of trees, and things that can be done to or in trees.

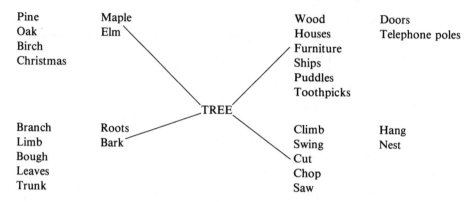

Pine	Maple	Wood	Doors
Oak	Elm	Houses	Telephone poles
Birch		Furniture	
Christmas		Ships	
		Puddles	
		Toothpicks	

TREE

Branch	Roots	Climb	Hang
Limb	Bark	Swing	Nest
Bough		Cut	
Leaves		Chop	
Trunk		Saw	

Once the semantic map has been completed and discussed, the teacher selects any one word from it and uses it to begin a new map:

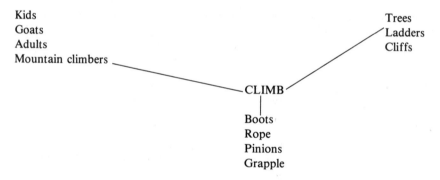

Kids	Trees
Goats	Ladders
Adults	Cliffs
Mountain climbers	

CLIMB

Boots
Rope
Pinions
Grapple

Semantic mapping provides an endless and rather intriguing way to expand vocabulary and it follows the principle of comprehension mentioned earlier—proceeding from the new to the known. It is an excellent way to learn words through classification.

Two related semantic activities are these. Give the students a word and ask them to list as many things as possible that can be done to or with it. For example, if the word is *meat*, children will immediately list:

cook it	roast it
eat it	buy it
fry it	sell it

But some children will list other less typical responses:

hunt it	saw it	burn it
season it	hit it (Rocky)	smell it
chew it	wrap it	taste it
cut it	freeze it	brown it

Depending on the target word, the lists can get quite lengthy and it is likely that many children will be adding new semantic attributes to their understanding of a rather common word.

Next one of the attributes given to the previous word (*meat*) can be selected; for example, "chew it." Now the task is for the class to list as many things as they can think of that can be chewed.

gum	food	meat	rugs
candy	fingernails	taffy	tables
nuts	cuds	lips	chairs

And this can go on and on—"What or who can chew?" "Girls, boys, people, bears, puppies, etc." "What can puppies do?" "Chew, bark, jump, growl, etc." Again, the point of all these activities is that new vocabulary is best learned when it is fit into the framework of experience and knowledge of the learner—building bridges from the new to the known.

To close this section, it seems appropriate to point out that vocabulary is the one aspect of language over which we never achieve mastery. The discrimination and articulation of phonology is completed for nearly all children by age six or seven. By early adolescence we have at our command nearly all the syntactic structures of English. But vocabulary and all the fine semantic shadings continue to expand and develop throughout life. The point, again, is that reading vocabulary instruction is a profitable and essential component of the reading program in the middle grades.

The dictionary and thesaurus

Dictionaries contain much more than the definitions of words. Spelling, pronunciation, formal, informal, the idiomatic usage, word derivations, and abbreviations are included in a good dictionary. Many English words have multiple meanings. While context will often provide the author's intended meaning of an unfamiliar word, the dictionary encourages vocabulary growth by listing all possible meanings. As an example, consider the word *run*. Most people would probably define *run* as some sort of human movement faster than a walk. Consulting a dictionary would show that *run* has many other meanings.

Jane made a home run.

She has a run in her nylon.

This was the bus driver's last run.

Birch Street runs past my house.

Mary will run for office.

Occasionally, consulting a dictionary will be necessary for word identification. This may be particularly true as children do required reading in the content areas of science, math, social studies, industrial arts, home economics, and English literature. However, since the other identification skills discussed previously usually operate more quickly, the dictionary will be used mainly for vocabulary development, pronunciation accuracy, or spelling reinforcement. Nonetheless, it cannot be denied that some middle grades children may need practice with alphabetization (*come, comic, cone, conic*), using guide words found in the top corners of dictionary pages, identification of synonyms and antonyms, levels of usage (formal, informal, technical, slang), pronunciation keys and symbols, word derivations (for example, *postmortem*), abbreviations, and foreign words.

Similarly, a thesaurus can be an outstanding vocabulary reference for both reading and writing. Unfortunately, except for college students taking freshman English, it is an often-neglected resource. Despite the availability of such imaginative thesauruses for young people as Patrick Drysdale's *Words to Use A Junior Thesaurus* (Wm. H. Sodlier, Inc., 1971), a great many middle grade students are completely unaware of the contents or the possibilities of a thesaurus. The basic difference between a dictionary and a thesaurus is that a dictionary presents the meanings of alphabetically listed words while a thesaurus presents the synonyms (and in some cases antonyms) for a given meaning or concept. Thus, a dictionary goes from word to meaning and a thesaurus goes from meaning to word. Middle graders need to be aware of the possibilities both references have to offer and the ways they can be used to expand their reading and writing vocabularies.

A Final Word

During the course of this chapter, we have tried to indicate that word identification and reading vocabulary development should not be thought of as separate entities. Many middle grade children who fail reading comprehension tests do so because of inadequate word identification skills and reading vocabularies. They stumble and sometimes skip over unfamiliar words. As a result comprehension is hindered by the lack of continuity in identifying words as well as by the semantic shortages they possess. Children with poor word identification skills and with limited vocabularies become frustrated with reading and some wish to avoid it entirely. The middle grade reading program that includes a strong word identification and reading vocabulary element can do much to help students improve their general reading abilities and interest in reading. To this end, we suggest the books by Johnson and Pearson (1978) *Teaching Reading Vocabulary*, and Dale and O'Rourke (1971) *Techniques of Teaching Vocabulary*. They are excellent resources for additional learning activities in word identification and reading vocabulary.

Something to Think and Talk About

At a middle school faculty meeting attended by all fifth-, sixth-, and seventh-grade teachers, Mr. Smith of X Publishing Company was the scheduled speaker. He had obviously taken a public-speaking course or he belonged to an after-dinner speaking club, for his delivery was witty, eloquent, and most convincing. His message was supported by judicious use of skillfully prepared audiovisuals, and the main thrust of his talk was the demonstration of a new set of reading materials written especially for middle grade youngsters.

In addition to interesting stories, vivid illustrations, and comprehensive teachers' manuals, the program contained a tightly sequenced, thorough word identification component. Every story was followed by word identification exercises keyed to words within the story. The teachers' manuals contained explicit instructions for relating the story and exercises to appropriately sequential workbook pages. Teachers were admonished not to skip any pages since all skills built upon previous ones and paved the way for subsequent ones.

After Mr. Smith's presentation, a faculty committee was appointed to decide whether or not to purchase the program. After careful comparisons with the presently used materials, it was concluded that the major difference was the comprehensive word identification component of Mr. Smith's program.

What decision should the committee reach? (See Appendix 3 for Authors' Response to "Something to Think and Talk About.")

References

Berdiansky, Betty, Bruce Cronnell, and John J. Koehler (1969). *Spelling Sound Relations and Primary Four Class Descriptions for Speech-Comprehension Vocabularies of 6–9 Year Olds*. Englewood, California Regional Lab of Educational Research and Development.

Chall, Jeanne (1967). *Learning to Read: The Great Debate*. New York: McGraw-Hill.

Dale, Edgar, and Joseph O'Rourke (1971). *Techniques of Teaching Vocabulary*. Palo Alto: Field Enterprises Publications.

Durkin, Dolores (1972). *Phonics, Linguistics and Reading*. New York: Teachers College Press.

Durkin, Dolores (1976). *Strategies for Identifying Words*. Boston: Allyn and Bacon.

Ekwall, Eldon E. (1970). *Locating and Correcting Reading Difficulties*. Columbus, Ohio: Charles E. Merrill.

Emans, Robert (1970). "Use of Context Clues." *Teaching Word Recognition Skills.* Newark, Delaware: International Reading Association, 1971, pp. 181–187.

Johnson, Dale D. (1973). "Suggested Sequences for Presenting Four Categories of Letter-Sound Correspondences." *Elementary English* **50**: 888–896.

Johnson, Dale D., and P. David Pearson (1978). *Teaching Reading Vocabulary.* New York: Holt.

Mazurkiewicz, Albert J. (1976). *Teaching About Phonics.* New York: St. Martin's Press.

Pearson, P. David, and Dale D. Johnson (1978). *Teaching Reading Comprehension.* New York: Holt.

Smith, Frank (1971). *Understanding Reading.* New York: Holt.

Spache, Evelyn B. (1976). *Reading Activities for Child Involvement*, 2d ed. Boston: Allyn and Bacon.

Venezky, Richard L. (1970). *The Structure of English Orthography.* The Hague: Mouton.

A TAXONOMY OF READING COMPREHENSION AND RELATED TEACHING STRATEGIES

What we have to say about the teaching of reading comprehension is based upon three interrelated assumptions. *First,* reading does not take place unless comprehension occurs; therefore, the teaching of reading comprehension is fundamental at all levels of education. *Second*, in order to make intelligent curricular and instructional decisions, teachers must have a way of conceptualizing reading comprehension. *Third*, teaching strategies and tactics that grow out of a sound conceptualization of reading comprehension can facilitate students' abilities to think about, respond to, and use in different ways the information they gain through reading. It is with these three assumptions in mind that we present a taxonomy of reading comprehension, a logically derived schema for practical use by teachers, and the related teaching strategies and tactics which follow.

A Taxonomy of Reading Comprehension

Some time ago Guszak (1967) conducted an investigation that has contributed to our thinking about the teaching of reading comprehension. The purpose of this often-quoted study was to determine the types of questions teachers used to stimulate their students' reading comprehension. To accomplish this objective Guszak observed and tape recorded reading classes at the second-, fourth-, and sixth-grade levels. He then transcribed the recordings into written protocols and categorized the teachers' questions and students' responses according to a Reading Comprehension Question-Response Inventory he devised.

Three of Guszak's findings have significance here. First, the vast majority of the teachers' questions, overall and at each grade level, were literal; that is, they called for the recognition or recall of explicit information in the selection read.

Although the proportion of such questions decreased as the grade level increased (78.3 percent, 64.7 percent, and 57.8 percent for grades two, four, and six, respectively), it is safe to say that literal comprehension was emphasized during the reading classes observed. Second, although evaluation questions requiring judgments on the part of students were the next most frequently asked, Guszak indicated that the majority of such questions required only yes or no responses. Third, he found that inferential questions—that is, conjecture and explanation combined—were third in order of frequency, although the materials used in the classes were amenable to more emphasis on questions of this nature.

On the basis of his findings, Guszak drew two pertinent conclusions. First, teachers in the study placed excessive emphasis on literal questions, regardless of the nature of the materials or the ability levels of the readers involved. Second, teachers did not use inferential and evaluative questions to a greater extent because Guszak found that they did not have a clear conceptualization of reading comprehension from which to work.

We agree with Guszak's conclusions not only because of his findings but because of our experiences in working with teachers in this area of reading instruction. We have found that teachers must have a clear and manageable blueprint of reading comprehension in their minds' eye in order to make intelligent curricular and instructional decisions in this area; decisions that have a bearing on the objectives, materials, assessment procedures, and strategies used to teach reading comprehension.

It is because of this conviction that the Taxonomy of Reading Comprehension (Taxonomy) presented in Table 4.1 was developed.[1] As shown in the table, the Taxonomy defines and classifies reading comprehension into four major abilities and provides examples of tasks that we feel will contribute to the development of each of the four abilities.

Four principles governing the use of the Taxonomy

First, it is important to think of the Taxonomy (Table 4.1) as a teaching tool and not as a complete classification of comprehension abilities and tasks. The four major categories are literal recognition or recall, inference, evaluation, and appreciation. They were logically derived and represent the spectrum of interrelated comprehension abilities we feel students should have at their disposal and be able to demonstrate.

Other authors take a somewhat different point of view in terms of the abilities to be classified. For example, Ruddell and Bacon (1972) developed a communication model, derived from a psycholinguistic research base, in which identification and recall, analytical, integrative, and evaluative abilities are classified within the interpretation process category. More recently, Pearson (1977)

---

1. The Taxonomy is based on a synthesis of the work of Bloom (1956), Guilford (1958), Sanders (1966), and Guszak (1967), as well as our logical analysis of reading comprehension.

proposed a schema for conceptualizing reading comprehension abilities and tasks that takes the form of a three-dimensional cube. The first dimension specifies the size of the linguistic unit involved in the task; for example, word, sentence, paragraph, or passage. The second dimension specifies six logical relationships that only exist between linguistic units; for example, subordinate–holstein is a type of cow. The third dimension is called textual explicitness but is not yet developed in complete detail for various reasons. Nevertheless, Pearson believes his schema can classify almost any comprehension task in captivity and can be used by researchers and practitioners alike.

Table 4.1 *Taxonomy of Reading Comprehension*

1.0 *Literal Recognition or Recall.* Literal comprehension requires the recognition or recall of ideas, information, and happenings that are explicitly stated in the materials read. *Recognition Tasks*, which frequently take the form of purposes for reading, require the student to locate or identify explicit statements in the reading selection itself or in exercises that use the explicit content of the reading selection. *Recall tasks* demand the student to produce from memory explicit statements from a selection; such tasks are often in the form of questions teachers pose to students after a reading is completed. Two additional comments seem warranted with regard to literal comprehension tasks. First, although literal comprehension tasks can be overused, their importance cannot be denied, since ability to deal with such tasks is fundamental to ability to deal with other types of comprehension tasks. Second, all literal comprehension tasks are not necessarily of equal difficulty. For example, the recognition or recall of a single fact or incident may be somewhat easier than the recognition or recall of a number of facts or incidents, while a more difficult task than either of these two may be the recognition or recall of a number of events or incidents and the sequence of their occurrence. Also related to this concern is the hypothesis that a recall task is usually more difficult than a recognition task, when the two tasks deal with the same content and are of the same nature. Some examples* of literal comprehension tasks are:

1.1 *Recognition or Recall of Details.* Students are required to locate or identify or to call up from memory such facts as the names of characters, the time a story took place, the setting of a story, or an incident described in a story, when such facts are explicitly stated in the selection.

1.2 *Recognition or Recall of Main Ideas.* Students are asked to locate or identify or to produce from memory an explicit statement in or from a selection which is the main idea of a paragraph or a larger portion of the selec-

1.3 *Recognition or Recall of Sequence.* Students are required to locate or identify or to call up from memory the order of incidents or actions explicitly stated in the selection.

---

*Although the examples in each of the categories are logically ordered from easy to difficult, it is recognized that such a finite hierarchy has not been validated. Therefore, the user of the Taxonomy should view the examples as some of the tasks that might be used to help students produce comprehension products that relate to the type of comprehension described in each of the four major categories of the Taxonomy.

Table 4.1 *(continued)*

1.4 *Recognition or Recall of Comparisons.* Students are requested to locate or identify or to produce from memory likenesses and differences among characters, times in history, or places that are explicitly compared by an author.

1.5 *Recognition or Recall of Cause and Effect Relationships.* Students in this instance may be required to locate or identify or to produce from memory reasons for certain incidents, events, or characters' actions explicitly stated in the selection.

1.6 *Recognition or Recall of Character Traits.* Students are requested to identify or locate or to call up from memory statements about a character which help to point up the type of person he or she was when such statements were made by the author of the selection.

2.0 *Inference.* Inferential comprehension is demonstrated when the student uses a synthesis of the literal content of a selection, personal knowledge, intuition, and imagination as a basis for conjectures or hypotheses. Conjectures or hypotheses derived in this manner may be along convergent or divergent lines, depending on the nature of the task and the reading materials involved. For example, inferential tasks related to narrative selections may permit more divergent or creative conjectures because of the open-ended possibilities provided by such writing. On the other hand, expository selections, because of their content, may call for convergent hypotheses more often than not. In either instance, students may or may not be called upon to indicate the rationale underlying their hypotheses or conjectures, although such a requirement would seem to be more appropriate for convergent rather than divergent hypotheses. Generally, then, inferential comprehension is elicited by purposes for reading, and by teachers' questions which demand thinking and imagination which are stimulated by, but go beyond, the printed page. Examples of inferential tasks related to reading are:

2.1 *Inferring Supporting Details.* In this instance, students are asked to conjecture about additional facts the author might have included in the selection which would have made it more informative, interesting, or appealing.

2.2 *Inferring the Main Idea.* Students are required to provide the main idea, general significance, theme, or moral which is not explicitly stated in the selection.

2.3 *Inferring Sequence.* Students, in this case, may be requested to conjecture as to what action or incident might have taken place between two explicitly stated actions or incidents; they may be asked to hypothesize about what would happen next; or they may be asked to hypothesize about the beginning of a story if the author had not started where he or she did.

2.4 *Inferring Comparisons.* Students are required to infer likenesses and differences in characters, times, or places. Such inferential comparisons revolve around ideas such as: "here and there," "then and now," "he and he," "he and she," and "she and she."

2.5 *Inferring Cause and Effect Relationships.* Students are required to hypothesize about the motives of characters and their interactions with others and

Table 4.1 *(continued)*

with time and place. They may also be required to conjecture as to what caused the author to include certain ideas, words, characterizations, and actions in this writing.

2.6 *Inferring Character Traits.* In this case, students may be asked to hypothesize about the nature of characters on the basis of explicit clues presented in the selection.

2.7 *Predicting Outcomes.* Students are requested to read an initial portion of selection, and on the basis of this reading to conjecture about the outcome of the selection.

2.8 *Inferring about Figurative Language.* Students, in this instance, are asked to infer literal meanings from the author's figurative use of language.

3.0 *Evaluation.* Evaluation is demonstrated by students when they make judgments about the content of a reading selection by comparing it with external criteria— for example, information provided by the teacher on the subject, by authorities on the subject, or by accredited written sources on the subject; or with internal criteria—for example, the reader's experiences, knowledge, or values related to the subject under consideration. In essence, evaluation requires students to make judgments about the content of their reading, judgments that have to do with its accuracy, acceptability, worth, desirability, completeness, suitability, timeliness, quality, truthfulness, or probability of occurrence. Examples of evaluation tasks related to reading are:

3.1 *Judgments of Reality or Fantasy.* Students are requested to determine whether incidents, events, or characters in a selection could have existed or occurred in real life on the basis of their experience.

3.2 *Judgments of Fact or Opinion.* In this case, students are asked to decide whether the author is presenting information which can be supported with objective data or whether the author is attempting to sway the reader's thinking through the use of subjective content that has overtones of propaganda.

3.3 *Judgments of Adequacy or Validity.* Tasks of this type call for the readers to judge whether the author's treatment of a subject is accurate and complete when compared to other sources on the subject. In this instance, then, the readers are called upon to compare written sources of information with an eye toward their agreements or disagreements, their completeness or incompleteness, and their thoroughness or superficiality in dealing with a subject.

3.4 *Judgments of Appropriateness.* Evaluation tasks of this type require the students to determine whether certain selections or parts of selections are relevant and can contribute to resolving an issue or a problem. For example, students may be requested to judge the part of a selection which most appropriately describes a character. Or they may be called upon to determine which references will make significant contributions to a report they are preparing.

Table 4.1 *(continued)*

3.5 *Judgments of Worth, Desirability, or Acceptability.* In this instance, students may be requested to pass judgments on the suitability of a character's action in a particular incident or episode. Was the character right or wrong, good or bad, or somewhere in between? Tasks of this nature call for opinions based on the values the readers have acquired through their own personal experiences.

4.0 *Appreciation.* Appreciation has to do with students' awareness of the literary techniques, forms, styles, and structures employed by authors to stimulate emotional responses in their readers. Obviously, tasks which fall into this category will require varying degrees of inference and evaluation, but their primary focus must be on heightening students' sensitivity to the ways authors achieve an emotional as well as an intellectual impact on their readers. More specifically, appreciation involves cognizance of and visceral response to: (a) the artistry involved in developing stimulating plots, themes, settings, incidents, and characters, and (b) the artistry involved in selecting and using stimulating language, in general. Examples of tasks that involve appreciation are:

4.1 *Emotional Response to Plot or Theme.* Tasks of this type are based on the assumption that the plot or the theme of a given selection has stimulated and sustained a feeling of fascination, excitement, curiosity, boredom, sentimentality, tenderness, love, fear, hate, happiness, cheerfulness, or sadness. Provided this assumption is met, the students may be requested to determine what the author did in the process of developing the plot or theme that elicited a given emotional response.

4.2 *Identification with Characters and Incidents.* Some appreciation tasks should require students to become aware of the literary techniques and devices which prompt them to sympathize or empathize with a particular character, or to reject the character, for that matter. Other tasks should require students to consider the placement, nature, and structure of events or incidents which cause them to project themselves into the action.

4.3 *Reactions to the Author's Use of Language.* In this instance, students are required to recognize and respond to the author's craftsmanship as reflected in his or her selection of and use of words. Such tasks may deal with the connotations and denotations of selected words and the influence they have on a reader's feelings. In addition, students should at times note figures of speech; for example, similes and metaphors, and the effect their use has on the reader.

4.4 *Imagery.* Tasks of this nature require the reader to recognize and react to the author's artistic ability to "paint word pictures." In other words, students should become sensitive to the techniques an author uses in order to enable them to see, smell, taste, hear, or feel things through reading.

Source: Thomas C. Barrett, "Taxonomy of Reading Comprehension," *Reading 360 Monograph* (1972). Lexington, Massachusetts, Ginn and Company. A Xerox Company. Reprinted by permission.

A second principle governing the use of the Taxonomy is that the tasks listed within each category should not be thought of as discriminate comprehension subabilities. Rather, they should be viewed as examples of tasks that will contribute to the development of the ability used to designate a category. It should also be understood that the tasks listed are illustrative and not exhaustive. Others can be added.

A third principle for users is that the order of the categories in the Taxonomy does not mean that tasks in category 4.0 will always be more difficult than those in category 3.0, and so on across the categories. Although students must have a literal understanding of what they read before teachers can expect them to respond in other ways, it is not inconceivable that some literal tasks may be more difficult than some inferential tasks. Another way of putting the principle is to suggest that the learning tasks for any category can range from easy to difficult. Difficult tasks from one category, therefore, may be more linguistically and intellectually demanding than the easy tasks from another category, regardless of the apparent hierarchical ordering of the categories within the Taxonomy.

Finally, users must keep in mind that the thrust of a task, in terms of the response it is intended to stimulate, is the primary criterion for placing it in a category. Certainly, there is overlap among the categories. Appreciation may very well involve inference and evaluation, while evaluation may require inference. In fact, there are those who would argue that these three classifications may be thought of as three types of inference. Nevertheless, the best way to classify a seemingly ambiguous comprehension task is to determine the primary intent of the task, in terms of the behavior it calls for, and to label it according to the category whose description best matches its intent.

Three uses for the Taxonomy

The Taxonomy (Table 4.1) is intended to provide teachers with an understandable and manageable framework for planning, teaching, and evaluating reading comprehension. Keeping in mind the principles just discussed, let us briefly consider some ways such an instrument can be used in relation to these purposes.

Evaluation of comprehension tasks in teachers' guides. The Taxonomy can be a useful tool for determining the relative emphases teachers' guides give to various types of comprehension tasks (a) across different programs, (b) across levels within a program, and (c) within a program for a particular level or a specific selection. As a matter of fact, it has been employed for these purposes on a number of occasions. Textbook selection committees have used the Taxonomy as an aid in arriving at final decisions about which programs to recommend for purchase. Teachers within a single school have studied the reading programs they use to see how they deal with comprehension across levels. More specifically, many teachers have applied the Taxonomy to the comprehension tasks suggested in the teachers' guide for particular stories to determine which tasks would be most appropriate for their students. In summary, the Taxonomy can be used to evaluate the comprehension tasks proposed in teachers' guides within and across reading programs. Such information can be of paramount importance in a time when teachers are being held accountable for their students' achievement in this area.

Evaluating current and designing new classroom comprehension tasks. As we stated earlier, teachers sometimes fall into the trap of being unidimensional in their selection of comprehension tasks; that is, they place excessive emphasis on literal comprehension regardless of the needs and abilities of their students. The Taxonomy can help teachers to avoid this pitfall if it is used: (a) to evaluate teacher-created comprehension tasks currently being implemented in the classroom and (b) to design new comprehension tasks. Such devices as the purposes teachers set for their students prior to reading and the questions they ask during and after reading are amenable to these procedures, for example. The point here is that the tasks used by teachers to stimulate and develop comprehension, whatever they are, should help students think about, respond to, and utilize what they read in diverse and expanding ways. The Taxonomy can help teachers accomplish this important objective.

Evaluating and designing comprehension tasks are, from our perspective, probably the Taxonomy's most important reasons for being. Our experience in helping teachers to use the Taxonomy for these purposes suggests that a clear understanding of the definitions and descriptions contained in the instrument is fundamental. Teachers must have such an understanding in order to distinguish literal, inference, evaluation, and appreciation tasks one from the other.

Beyond a clear understanding of the definitions in the Taxonomy, teachers must have a mind set, a predisposition, if you like, to employ comprehension tasks which require responses beyond the literal level. This predisposition must be invoked whenever the reasons for reading, the materials, and the students make such tasks possible. Suffice it to say that the development across the four reading comprehension abilities described in the Taxonomy must be viewed as the goal of instruction in this area. It is a goal that will be achieved by students through exposure to diverse comprehension tasks related to many and varied reading selections.

Designing comprehension tasks that complement the materials being read. The third instructional use of the Taxonomy is to aid teachers in designing comprehension tasks that place emphasis on the strength of a particular reading selection. In other words, some selections are more conducive to certain comprehension tasks than they are to others.

For example, mystery stories and stories with intricate plots permit, even encourage, emphasis on inference. Such writing almost demands the reader to conjecture about: "What will take place next?" "Who will do what?" "Why did someone do what he or she did?" On the other hand, biographies, historical accounts, and even some pieces of historical and science fiction can provide the basis for having readers evaluate the selection in terms of its accuracy, completeness, or objectivity. Such tasks may require students to compare a selection or parts of a selection with other sources on the topic, to interview an expert on the topic, or to do library research on the topic before final judgments are made. Fiction can add yet another dimension, depending on the artistry of the author, by providing the stimulus for different appreciational responses on the part of the reader. What this attempts to suggest is that teachers must have enough confidence to permit them to rely on their own judgments about what a particular selection has to offer for the development of students' comprehension abilities.

Teaching Strategies and Tactics

The remainder of the chapter will devote attention to selected strategies and tactics for teaching reading comprehension. The strategies and tactics will be organized according to the four major categories of the Taxonomy and will clarify ways in which the abilities discussed in the Taxonomy can be viewed and developed.

Literal recognition or recall

As defined in the Taxonomy, literal comprehension requires the recognition or recall of explicit items of content from the reading material. Recognition tasks are usually presented in the form of purposes for reading, while teachers' questions are the predominant stimuli for encouraging recall behaviors. The critical thing to remember with respect to either of these types of task is that the students' responses can be judged right or wrong by referring to the explicit statements of the author.

Literal comprehension is fundamental. Although reading authorities have warned against too much emphasis on literal comprehension in our reading programs, the fact remains that literal comprehension is fundamental. Teachers must be certain their students possess this basic ability before presenting them with tasks which require other kinds of comprehension abilities. This principle is particularly important for teachers in the middle grades, since the reading materials increase in difficulty during this period and middle grade students are divergent in the reading skills and abilities they possess.

To put it another way, the degree of emphasis given to literal comprehension tasks in the middle grades should vary across groups and individuals and should reflect the teacher's knowledge of students' comprehension abilities and the reading materials being used. With students who are known to possess literal comprehension abilities, for example, the oral or written questions a teacher uses to stimulate a follow-up discussion over a selection should place little or no emphasis on literal comprehension; rather, they should focus on inference, evaluation, or appreciation, depending on the nature of the selection. On the other hand, a particular teacher may have to dwell on literal recognition and recall tasks before attempting other types of tasks when students are less capable in literal comprehension.

One final comment warranted here concerns those *middle grade students who are extremely deficient in literal comprehension.* Although not a happy circumstance, it does exist. For example, some students in grades four through eight can pronounce the words in a reading selection but cannot demonstrate even a modicum of literal comprehension. What can be done for such students will undoubtedly depend on the instructional personnel available and the ability of those persons to deal with the needs of such students. Nevertheless, to attack this type of problem one has to begin with the literal comprehension of sentences.

A basic activity here would be to require such students to read and respond to one-sentence directions which may be as simple as: "Draw two circles." "Write your name in the upper left-hand corner of this page." "Write the color of your shoes." "Draw a map of the way you walk to school." Next the directions can be expanded into two and three sentences which require a series of related responses. For example:

"Draw two circles.
Color one black and one red."

"Write your name in the upper left-hand corner of this page. Write your address under it. Write the data in upper right-hand corner of this page."

Although such activities may seem too simple for fourth- to eighth-grade students, they are needed by some. One way or the other, the beauty of directions is that the students' literal comprehension can be verified by their responses. The Gates-Peardon reading exercises, although somewhat dated, and the Barnell-Loft materials expand upon this idea, but both go beyond the one- or two-sentence format.

Simons (1971), who studied the ability of students to recover the deep structure of sentences, designed some tasks that may help students who need work on literal comprehension. The first task requires the student to select one sentence out of three which is not a paraphrase of the other two. Simons's examples for this task are:

1 a) What the boy would like is for the girl to leave.

   b) For the boy to leave is what the girl would like.

   c) What the girl would like is for the boy to leave.

2 a) He painted the red house.

   b) He painted the house red.

   c) He painted the house that was red.

3 a) The girl asked the boy when to leave.

   b) The girl asked the boy when she should leave.

   c) The girl asked the boy when he should leave.[2]

The second measurement task proposed by Simons is related to the first and adds a cloze element; that is, the students are asked to make the second sentence have the same meaning as the first by placing the proper words in the blanks provided. Simons illustrates this as follows:

1 a) For the girl to leave is what the boy would like.

   b) What the _____ would like is for the ____ to leave.

2 a) He painted the house that was red.
   He painted the _____ _____.

3 a) The girl asked the boy when to leave.

   b) The girl asked the boy when ____ should leave.[3]

Simons's final measurement suggestion, another which may have instructional possibilities, requires students to provide paraphrases for written sentences presented to them. For example, a stimulus sentence might be: "It was Peter who repaired the bike." An appropriate paraphrase which would demonstrate literal comprehension on the part of a student might be: "Peter fixed the bike."

What is being said here is that the exercises cited by Simons do appear to provide instructional possibilities for middle grade students who need to begin with the sentence unit in order to develop their literal comprehension abilities. Obviously, the next step for such students would involve literal activities based on paragraphs.

Not all literal tasks are easy. Although it has been suggested that literal comprehension is basic, all literal comprehension tasks should not be assumed to be equally or unduly easy. There is no doubt such tasks can be developed to

---

2. Herbert P. Simons, "Reading Comprehension: The need for a New Perspective," *Reading Research Quarterly* **6**, 3 (Spring 1971): 359. Reprinted by permission.

3. *Ibid.*

progress from easy to difficult. For example, consider four questions which are logically sequenced from easy to difficult:

1   Who was the story about?

2   What were two events which took place in the story?

3   What are the three things Harry did in the story and the order in which he did them?

4   Can you tell us three events that led to the discovery of America, including where they took place, when they took place, who was involved, and how they were related?

The logic of this sequence is based on two principles. First, the more bits of information we ask a reader to identify or recall, the more difficult the task. (It might be added that recall tasks appear to be more difficult than counterpart identification tasks.) Second, tasks, particularly recall tasks requiring sequencing or ordering of events, are more difficult than those requiring the recall of a number of events in any order. Of course, the author's style, the student's background of information, and the concept load of the materials, among other things, interact with the task in determining its degree of difficulty.

Nevertheless, middle grade teachers can and should vary the degree of difficulty of the literal comprehension tasks they employ with the idea of helping all students to grow in this ability.

The why and how fallacy. Although the point to be made here might have been included with the general principles governing the use of the Taxonomy, it will be presented now because it is of specific importance to the teaching of literal comprehension. The "why and how fallacy" relates to the commonly accepted assumption that questions which begin with *why* or *how* are automatically more intellectually demanding than questions which begin with *what, where, when,* or *who.* As Sanders (1966) has indicated, however, one cannot classify a comprehension task on the basis of what the task appears to demand of the reader. For example, it is possible that several *why* or *how* questions might appear to demand inference or evaluation, when, in fact, they are literal because the author has explicitly answered the questions. To avoid the "why and how fallacy" teachers must be totally familiar with the reading materials their students are using, since any question the author explicitly answers is a literal comprehension task, regardless of its surface appearance.

Inference

As described in the Taxonomy in Table 4.1, inference is demonstrated by students when they use a synthesis of the literal content of a selection and their personal knowledge, intuition, and imagination as bases for conjectures or hypotheses. It is further suggested that the conjectures or hypotheses may be convergent or divergent, depending upon the nature of a given task and the reading materials involved. The remainder of this section will be devoted to differentiating between these two dimensions of inference and will provide some instructional strategies and tactics related to them.

Convergent inference. There should be times in the reading program when students are involved in drawing what we will call convergent inferences. Such inferences are based primarily upon the data or information provided by the author and the logic and imagination of the student. Moreover, tasks requiring this ability will produce inferences or conjectures which students and teacher will agree upon and which ultimately can be confirmed by the information provided by the author. Tasks that require this ability should aid students in drawing logical conclusions from given data or premises and should aid them in reading in the content areas where this ability becomes increasingly important in the middle grades. Furthermore, tasks devoted to stimulating convergent inferences can help students to better analyze and synthesize information, particularly if they are required to provide rationales for their hypotheses or conjectures.

One of the values of working on convergent inferences is that the procedures students are guided through provide a sound model for their independent reading. Take as an example the task of predicting outcomes utilized as a strategy by a teacher with a group of eight seventh graders as they read *The Magnificent Failure* by Robert Falcon Scott.[4] The selection is an excerpt from Scott's diary which deals with the last 29 days of his party's return from the South Pole after they found that Roald Amundsen had reached the goal first. The teacher and students worked together in the following manner:

Teacher: After writing the title of the selection on the board, she asked the students what they thought a selection with such a title might be about.

Student 1: It might be about someone who built an airplane that wouldn't fly. You know the movie *The Magnificent Men and Their Flying Machines*, or something like that.

Student 2: Maybe it's about a man who ran for President but didn't get elected.

Student 3: Maybe it's about someone like that girl in the last Olympics who tried so hard to win a gold medal in swimming but didn't make it.

Student 4: I bet it's about someone who tries to help other people but always fouls up.

While the students responded the teacher paraphrased their conjectures and recorded them on the board. When none of the remaining four students had anything to add, she asked each of them to bet on one of the predictions listed on the board.

---

4. Found in Helen M. Robinson *et al.*, *Challenges*. Glenview, Illinois: Scott, Foresman, 1967, pp. 332–343.

Next, she asked the students to open their books to page 333 and place a piece of paper over page 332. This was done because an introductory paragraph above a picture of Scott's party on page 332 gives away the outcome of their adventure. After the papers were in place, she asked the students to slide them up far enough so they could study the picture. Then she asked them to reconsider their predictions in light of the new evidence.

Student 5:   I don't think any of the ideas we have on the board fit. The guys in the picture are all bundled up and they look like they are in a lot of snow. Maybe they are mountain climbers who failed to reach the top of Mount Everest or something.

Student 6:   You know, I think this might be about those guys who snowmobiled to the North or South Pole, but I thought they made it and there aren't any snowmobiles in the picture.

At this point, the teacher explained Scott's disappointment in not reaching the South Pole first, and told the group that they were going to read the entries in his diary as the party returned from the Pole. She then asked them to read the first two entries in the diary recorded on page 333 and to predict how the party's return from the South Pole would come out.

Student 3:   The entry for March 1 made it sound like they would have smooth sailing, but the entry for the next day doesn't sound so good. Maybe they are going to have a lot of trouble.

Student 5:   I don't know, but I think another group will come down with dog sleds and help them get back.

Since the rest of the group thought these were pretty good possibilities, the teacher asked them to read the entries in the diary through March 10 and to reconsider the conjectures they had recorded on the board.

Student 5:   I still think they are going to be rescued.

Student 3:   I still think they are going to make it on their own.

Student 8:   I don't know but it sounds like Oates is going to die. Maybe none of them will get back.

After the students had read the diary entry of March 19, they reconsidered their predictions for the last time. At that point, the data were overwhelmingly in support of predicting that all of Scott's party would perish. All of the students converged on this conclusion and confirmed it by reading the remaining entries in Scott's diary.

There is no doubt the teacher could have asked the students to provide more in the way of rationales for the hypotheses they put forward during the reading of *The Magnificent Failure*. Nevertheless, the value of the strategy used by the teacher was that it provided a model for the kind of behavior her students should use when they read independently.

What is proposed here is not dissimilar in intent from one form of Stauffer's (1975) group-directed-reading-thinking-activity in which students actively predict, read, and prove while the teacher acts as a facilitator. Over the years Stauffer has argued that such an approach is superior to the usual basal series' approach to teaching a selection; that is, the teacher sets the purposes and the students read to achieve the purposes set for them. He feels this is the case because the directed-reading-thinking-activity involves students in actively setting their own purposes and achieving them. This is, of course, what they should do when they read independently.

Singer (1976) is another person who supports the notion of helping students to become actively involved in setting their own purposes or questions for reading. His active comprehension approach involves teaching students to ask their own questions so that they can become independent in their efforts to derive meaning from written messages. Singer's point, along with those of Stauffer and our own, supports the notion that active personal, inferencing, hypothesizing, predicting, or questioning facilitates the ability of students to become effective, independent comprehenders.

Divergent inference.[5] While the purpose of convergent-inference tasks is to have students come to an agreed-upon hypothesis, which may be a verifiable conclusion based on the data supplied by an author, divergent inference calls for the use of the reader's imagination or creativity. Thus, the primary thrust in this area should be to use reading materials, particularly literary materials, as stimuli for the students to produce divergent conjectures or hypotheses which cannot be judged right or wrong. The need for this thrust is that the curriculum in the middle grades provides few situations where the youngsters can use their imaginations without their thought products undergoing such judgments. If the development of creative thinking is a viable goal of education, and we feel that it is, reading tasks calling for divergent inference can contribute to this cause.

To illustrate some of the ways in which divergent or creative conjectures might be stimulated, consider how some of the tasks under "Inference" in the Taxonomy might be related to the short story "Cemetery Path" by Leonard Q. Ross. "Cemetery Path" concerns a timid little man named Ivan who frequented a saloon on the edge of the village cemetery. On the night in question, a lieutenant and some of his cronies had been taunting Ivan. Finally, the lieutenant pulled out his saber and challenged Ivan, who was frightened of the cemetery, to take it, walk into the cemetery, and stick it in the ground at the foot of the largest tomb in the center of the cemetery. If the lieutenant found his saber in the designated spot in the morning, he told Ivan he would pay him five gold rubles. Unexpectedly, yet for a variety of reasons, some subtle and some not so subtle, Ivan took the saber,

---

5. Although Chapter 7, "Using Reading to Foster Creativity," details many teaching-learning activities related to divergent thought production, the tasks mentioned in the Taxonomy, which stimulate this type of thinking, will be highlighted here.

left the saloon, entered the cemetery muttering supportive comments to himself, reached his destination, kneeled, and plunged the saber into the ground. As Ivan began to rise, he felt something holding him in place. He became panic stricken. Try as he might, he could not stand up. The next morning he was found dead, with the saber pounded into the ground through the folds of his long coat.

Ross's story provides many possibilities for stimulating divergent conjectures which youngsters might demonstrate through such oral, written, or dramatic responses as:

Students could be asked to write, tell, or dramatize a sequel to the story. Such efforts could focus on the effects Ivan's death had on the lieutenant, on activities at the saloon, or on other people in the village.

Students could conjecture about events that took place before the fateful night. Obviously, Ross had to start somewhere, but the reader can imagine what may have transpired before the story began.

Students may be called upon to hypothesize about things that occurred in the early lives of the lieutenant and Ivan that made them the men they were.

Students could conjecture about events that may have occurred during the story which Ross did not include. For example, what things—not mentioned by Ross—might have happened to Ivan as he crossed the cemetery?

To further illustrate the opportunities that literature provides as a stimulus for the production of divergent inferences, consider a lesson one of the authors observed in an eighth-grade classroom. In this instance the teacher had the students read "Cemetery Path" to the point where Ivan reached the tomb, kneeled, and plunged the saber into the ground. When the reading reached that point the teacher asked each of the students to write an ending for the story. A limited sample of the endings produced illustrates the rich potential of such an activity.

Ivan, timid yet not so fearful, freezing yet not so cold, left the cemetery anxious to face his enemies on the next day.

Slowly Ivan got up and began to walk toward his little shack. The wind did not blow so hard and the cold did not cut. He would go to the saloon tomorrow, like a hero, and collect his five gold rubles. But for now he knew he did need them. For this moment, he was complete.

Ivan stood and thought aloud. "I've been the brunt of their jokes too long. Now I'll show them by waiting here to meet their taunts and get the money." Ivan was found the next day frozen to death.

What Ivan didn't know was that the lieutenant and a few of his friends had set a trap at the grave. They had stationed a person behind the tombstone. When Ivan drove the saber into the ground, the man hidden behind the tombstone groaned and then came at Ivan. Ivan was terrified. He tried to run but he couldn't. Then he awoke from his terrible dream.

The morning dawn reflected a bright flash from the saber's handle. Ivan won the bet, but the five golden rubles would not be his, for the lieutenant was not brave enough to come after the saber, not even in the full light of day.

The next morning Ivan approached the small band of men gathered silently around the partially exposed hilt. He seemed to be somewhat taller, somewhat bolder, and, in a way, relieved. "Ah, Lieutenant, my rubles," he demanded with a glint in his eyes. "Ivan the Terrible is here!"

After the students completed their writing, they shared their endings to see how many different ideas they had produced. The important thing here was that the teacher did not place emphasis on the quality of the writing or the plausibility of an ending. Even when the students read Ross's ending to *"Cemetery Path"* the teacher did not encourage the group to see whose ending was most accurate; rather, the class discussed the idea that the story could have ended in many ways and that some of their endings were possible alternatives. All in all, the efforts in this lesson on predicting outcomes were a step in the direction of encouraging youngsters to use their imaginations, to produce divergent inferences, without concern for being right or wrong.

Evaluation

As described in the Taxonomy (Table 4.1) evaluation involves the act of judging. Some authors call this critical reading; however, the term critical seems to carry a connotation of fault finding or of judging things negatively. While readers are required to do this at times, it should not be the main thrust of work in this area. On the other hand, the term evaluation seems to us to have a broader connotation which implies the making of both positive and negative judgments. Moreover, the term evaluation seems to imply a process—a process which should place emphasis on such ideas and actions as: (a) the importance of being systematic, logical, and objective when one is evaluating what is read; (b) the need for the reader to reserve judgment until adequate data are available; that is, the avoidance of leaping to conclusions, opinions, or overgeneralizations; (c) the understanding that judgments can be and are influenced by the reader's values; (d) the awareness that writers' values often influence what and how they write. For these reasons we feel evaluation is appropriate for designating the types of comprehension we are concerned with here.

The Taxonomy also suggests that evaluation tasks require the reader to make judgments about the content of a selection or selections by comparing it to *external* or *internal criteria*. Before going on to some practical suggestions for teaching evaluation in the middle grades, let us consider these two types of criteria, since the teacher will often find them the most difficult elements to deal with when working on evaluation in the middle grades.

External criteria may be in the form of information provided by the teacher, an outside authority on a given subject, or an accredited written source on the subject. For example, a sixth-grade class which one of the authors observed was in the process of completing its study of bees. As a culmination and evaluation session for their study a beekeeper from a neighboring university was invited to share his knowledge with the class for an afternoon. In the process the beekeeper confirmed, augmented, and clarified much of the information the class had gained through its research on bees. After the beekeeper left, the teacher and the class spent time in a final evaluation session. Using the observations and information the beekeeper had provided as criteria, the class made judgments about the adequacy, validity, and appropriateness of the information they had gained through their study of bees.

Another example of using external criteria as a basis for judgment was illustrated by fifth graders who read a brief account of the life of Thomas Jefferson. In this instance the teacher wanted the students to realize that the account was somewhat limited so she had the class compare it with the information provided on Thomas Jefferson in two encyclopedias. In so doing, the class made judgments about the completeness, accuracy, and appropriateness of the information obtained about Thomas Jefferson from the selection they had read.

Internal criteria, on the other hand, are within the reader and are based on his or her knowledge, experience, or values. For example, a student who has studied a topic in detail and knows a great deal about it is in a better position to make objective judgments about the completeness, accuracy, or appropriateness of a written piece on the topic than is a student without such background information.

Values are also used as internal criteria. For example, when students are asked to make judgments about the suitability or acceptability of a character's actions, opinions or judgments very often are based on the values the reader has acquired through personal experiences. Often such judgments or opinions are tinged with emotion, and students should be helped to see that people may have different opinions because of different feelings or values.

There is no doubt middle grade teachers face a problem with respect to the amount of knowledge their students have on any given topic. In other words, they will constantly have to be concerned as to whether their students have enough background information to make logical, objective judgments about what an author has written on a given topic.

Although this may be a problem, we feel much can be done in the middle grades to help students to be objective, to avoid leaping to conclusions or overgeneralizations, to be aware of the influence their values or feelings have on their judgments, and to be sensitive to the influence authors' values or feelings have on their writing. We know that a few scattered lessons here and there will not do the job, but we feel that the middle grades are the time to start emphasizing evaluation abilities.

Developing evaluation abilities in the middle grades. Much of what follows in this section is derived from an unpublished action research report authored by Nancy Nelson (1968), who was a teacher in a combination fifth-sixth grade classroom at the time she conducted the study. The intent of presenting some of the activities and tasks she employed in her study is to provide the reader with some concrete suggestions for ways of working on evaluation abilities in middle grade classrooms. The activities and tasks to be discussed are by no means foolproof, but they do represent what an industrious middle grade teacher can do.

1   The first task the students were involved in was the comparative reading of portions of different biographies dealing with the early lives of such people as Helen Keller, Abraham Lincoln, and Theodore Roosevelt. In making comparisons, students attempted to determine whether the references contained the same information, whether there were disagreements in the accounts, and whether there might be reasons for differences in the sources due to such things as authorship. In essence, the students categorized likenesses, differences, and disagreements and attempted to make objective judgments about the reasons for their findings. Finally, the portions of the biographies studied were compared to encyclopedia accounts, which the class considered to be factual.

2   The next area Nelson emphasized had to do with the judgments involved in making summaries. First, students were asked to condense the information contained in a paragraph into a single sentence. At first, they compared their products and worked together with the teacher to develop a composite summary sentence which they could accept as valid and could justify. This activity was continued until the students could make independent judgments about the most important parts of paragraphs for inclusion in summary sentences. The activity was then expanded to reducing an entire page to a single paragraph. Nelson noted that her fifth- and sixth-grade students found this latter activity to be much more difficult.

3   A third activity used to stimulate evaluative reading on the part of the students involved advertisements and commercial slogans gathered from radio, television, newspapers, and magazines. Once these items were organized, the class made judgments about, among other things, the audience to whom the ad was directed, the emotion, desire, or feeling the ad elicited, the occurrence of unsubstantiated claims, and the words or ideas used to impress the reader. The class found that ads in magazines and newspapers used visual gimmicks, such as putting important facts in small print; for example, GENUINE artificial LEATHER BAG! Finally, the students rewrote ads and slogans with the objective of making them true; for example, Pepsi, a soft drink for anyone.

4   Nelson found that newspapers provided great opportunities for developing evaluative reading abilities. To begin, the students determined how they read newspapers and their general knowledge of what a newspaper contained. Following this survey, they established what the functions of a newspaper should be. Keeping these functions in mind, they proceeded to do a comparative study of individual parts of several newspapers. In the process, they found that the inclusion or exclusion of a single word can influence the reader; for example, the youth was arrested for speeding vs. the longhaired youth was arrested for speeding. They also found that newspaper reporters are guilty of overgeneralizing at times. This finding led the class to consider the logic of such statements as: Harry and Dale are brothers; Harry is bad; therefore, Dale is bad. Next, the students made judgments about relevant and irrelevant material included in selected articles. They then worked on eliminating the irrelevant ideas to see how such editing might alter the impact of the original article on the reader.

In general, sections of the newspapers were analyzed separately. Headlines were discussed and compared from the point of view of type size, position on the page, and word choice. Comics were studied and differentiated into categories. This led to questions about why one paper carried certain comic strips while another did not. Political cartoons, editorials, and letters to the editor were studied and compared across newspapers. This latter activity resulted in a number of "letters to the editor," some of which were published in one of the local newspapers. Nelson observed that this part of her unit appeared to be most enjoyable and profitable for the class.

5 The final phase of Nelson's effort dealt with propaganda devices. Twelve such devices or techniques were isolated and illustrated, and the class then attempted to use them to evaluate written materials and speeches of various political persuasions. On the whole, Nelson found this area of study to be most difficult for her fifth and sixth graders and concluded that the concept load of the materials used seemed to be beyond the students. She did observe, however, that the exposure to persuasive literature and the awareness of some propaganda techniques seemed to make the students more evaluative when they read such materials.

Comparative reading. For too long in too many classrooms the "one-textbook approach" has been the accepted instructional mode. In the process, it has subtly conditioned many students to be unanalytical, unquestioning, unevaluative readers. To put it another way, the one-textbook approach has produced readers who believe anything they read. What can the middle grades do to reduce the number of readers of this type? We feel the answer, in part, can be found in comparative reading activities.

There are four reasons for making this recommendation. First, comparative reading provides an avenue for making students aware of the differing treatments authors give to a topic even though essentially the same information was available to them. Second, comparative reading activities can develop and sharpen abilities in analysis by requiring students to locate and categorize the likenesses and differences in the facts and opinions contained in selections on the same topic. This ability, it should be noted, is fundamental to evaluation. Third, such reading activities highlight the importance of consulting more than one source on a topic before making judgments about the completeness or accuracy of the information available. Finally, while the one-textbook approach tends to cut off an important avenue for building background information which may be incorporated into the criteria one uses for making judgments, comparative reading contributes to the acquisition of such information.

To our way of thinking, there are at least *two approaches to comparative reading in the middle grades.* One of these is the *unit-of-study approach* many people suggest for use in science and social studies. In brief, this approach involves the following steps:

Students develop questions about a topic with the assistance of the teacher.

Individuals or small groups of students select questions they will answer.

Students refer to multiple sources using appropriate research techniques to answer the questions.

Students pool their findings through sharing activities which take on various forms in a culmination and evaluation period or periods.

One of the important responsibilities middle grade teachers have when conducting units of study is to demonstrate the way research using multiple resources is done before students are required to be independent researchers. Too often, middle graders are expected to demonstrate research skills which they have not been taught. Nevertheless, the unit-of-study approach does provide an avenue for comparative reading.

The second approach, for want of a better label, will be called *the specific comparative reading activities approach.* This approach can be used in any area of the curriculum and requires teachers to provide such specific comparative reading activities as:

1 Comparison of treatments of scientific phenomena or historical events found in textbooks for a given grade or various grade levels.

2 Comparison of treatments of a current event by a newspaper reporter, a news magazine reporter, an editorial writer, and a political columnist.

3 Comparison of accounts of an historical event; for example, the Battle at Lexington, written from opposing points of view.

4 Comparison of biographies and fictionalized stories, biographies and autobiographies, or biographies about a famous person written for different audiences or age levels.

5 Comparison of a fictionalized account of an event with a factual account of the same event; for example, Custer's last stand.

6 Comparison of original versions of classics with adapted or modified versions.

7 Comparison of official statements made by prominent people on the same topic over time; for example, Presidents of the United States on almost any topic at almost any time.

8 Comparison of how medical discoveries have influenced the treatment of prevention of a particular disease over time; for example, polio as discussed in various editions of the *World Book Encyclopedia.*

9 Comparison of news reports or editorials on a given topic or event in two or more newspapers.

For the comparative reading activities suggested and for any others an industrious teacher might develop, students should ask and categorize the answers to such questions as:

What statements of fact are alike?

What statements of opinion are alike?

What statements of fact are different?

What statements of opinion are different?

Hopefully, an analysis of this type should lead to questions about the reasons for the likenesses and differences observed; for example, the dates of the writings, the points of view of the authors, the nature of the times when the writings took place, the nature of the media in which the writings were found, and the nature of the audiences to whom the writings were directed. Whether the answers to these latter types of questions can be found will vary with the resources available to teachers and students. Nevertheless, they are the types of questions that contribute to the making of objective judgments and that is what comparative reading activities will help prepare youngsters to do.

Appreciation

As defined in the Taxonomy (Table 4.1) appreciation has to do with the development of awareness of and regard for the devices and techniques an author employs in order to elicit emotional responses from readers. No doubt learning tasks designed to heighten appreciation will require some inference or evaluation on the part of the reader. Their distinctive characteristic, however, should be that they focus the reader's attention on the author's artistry in developing emotionally stimulating plots, themes, settings, incidents, or characters, and his or her craft in selecting and using stimulating language.

Catterson (1970) illustrated appreciation by comparing the way in which two people might view a painting. The first viewer might be able to detect only the painter's purpose or message. The second viewer may grasp the painter's message, but be emotionally stimulated by the painting in addition. Moreover, the second viewer may be aware of the painter's use of design, color, and technique which caused the emotional response. Because of his or her awareness of and sensitivity to the painter's skills, Catterson would see the second person as appreciating the painting. In other words, appreciation, as she defines it (and as we do also), goes beyond a mere cognitive response. It involves an emotional response, an awareness of how an artist or writer accomplished the effect.

Although the foregoing comments might be viewed as an endorsement for emphasizing the type of literary analysis in which every sentence in a selection is dissected in search of some obscure nuance, this is not the intent. Rather, the middle grades are seen as a time for developing awareness of the fact that writers place emphasis on different literary dimensions and devices in order to achieve the emotional effects they desire.

Emphasize an author's strength. One way to approach the development of appreciation in the middle grades is to have students focus on an author's particular strength; for example, theme, characterization, plot, setting, or imagery. By approaching reading selections in this way, students can direct their undivided attention to developing awareness of and sensitivity to the techniques and devices a particular author uses to gain the desired emotional response.

The assumptions upon which this approach is based are threefold. First, it is assumed that different authors will have different strengths and that teachers will be able to detect such strengths and will be able to judge which ones will have appeal to the students' emotions. Second, by having students focus on a single literary dimension at a time, it is assumed there is a better chance to avoid superficiality in this area. Finally, by approaching the development of appreciation in this way, it is assumed that over time students will become aware of the different ways authors approach their work and the different emphases they give to various literary dimensions in order to achieve the emotional effects they desire.

Obviously, one can argue with these assumptions. To allay such arguments, at least in part, two comments must be made at this point. First, we do not mean to imply that every piece of literature has a strength worthy of emphasis. As we all know, some selections do not, for a variety of reasons, have an emotional impact on the reader. Second, we are not suggesting that teachers should employ this approach with every suitable selection. Obviously, there are times when teachers should direct students' appreciation activities and times when they should encourage students to apply such abilities on an independent basis.

Specific tasks[6] for developing appreciation abilities. Although emphasis on authors' strengths will contribute to the development of appreciation abilities in the middle grades, there is a need to consider specific appreciation tasks which will contribute to the development of the appreciation abilities in the Taxonomy. The specific activities listed below are examples of these types of tasks for use in the middle grades:

1 Have the students note incidents which depart from linear chronological sequencing in the plot, determine the effect they have on the reader, and deduce what the author intended to evoke in the reader by including them.

---

6. A number of the ideas included here are drawn from Catterson's (1970) work. The reader is urged to read her discussion of appreciation for additional ideas and insights.

2   Have readers note whether events are just thrown in to create activity or whether they contribute to the development of the plot, the theme, or a character.

3   Since an author has to select a time and place for the story, have students determine why he or she made a specific choice and how effective it was in terms of providing a base for events, action, or characterizations which had an emotional impact on the students.

4   Once students have identified an author's theme and its impact, have them determine whether and how the author used incidents, characters, setting, and imagery to achieve the objective.

5   Compare the way identical themes are treated in different books. Compare the theme of accepting responsibility as presented in Rawlings's *The Yearling* and Speery's *Call it Courage.*

6   Have students become aware of the devices authors utilize to develop their characters; for example, their thoughts, actions, statements, physical and emotional characteristics, how others react to them, what others say to them or say about them when they are not present, etc.

7   Have students compare the main characters from different selections to see how they are alike or different. How did they affect different students?

8   Compare the way in which the same author has developed characters in two or more of his or her other selections; for example, Marguerite Henry's *King of the Wind* and *Misty of Chincotique.*

9   Have students respond to an author's use of language. Have them deduce the author's purpose in choice of sensory images, figures of speech, nouns, verbs, and adjectives, and the effect intended. Where possible, have students consider the connotations certain words have and how replacing them with other words could influence a sentence or passage.

10   Analyze titles of reading selections and discuss why authors chose the titles they did. Have students compose new titles to see what other words might have been used and whether the new titles produce the same types of effect as the original ones.

11   Make a list of sentences using metaphors drawn from a variety of sources. Be certain students grasp the literal meanings of the metaphors, then have them give opinions as to why they were useful to the author in a particular context. To highlight the impact of metaphors, have the students rewrite the sentences without the metaphors to see if they are able to produce the same effect.

12   Locate passages which elicit sensory images on the part of the readers. Have students determine how the writer has designed passages which have had this effect on them.

13 Explore several writings of the same author to determine how his or her interests and viewpoints, characters, settings, and language (expressions) are similar from one selection to another and whether his or her techniques have changed over time; for example, John Krumgold's books. . . *And Now Miguel, Onion John,* and *Henry 3.*

Obviously, other tasks can be added to the list. Because of this, it is important that the ones suggested not be viewed in a sequential, programmatic way. Rather the tasks listed, and others which might be designed, should be used to highlight a particular aspect of appreciation of which students should be more aware. In general, then, specific appreciation tasks can be related to the approach of placing emphasis on the particular strengths of various authors.

A Final Word

The Taxonomy and the related teaching strategies just presented are intended to help middle grade teachers help their students improve and broaden their reading comprehension. Of course, the teacher is the critical factor here. Nothing positive happens in any area of study in any classroom unless the teacher has a grasp of the content and the necessary teaching strategies and tactics to make the content come alive for students. The area of reading comprehension is no exception to this rule.

Something to Think and Talk About

A survey conducted by the reading consultant in the Wioka School System indicated that one of the problem areas for middle grade teachers was teaching reading comprehension. Although the teachers' concerns were varied, an analysis of their responses revealed agreement on four basic problems which are illustrated by the following statements:

1 My students' median grade score on the comprehension section of our standardized reading achievement test was well above the national norm, but most of them don't perform that way in the classroom.

2 My students comprehend adequately when I am guiding them, but they have a great deal of trouble understanding what they read independently.

3 My students comprehend pretty well during reading period, but they don't do as well in science and social studies, particularly when they are reading and doing research for individual or small group reports.

4 I have attempted to determine what our basal series emphasize in comprehension because I think it is so important at this level, but I find little agreement among the three we are using.

As a result of the survey, the middle grade teachers decided to focus on the area of comprehension as an in-service project, using problems 2 and 3 as points of departure. Where should the teachers begin in order to resolve these two problems? (See Appendix 4 for Author's Response to "Something to Think and Talk About.")

References

Barrett, Thomas C. (1972). "Taxonomy of Reading Comprehension." *Reading 360 Monograph.* Lexington, Massachusetts: Ginn, A Xerox Education Company.

Bloom, Benjamin S., ed. (1956). *Taxonomy of Educational Objectives: Handbook 1, Cognitive Domain.* New York: McKay.

Catterson, Jane H. (1970). "Interpretation and Appreciation: The Mind Set for Reading Literature." In *Children and Literature,* edited by Jane H. Catterson. Newark, Delaware: International Reading Association, pp. 98–104.

Guilford, J. P. (1958). "Three Faces of Intellect." *American Psychologist* **14**: 469–479.

Guszak, Frank James (1967). "Teachers' Questions and Levels of Reading Comprehension." In *The Evaluation of Children's Reading Achievement,* edited by Thomas Barrett. Newark, Delaware: International Reading Association, pp. 97–110.

Nelson, Nancy (1968). "A Study in Critical Reading Instruction." A mimeographed paper. Madison: University of Wisconsin.

Pearson, P. David (1977). "Operationalizing Terms and Definitions in Reading Comprehension." An unpublished paper delivered at the Annual Convention of the International Reading Association, Miami, Florida.

Ruddell, Robert B., and Helen G. Bacon (1972). "The Nature of Reading: Language and Meaning." In *Language and Learning to Read,* edited by Richard E. Hodges and E. Hugh Rudorf. Boston: Houghton Mifflin, pp. 169–188.

Sanders, Norris M. (1966). *Classroom Questions.* New York: Harper & Row.

Simons, Herbert D. (1971). "Reading Comprehension: The Need for a New Perspective." *Reading Research Quarterly* **6** (3): 338–363.

Singer, Harry (1976). "Active Comprehension: From Answering to Asking Questions." A paper delivered at the International Reading Association Sixth World Congress on Reading. Singapore, August 1976, pp. 1–16.

Stauffer, Russell G. (1975). *Directing the Reading-Thinking Process.* New York: Harper & Row, pp. 31–72.

5

TEACHING READING STUDY SKILLS IN THE MIDDLE GRADES

Perhaps the most opportune time in the school curriculum to teach reading study skills is during the middle grades. Most students in grades four through eight develop consuming, albeit short-lived, interests in subjects that they can learn about by reading. The middle grader for whom interesting, "researchable" topics cannot be found at regular intervals throughout grades four through eight is rare indeed. Furthermore, the importance of teaching middle graders the skills needed to find and organize information in printed materials cannot be overemphasized. The study skills and habits students learn between the primary grades and the senior high school are likely to be the skills and habits they rely upon in the senior high school and beyond.

We purposely do not provide a formal scope and sequence chart which pinpoints what should be introduced in which grades and in which curriculum areas. Such a chart would be too prescriptive for teaching the skills and habits that need to be introduced, taught, and practiced throughout the middle grades and in all curriculum areas when opportunities are present. We would not want study skills to be thought of as something to be taught as a separate entity or as a subject in itself. Study skills are taught best when they are taught within the context of meaningful units of study in content area classes and in reading classes. We agree with Mattleman and Blake (1977), ". . . the most effective way to learn study skills is to learn and to use them in a functional setting." (p. 925)

Basically, our position relative to teaching reading study skills in the middle grades is that students learn by doing. While this position can be stated simply and clearly, the implications for middle grades teachers are not quite so simple. However, they can be delineated as follows:

Teachers must:

a) help students identify topics they want to find information about.

b) help students discover the wide variety of resources available to them for getting information.

c) teach students how to use the many resources available to them.

d) provide opportunities for students to communicate orally and/or in writing the information they have found by reading.

Norton (1977) has described a unit of study she calls "A Web of Interest" which is a good illustration of how a teacher might implement the four steps above. Using "water" as the center of the web, Norton guided students to the study of topics related to water, such as "pollution," "conservation," "treasures from the sea," and "waves and tides." Certainly, Norton's unit is only one possibility. Imaginative teachers will find many organizational frameworks for getting students actively involved in finding and using information in print.

Obviously, the emphasis in the approach we recommend is upon getting students to actively find and use information. We feel that instructional units on how to study, sections in workbooks or kits that tell students how to study, or other teaching approaches that rely upon telling students how to rather than plunging them into the process are relatively ineffective. Reading study skills are developed over many years of practice. The key in the middle grades is to guide the practice so the skills and habits are learned properly and to supply topics and related activities that students find meaningful. Too often students either reject or quickly forget the teaching of reading study skills because the what and how of the teaching are couched more in contrivances than in meaningful study. Motivation to learn, good instruction, and plenty of guided practice are the basic ingredients of reading study skills instruction in the middle grades.

We believe that middle grades teachers should guide students to the most frequently used resources available to them for getting information and give them plenty of practice using those resources efficiently. In senior high school and beyond the more esoteric resources available to students can be introduced. We have so many resources available in libraries of even modest size that trying to teach middle grades students everything there is to know is unrealistic and probably counterproductive to their learning the basics of study skills. The objective in the middle grades should be to make students comfortable with the searching-out process, not to have them memorize long lists of specific resources they might want to or be required to use someday.

We firmly believe that no teacher should be exempt from teaching study skills. While the teaching of study skills may be given a sharper focus and be approached more explicitly in reading classes, teachers in other curriculum areas should also teach students how to search for, organize, and report information relative to their curriculum areas. In the remainder of this chapter we present what we believe to be a reasonable study skills curriculum for the middle grades. The remainder of this chapter will be most helpful if every teacher considers himself or herself responsible for contributing to students' growth in study skills and selects from our presentation the information that seems most useful for his or her teaching assignment.

Inventories and Teaching Suggestions

Most people enjoy self-diagnosis, and middle graders are no exception. Therefore, we are presenting inventories that will help students and teachers know each student's present status in regard to different aspects of study skills development. The inventories may be used together to obtain a fairly complete picture of students' skills and habits or they may be used separately for different purposes at different grades or in different curriculum areas. Some teachers may prefer to select items from among the inventories, perhaps add some of their own items and create an inventory that meets their particular needs. Notice that the formats of the inventories are designed to allow students to indicate how much they already know as well as with how much they can still learn.

Inventory 1: Parts of textbooks

Which of the following do you usually use when you get information from textbooks? Which parts do you usually ignore? Put "U" before each of the following you usually use and "I" before those you usually ignore.

_____ The title of the book
_____ The name of the author(s)
_____ The table of contents
_____ Chapter titles
_____ Headings
_____ Subheadings
_____ Questions or statements at chapter beginnings
_____ Summaries at ends of chapters
_____ Suggested additional readings
_____ Color keys, underlining, or other format aides
_____ Footnotes
_____ Charts and graphs
_____ Maps
_____ Appendixes
_____ Glossary
_____ Index
_____ Other (examine one or more textbooks to discover any other information-getting aids you frequently use or frequently ignore)

Teaching suggestions for Inventory 1. A suggestion for teachers using the inventory above, with or without modifications, is to use it as a teaching tool after students have responded to it. Students may compare their responses and tell why they tend to use certain parts of textbooks and ignore others. The teacher may also ask students which parts of textbooks on the inventory they did not know about. Teachers may also want to show and describe how to use all or selected items on the inventory. Teachers and students might also analyze together some footnotes, maps, end-of-chapter summaries or other textbook parts to discover how each provides information or guidance helpful in getting information from textbooks. Finally, teachers and students might examine the textbooks they are presently using to find how many of the parts listed on the inventory are included in their own textbooks and how they can be used more efficiently.

Inventory 2: Resources in the library or Instructional Materials Center (IMC)

(*Note:* This inventory will be most appropriate and helpful if librarians or IMC personnel adapt it in accord with the resources in their particular schools). Put a "+" before each of the library or IMC resources below you have already used. Put a "−" before those you have not yet used.

____	Dewey Decimal System	____	Phonograph records
____	Card catalog	____	Audio tapes
____	Films	____	Video cassettes
____	Filmstrips	____	Magazines
____	Encyclopedias	____	Newspapers
____	Unabridged dictionary	____	Textbooks
____	Maps	____	Other resources
____	Atlases		

Teaching suggestions for Inventory 2. One suggestion for teachers using the inventory above is to shorten it and have each student complete the inventory ("Other resources") in the library or IMC. Another suggestion is to have students compare their responses and tell why and how they used the resources marked with a "+". Still another suggestion is to use students' responses for planning a guided tour of the library or IMC, preferably accompanied by the librarian or IMC director. A final suggestion is to ask students to formulate questions or research topics which could be answered or investigated by using specified resources in the library IMC.

Inventory 3: Places and times for studying

Where and when do you study most efficiently? Check the places and times below that you think are good study places and study times for you. (*Note:* This inventory will probably require modification according to individual school physical plants and policies.)

At School (places)

_____ Study hall
_____ Library
_____ IMC
_____ School steps
_____ School yard
_____ Leaning against a wall
       in the hallway
_____ Full classroom

_____ Empty classroom
_____ Students' lounge
_____ Gym bleachers
_____ Locker room
_____ Lunchroom
_____ Auditorium
_____ Study carrel
_____ Other

At School (times)

_____ Before school starts
       (morning)
_____ Right after school starts
       (morning)
_____ Just before lunch
_____ During lunch
_____ Right after lunch
_____ Mid-afternoon
_____ Right after school
_____ Immediately before a
       class starts

_____ Immediately after a
       class ends
_____ During the first part of the
       class (study time given by
       the teacher)
_____ During the last part of the
       class (study time given by
       the teacher)
_____ Other

Outside School (times)

_____ Sunday
_____ Monday
_____ Tuesday
_____ Wednesday
_____ Thursday
_____ Friday

_____ Saturday
_____ Early morning
_____ After school
_____ After evening meal
_____ Late evening
_____ Other

Outside School (places)

_____ Bedroom
_____ Kitchen
_____ Family room
_____ Living room
_____ Dining room
_____ Patio
_____ Porch
_____ Public library

_____ Restaurant
_____ Park
_____ Bus stop
_____ Bus
_____ Subway
_____ Friend's house
_____ On the job (babysitting)
_____ Other

Teaching suggestions for Inventory 3. A suggestion for using Inventory 3 is to
ask students to analyze their responses and make a composite list of the times and

places they presently use for studying. Each student's composite list might be evaluated in terms of the advantages (for example, suitable furniture, quiet, using time that would otherwise be wasted) and disadvantages (for example, distractions, not enough time) of present places and times used for study. Another suggestion is for students to experiment with alternative places and times for a week or two to discover the most productive arrangements suitable to their schedules and life styles. The objective is to get students thinking about the variety of study places and times available to them and to help them understand that some places and times may be more advantageous to their learning than others.

Inventory 4: Strategies for study-type reading

Answer "yes" or "no" to each of the following questions. "Yes" answers indicate good strategies for study-type reading.

1   When you read for information, do you have some questions in mind you are trying to answer; for example, "What are several different ways meat can be preserved?"

2   Do you sometimes read the questions at the end of a chapter before you read the chapter to help you direct your reading?

3   Do you pause after reading a title, subhead, or paragraph and try to guess what the next paragraph will be about or what question(s) it will answer?

4   Do you read textbooks and other study-type materials more slowly than materials you read for recreation?

5   Do you keep a notebook of key words and their definitions for subjects that have a specialized vocabulary—words like "circumference," "photosynthesis," "humanist," "alliteration?"

6   Do you use the glossary or a dictionary to be sure you know the meanings of words you're not sure of?

7   Do you read some sentences or paragraphs more than once if you're not sure you understood the ideas?

8   Do you try to form pictures in your mind of people, places, or procedures described in the material you're reading?

9   Do you sometimes whisper to yourself words, sentences, or paragraphs you don't understand to see if saying them aloud helps to understand them?

10   Do you take notes on or underline the important ideas in a selection you are studying?

11   Do you pause occasionally as you are reading and think back over what you just read?

12 When you have finished reading study-type material, do you try to give a short speech to yourself about what you just read to see how much you remember?

13 Do you jot down questions to ask your teacher about ideas or words you don't understand?

14 Do you usually look a chapter or selection over quickly to get an idea of what's in it before you read it carefully?

15 Do you have a "best" place and time for studying?

16 When you find your mind wandering while you're reading, do you try to find out why you're having trouble concentrating and correct the problem?

Teaching suggestions for Inventory 4. We have made one or more teaching suggestions for each question on Inventory 4. The sixteen questions (abbreviated) and the suggestions for each appear below. In sum, we believe the suggestions comprise a fairly complete program for teaching strategies for study-type reading to middle graders.

1 When you read for information, do you have some questions in mind you are trying to answer? *Give students one or more questions to answer as they read an assigned selection.* The questions may ask them to find specific facts, to be able to recall a particular sequence of steps in a process, or to locate main ideas. The questions may be written on the chalkboard or typed on a handout. Obviously, teachers must read beforehand the materials about which they ask questions so that the questions are meaningful and important to the understanding of the selection. Teachers should be careful not to ask so many prereading questions that the normal reading process is interfered with or that students develop negative attitudes toward reading for specific purposes. Two or three questions per reading assignment are usually sufficient. Of course, students should be held accountable, through class discussion or in writing, for answering all prereading questions supplied by the teacher. A good description of one teacher's success with helping students become aware of the importance of questioning in their lives and helping them transfer their ability to generate questions to reading and writing activities is given by Ortiz (1977).

2 Do you sometimes read the questions at the end of a chapter before you read the chapter? *Unless the questions at the ends of chapters are going to be used to test comprehension, they may be used as prereading questions to direct students' reading.* In most cases, we think questions formulated by classroom teachers are superior to questions in the published material because teachers can match the difficulty level of the questions to their students' abilities, and they can ask questions that help in the attainment of their particular course objectives. Furthermore, teachers can add some humor, specific relevance, or some other personal touch to the questions they create to add enthusiasm and interest as well as direction to students' reading. However, students should know that in the absence of teacher-provided questions the questions that publishers often provide at the end of reading assignments may be used effectively to help them read for specific purposes.

3 Do you pause after reading a title, subhead, or paragraph? *Teach students to formulate their own prereading questions by analyzing titles, subheads, or first paragraphs of selections.* Students should learn that they can anticipate authors' messages on the basis of minimal cues. The more independent students become of questions provided by someone other than themselves the better able they are to use the many resources available to them for their own personal interests and purposes.

Teachers might ask a class to study a chapter title or read one or two paragraphs and then suggest questions they think might be answered in the material that follows. After reading, the class can identify the clues that were used for correct anticipations. During the middle grades students can become quite adept at setting their own reading purposes.

In regard to suggestions 1, 2, and 3, teachers should be aware that giving students specific information to look for in their reading will help them to find the specified information; however, it is likely to detract from their finding of information that is not specified. Therefore, teachers should avoid using suggestions 1, 2, and 3 when they want their students to obtain an overview of the material assigned or to decide after reading what is and is not important in the selection.

4 Do you read study-type materials slowly? *Teach students to read slowly and carefully for study-type reading unless they are reading about a subject with which they are very familiar.* Good readers are flexible in regard to their reading rates. They change their rates according to the difficulty of the material they are reading and their purpose for reading it. Gibson and Levin (1976) point out that ". . . there are large individual differences in reading speed . . . the same individual may read slowly on some occasions and rapidly on others, for a great variety of reasons." (p. 539) Study-type materials for middle graders are usually relatively difficult and the purpose for reading them is to learn and retain most of the information presented. Therefore, students should be explicitly informed that if they expect to get more than a superficial understanding, they will have to read slowly and allow more time for their reading.

It follows that teachers should take the importance of slow reading for most study-type reading assignments they make into consideration when they determine the length of the assignment.

During the middle grades is not too early to disabuse students of the belief that "speed reading" is appropriate for study-type reading. Promoters of speed reading instruction have generally not made clear that the techniques of speed reading are helpful only for the reading of certain materials for certain purposes and that they are inappropriate techniques for most study-type reading, especially for middle graders whose basic word identification and comprehension skills are still developing.

5 Do you keep a notebook of key words and definitions? A major characteristic of study-type materials, and one that makes them difficult for students to read, is the specialized vocabulary in them. As a matter of fact, a major purpose of studying a subject in the middle grades is to learn the vocabulary of that subject. Thomas and Robinson (1972) say, "If you are a subject matter teacher—in contrast to a specialist in the field of reading—you may have little or no idea of what an important contribution you can make to the reading of your students. And in no area of reading are you likely to be more effective than in vocabulary." (p. 9)

In addition to introducing specialized words prior to students' encountering them in a reading assignment, teachers might encourage or require students to keep a notebook of key words for understanding a particular subject. The teacher could tell students which words to include in their notebooks and test them periodically on their vocabulary development. From the very beginning of their study skills and reading efficiency training in the middle grades students should be impressed with the importance of correct interpretation of specialized vocabulary.

6 Do you use a glossary or dictionary? Closely alligned with suggestion 5 is the suggestion that teachers teach students how to use glossaries and dictionaries and encourage students to use them.

If students have not learned how to use glossaries and dictionaries for vocabulary development in the primary grades they should be taught in grade four how to use them. They should be taught the following:

a) Dictionaries and glossaries are both sources of definitions for words whose meanings are not clear from their contexts.

b) Dictionaries are more generalized sources while glossaries are specialized for the books in which they are contained. Dictionaries may not include words that appear in a glossary and glossaries certainly do not contain all of the words in a dictionary.

c) The words in dictionaries and glossaries are alphabetically arranged.

d) The guide words at the tops of dictionary pages tell users the alphabetical range of the words on those pages.

e) A dictionary entry may contain more than one definition for a word, and users must decide which definition fits in the context they are trying to interpret.

f) Diacritical marks will help them to pronounce the word.

The best way to teach dictionary and glossary use is to give students practice in finding definitions for words provided by the teacher. A good exercise is to ask students to determine what kinds of books or in what subjects words such as those on the following list would be used:

saxifrage	gherkin	tabloid
scimitar	gibbet	symmetry
incalculable	cordon	postmortem
devot	bourgeois	myth
ophthalmia	arterial	
Olympus	quoit	

Teachers can easily browse through a dictionary to create a list that is interesting and instructive for their students to use in practicing dictionary skills. The same list can be used for practice in using diacritical marks.

Another good activity is to select passages from the students' textbooks which contain words with multiple meanings. Students may be asked to find the words in a dictionary and be prepared to tell which of the definitions given best fits the word in the passage that was assigned.

Middle grades teachers should remember that their objective is to give their students the skills they need to look up words they don't know and get them in the habit of using dictionaries and glossaries. Their objective is not to teach their students everything there is to know about dictionaries and glossaries. The uses of a dictionary we have not included here are more important for teaching writing skills or better taught in later grades. In the middle grades, for reading study skills, the focus should be upon finding the definitions and perhaps the pronunciation of unknown words encountered in study-type materials.

7   Do you read some sentences or paragraphs more than once? Students may get in the habit of skipping over words or ideas they don't comprehend upon first reading. Sometimes reading further in the text clarifies the author's message. Other times students become hopelessly lost. *Periodically, teachers should remind students that good readers occasionally have to re-read material they didn't understand upon first reading.* Students should learn that occasional re-reading is acceptable and even desirable for study-type reading.

8   Do you try to form pictures in your mind? *Teach students to create mental pictures of people, places, objects, and procedures they read about.* Many times students don't take the time to visualize descriptions that must be visualized to be understood. Teachers should have students mark specific passages that need mental imagery to be fully comprehended and remembered. Unless students are told, "Try to picture this procedure in your mind," they are not likely to do so. Students who are reminded frequently before they read to create mental pictures may develop the habit of doing that while reading study-type material and thereby improve their comprehension and retention.

9   Do you sometimes whisper to yourself words, sentences, or paragraphs you don't understand? Sometimes vocalizing words, sentences, or paragraphs that are hard to understand helps the reader to understand them. *Teach students to use the meaning cues in the intonation patterns of the language.* Of course, if students are found vocalizing more than a few paragraphs in a reading assignment, the material is obviously too difficult and the information should be given to the students in some other form.

10   Do you take notes on or underline important ideas? *A good procedure for helping students learn how to underline or notate important ideas in a reading selection is to show them some models of good underlining or good notes.* Either an opaque projector or overhead projector transparencies can be used to show students samples of good underlining and/or notetaking. Then students should be asked to read a selection and underline or take notes on the important ideas in it for the purpose of comparing their underlining or notetaking with their teacher's and other students'. If students are asked periodically to underline or take notes on assigned readings and to compare their underlining or notes with other students' and their teacher's products, they will learn how to identify important ideas for purposes of retaining them and having them recorded for future study. The job of the teacher, then, is to provide good models and give students periodic guided practice throughout the school year.

11   Do you pause and think back? *Teach students to pause at transitional places in their reading (for example, at the end of a subsection) and to reflect upon what they just read by guiding them through the process via class discussion.* The teacher might assign the class part of a chapter to read with the instruction that after a reasonable period of time all students will close their books and, as a group, recall as many ideas from their reading as they can. After reading the assigned passage and closing their books students individually volunteer bits of information from the passage. When the students begin repeating themselves, the teacher asks them to look back over the passage to see if they forgot anything. This activity can be repeated periodically so that students become habituated to recalling information they have just read.

After students have had some guided experience with pausing and reflecting, teachers can help them practice this strategy by telling them where to place small marks throughout reading assignments to remind them to pause and reflect at appropriate places.

12   Do you try to give a short speech to yourself about what you just read? *A variation on teaching students to pause and reflect is to suggest that they put the words of the author into their own personal language by pretending they are making a short speech about what they just read.* This strategy is good for clarifying the information and for helping to recall it later on.

13   Do you jot down questions to ask your teacher? *Students should be taught to jot down questions as they read about things they would like clarified or* *expanded upon by their teacher.* Teachers can encourage students to do this by asking for questions about reading assignments as a part of discussing the assignment. Teachers who are explicit about the value they place on students' questions relative to their reading assignments will foster in students the habit of jotting down questions that would otherwise be forgotten. Much learning can occur in the process of writing the question, asking it, and listening to the teacher's response. Hearing the questions other students ask and the teacher's responses to them is also highly instructive and interesting for middle grades students.

14   Do you look a selection over quickly to get an idea of what's in it? *Teach students some study-type reading strategies that include surveying a selection before careful reading and reviewing.* The most popular of these strategies is SQ3R (Robinson, 1961). The letters, SQRRR, are the first letters in five processes that in combination improve comprehension and retention of study-type materials: Surveying, Questioning, Reading, Reciting, Reviewing.

Surveying: Teach students to look over the entire reading assignment before reading it carefully. Title, subheads, pictures, summary, and questions at chapter end are examples of the items that should be looked at.

Questioning: Teach students to formulate questions they expect the reading selection will answer. For example, if the title of the selection is "Events that Shaped the Revolution," students might ask, "What were the events that shaped the revolution?" All questions should be written down.

Reading: Teach students to read the chapter, looking especially for the answers to the questions they wrote down.

Reciting: After the selection has been read, students should answer their questions, in writing or in class discussion.

Reviewing: Teach students to return to the selection to clarify, expand upon, or learn more about the questions they could not answer satisfactorily.

We have always felt that the SQ3R process expected too much of most middle graders, even good students. In our experience, the process has been more appropriate for highly motivated college students who are having difficulty in courses with reading assignments upon which they are examined. However, we think middle grades teachers should be aware of the process and modify it to meet the needs of their students. In our experience, the attention and interest of middle grades students are captured by having a study "formula." We think the formula could be effectively modified for middle graders by reducing it to SQR, Survey-Question-Read. We do see the surveying-before-reading process as being a very important study habit.

15 Do you have a "best" place and time for studying? *Help students discover the best place and time for them to study.* Students should be told that most people study more efficiently and comfortably in a certain chair, room, building, or whatever. Students should also be told that most people have a time (day and time of day) that they learn best. The teacher might share his or her best place and time for study and ask students to begin experimenting to find theirs. Inventory 3 and the teaching suggestion for it presented earlier in this chapter should be useful in helping students discover where and when they study best.

16 When your mind wanders, do you try to correct the problem? *Helping students ascertain the probable cause or causes of concentration problems is an important part of teaching study skills and reading efficiency, especially in the middle grades where concentration problems abound.* We do not recommend that teachers engage in deep psychological probing. Students with serious emotional problems are best referred to personnel better trained for emotional counseling than most teachers are trained. Rather, we recommend helping students look for the obvious and easily correctible causes of their concentration problems that they may have overlooked or avoided admitting. For example:

- Do you sit next to or try to study with someone who distracts you?
- Do you try to study in a place that is distracting or uncomfortable?
- Do you try to study with radio, TV, or phonograph playing? Might it be interfering with your concentration?
- Are you worried about a particular class? Might telling the teacher or a guidance counselor about your worries help?
- Is the material you are trying to study too hard? Might telling the teacher or a guidance counselor that you try but can't read the assignments help?
- Do you try to study when you're tired?
- Do you try to study for too long a period of time at one sitting?
- Do you put off your studying until the last minute and then feel rushed, guilty, or frightened?
- Do you save all of your studying for one time and end up feeling frustrated and overworked?
- Can you think of any other reasons that might be causing you to have trouble concentrating?

Topics for Students to Research

In keeping with our position that students learn study skills by ongoing instruction and much practice throughout the middle grades, we are including in this chapter 50 research topics for middle graders. The topics range in difficulty and in interest appeal. They are intended to be enjoyable as well as instructive, and they are intended to get students into the wide variety of printed materials available to them in most libraries. For example, the topics will enable teachers and librarians to acquaint students with bird identification books, maps, telephone books, newspapers, books of familiar quotations, magazines, thesaurases, textbooks, atlases, books of world records, almanacs, and a host of other materials that students may miss or give only cursory attention to in their visits to the library or IMC.

Our suggestion for using the topics is that teachers assign them to individual students, with the more able students receiving the more difficult topics. Librarians or IMC personnel should be given the topics in advance so they can be prepared to give students the help they need in finding and using the appropriate resources. The students should be required to report not only the information they found but the source or sources they used to find it. Teachers may want to list the resources on the chalkboard to impress students with the wide variety of printed resources available to them and to discuss or demonstrate certain resources, where to find them, and how to use them.

We are indebted to Suzanne Kaye Smith, News Director for radio station WOSH, Oshkosh, Wisconsin, for creating the following topics and ascertaining that all of the information asked for in them can be found in most libraries.

1   If your locker partner became ill suddenly and had to be taken to the *nearest* hospital, which hospital would he or she be taken to?

2   What was the President's horoscope the day he was elected?

3   If you wanted to break the world record for taking a shower—how long would you have to do it?

4   If you were driving from the city in your state with the largest population to the city with the second largest population, how many miles would you have to drive?

5   If you were making a gangster film in which the bad guy was killed, tied to a cement block, and thrown into the deepest lake in the country, where would you have to go to shoot this movie *on location?*

6   How much would it cost to pick up the phone at 10:00 A.M. Monday morning and talk to the governor of the state for three minutes? What is the governor's phone number?

7   If you made your science teacher a card on which you'd drawn his or her favorite wild flower, what would the card look like?

8   Your class field trip to the military base is scheduled for 1400 bells. What time is that?

9   If your teacher invited a limnologist to speak to the class, what would you learn about?

10 If your class were to put on a play set in America during the Korean War, what kind of costumes would you have to have for the leading lady?

11 If you were writing a play wherein the sidekick kept jumping up and saying, "*I* have an idea!" but you wanted him to substitute the word "idea" for another word that means the same, how many synonyms could you come up with? Or list as many synonyms for the word "idea" as you can find.

12 If you wanted to give a speech about television and how it affects children (from a student's point of view), what magazine articles written in the past year might you use to get ideas and gather facts?

13 More than 100 short stories about murder were published in 1975. List three of those you'd like to read—include the name of the author and where you could find the stories.

14 It's your best friend's birthday and unfortunately he or she is not feeling well and must stay in bed. If you wanted to cheer him or her up by reading a short story about birthdays which was published the year he or she was born, what would you have to choose from?

15 What does the Bible say about "school"?

16 If you went into the greeting card writing business and specialized in writing cards with familiar quotations about "love" on them, what would your favorite cards say?

17 What would you say was the biggest news story in 1976 about the industry of television?

18 If you wanted to take an excursion down the longest river in the country how many miles would the trip be and what river would you be on?

19 If a young man had to make good on his promise that he'd climb the highest mountain (in the United States) for his girlfriend, which mountain would he have to climb and where is it?

20 The country's largest water ski show is looking for the country's largest lake for their once-in-a-lifetime extravaganza. Where will they find it?

21 The advertising campaign for a new shampoo calls for Miss America to wash her hair in the highest waterfall in the United States. Where's the waterfall and who's Miss America?

22 Where is Soso, Mississippi?

23 Does Captain John Smith's Indian friend "Pocohontas" (from pilgrim days) have a city named after her?

24 If you were copying down an address but only got as far as the name, street, number, and city—how easy would it be to find the state if the city was "Stratford?" Or your friend says it's in Texas, you say Washington, and your father says Iowa—who's right?

25 What is the address for the American Society for the Prevention of Cruelty to Animals?

26 If you wanted to form a national association for, say—treasure hunters, how could you be certain there wasn't already one?

27 Did Americans watch the inauguration of President Calvin Coolidge on television?

28 You just overheard your parents talking about your famous Aunt Mary Elizabeth Cylens Lease. For what was she famous?

29 If you wanted to paint a picture of a "wire-tailed" manakin, what colors would you need?

30 Will you be able to take your driver's test on the day you become of legal driving age or will your birthday fall on a weekend when the motor vehicle department is closed?

31 Suppose you discovered a "1952 D" penny in your change from the grocery store. How much is it worth?

32 Suppose you're in the market for a used car and are seriously considering a 1975 Vega. What are some of the problems with 1975 Vegas that you might want to watch out for?

33 You and your friend are going camping and you know that your friend is allergic to bee stings and has a serious reaction when bitten. What kinds of first aid materials should you bring along just in case your friend is bitten?

34 The famous baseball player Lou Gehrig (1903–1941) (he played, 2,130 consecutive games and is the only player ever to hit for more than 400 total bases in five seasons) died at the age of 37 of the incurable disease of amyotrophic lateral sclerosis. What is amyotrophic lateral sclerosis?

35 Your mother is serving Welsh rarebit for supper. Considering the ingredients, do you think you'll like it?

36 About how many calories did you consume at breakfast this morning?

37 Suppose you have a ringing, buzzing, or hissing in your ear. What medical problem could be causing it?

38 What national park do you think would be the best one to go to if you were a spelunker?

39 You have been invited to a lute music recital. Considering the instrument, do you think you'll enjoy the evening?

40 Which took longer: Michaelangelo—a single artist—to paint the Sistine Chapel or thousands of men to construct the Panama Canal?

41 What American musical does the song: "Oh, What a Beautiful Mornin' " come from? How about "Everything's Coming Up Roses"? and "Button Up Your Overcoat"?

42 Are there any good used motorcycles for sale around your town? Where are they?

43 Suppose you accidentally spilled catsup on your mother's new tablecloth. What could you do to get it out—quickly!

44 Your parents say your family's spending this summer camping near La Crosse, Wisconsin. Which radio stations will you be able to listen to there?

45 Suppose you're writing a poem to a girl named Anna, and you need as many words as you can find that rhyme with "Anna"—make a list.

46 Taking into account the "do it yourself" instructions, would you even consider building your own speakers for a stereo system?

47 Your class is having a magic party on the last day of school and all of you must come up with a really good trick to perform. Find one you'd like to work on.

48 You're doing a radio news story on the September 21, 1977 resignation of United States Budget Director Bert Lance. One of the key figures in Lance's downfall was the Comptroller of the Currency. How is "Comptroller" pronounced?

49 You're filling in for the disc jockey at the local radio station on Thanksgiving. It's important that you have some Thanksgiving-type jokes to use on the air. Find some.

50 In the pursuit of vacation happiness, your family is going to Arkansas. What amusement parks, tours, things to do or see, and other points of interest will you find there?

Something to Think and Talk About

School X surveyed its eighth-grade students and teachers to discover their feelings about the importance of the school library in their studying and teaching. Seventy-eight percent of the students indicated that the school library was "unimportant" to their school achievement. Sixty-nine percent of the teachers said they "never" or "seldom" gave assignments that required students to use the library. Ninety-four percent of the students felt that learning how to use the library more efficiently would be "boring" but "valuable." Eighty-two percent of the teachers "never" or "seldom" used the school library themselves. The school library personnel felt their library had an "excellent" collection of resources for many subjects, a "good" collection for most subjects, and an "excellent to good" overall collection. The principal ranked "the library" near the bottom of her weekly concerns. The guidance counselors "never" or "seldom" had occasion to use the school library in their work and had "never" investigated the resources available in the library. Many of the respondents in completing the sen-

tence, "Our school library is a good place for students to _____."
wrote "goof off," "avoid work," "visit with friends," "look busy without
working," and other negative remarks.

How should the staff of School X feel about the results of the survey? Is any
action indicated? (See Appendix 5 for Author's Response to "Something to
Think and Talk About.")

References

Gibson, Eleanor J., and Harry Levin (1976). *The Psychology of Reading*. Cambridge, Massachusetts: The MIT Press.

Mattleman, Marciene S., and Howard E. Blake (1977). "Study Skills: Prescriptions for Survival." *Language Arts* **54** (8): 925–927.

Norton, Donna E. (1977). "A Web of Interest." *Language Arts* **54** (8): 928–932.

Ortiz, Rose Katz (1977). "Using Questioning As a Tool in Reading." *Journal of Reading* **21** (2): 109–114.

Robinson, Francis P. (1961). *Effective Study*. New York: Harper & Row.

Thomas, Ellen Lamer, and H. Alan Robinson (1972). *Improving Reading in Every Class* (abridged ed.). Boston: Allyn and Bacon.

THE AFFECTIVE DIMENSION OF READING

Much is written about word identification and comprehension, the perceptual and cognitive dimensions of reading. On the other hand, the affective dimension of reading, which has to do with the way interests, attitudes, and values are involved in and related to the reading act, is often passed over lightly or totally ignored. To avoid this pitfall, and because we feel it is so important, this chapter focuses on the affective dimension of reading by: (a) presenting a definition of reading which includes the affective dimension and its implications for instruction; (b) discussing affective behaviors using the model developed by Krathwohl *et al.* (1964) as the point of departure; (c) suggesting illustrative instructional strategies concerned with using and developing affective behaviors in and related to reading.

In essence, the chapter is built around two implicit theses. The first of these is that a student's interest in, attitudes toward, and valuing of reading will have an influence on how and when he or she reads. The second thesis is that one of the major goals of reading instruction is to develop capable readers who will value reading as a source of information and enjoyment, readers who will, at least at times, select reading as a leisure-time activity even when other equally enjoyable activities are available.

Four Definitions of Reading and Their Implications for Instruction

What is reading? This question has been asked and answered many times. There are several reasons why it is asked again in this context. First, it's important to realize that differing definitions of reading have differing implications for instruction. Second, the question provides an avenue for presenting a definition which recognizes the importance of affective behaviors in the reading act. Finally, the discussion will hopefully cause the reader to take an accounting of his or her definition of reading and its implications for instruction.

Of the three reasons, the last is most important, since the definition of reading a teacher consciously or unconsciously holds determines the goals of the reading program he or she implements. To put it another way, it is hypothesized that one can infer a teacher's definition of reading by observing and recording what goes on in his or her reading program over a period of time. Such aspects of a reading program as types of learning activities, types of materials, allotments of time, and organization and deployment of personnel provide clues as to what a teacher believes about reading. Whether such a hypothesis can be empirically validated may be academic; however, it is not academic to state, as will be demonstrated, that there are differing definitions of reading which do, in fact, have differing implications for instruction. To this end we offer four different definitions of reading. Each one expresses a perspective, implies a philosophy, and holds implications for instruction.

Reading is decoding

With the aid of Barnhart, Bloomfield (1961), more than anyone else, made people aware of decoding as a definition of reading. Put simply, decoding means the ability to produce the phonemes or sounds represented by graphemes or written letters in English. In other words, reading is the ability to pronounce words swiftly and accurately, nothing more and nothing less. Obviously, comprehension has no place in this definition, since meaning, according to Bloomfield, is not uniquely inherent to reading, but pervades all use of language. The possibility that affective behaviors might be involved in reading is not even alluded to, although Bloomfield suggests that students' success in breaking the code will induce them to persist at the task.

Because of its narrow, unidimensional nature, there can be little doubt about the implications decoding has for classroom practice. Obviously, one instructional emphasis in a reading program based on this definition would be the development of sound-letter associations within words, or what has been commonly recognized as *phonics*. In addition, one would undoubtedly see a good deal of unprepared oral reading, where classmates and teacher follow the reader in their texts to see if words are pronounced accurately. This type of oral reading has been given such labels as "round robin," "barber shop," or "page at a time." There would, of course, be little or no emphasis on comprehension or affect in a classroom where decoding, in its pure form, provided the basis for instruction.

One might argue that the decoding definition is applicable only to the beginning stages of reading and therefore is of no concern to middle grade teachers. To a degree such an argument is appropriate; however, the amount of "round robin" oral reading done in many of the middle grade classrooms we have observed would suggest that this definition is consciously or unconsciously acted upon by teachers long after the beginning reading stages have been passed.

Reading involves word identification and comprehension

The definition which, over the years, has emerged as the most widely accepted one, the one offered by many basal series, reading experts, and teachers, views reading as a two-dimensional act. Representative of this type of definition is one offered by DeBoer and Dallmann (1970):

In reading we employ visual symbols to represent auditory symbols. The basic task in reading is therefore to establish in the mind of the reader automatic connections between specific sights and the sounds they represent. Since the sounds themselves are symbols of meanings, the process of reading involves a hierarchy of skills ranging from auditory and visual discrimination to such higher-order mental activities as organizing ideas, making generalizations, and drawing inferences. [1]

As can be seen, this definition, as do others of this type, clearly includes word identification and comprehension as integral parts of reading. With respect to the meaning dimension of reading, DeBoer and Dallmann, as do others, hasten to suggest that readers bring meaning to the printed page and that their intent and their background of information permit them to develop new understandings and modify old concepts as a result of what an author writes.

The implications the two-dimensional definition holds for a reading program are far different from those projected by the decoding definition. Basically, it extends the concept of reading provided by the decoding definition, by placing strong emphasis on meaning and various types of comprehension. The two-dimensional definition, therefore, suggests that the classroom teacher should be concerned with word perception skills and with the ability on the part of the reader to interact with the author in a variety of thoughtful ways. If we were to observe a reading program based on this definition we would undoubtedly see some of the things we would see in a decoding classroom, but we would also see emphasis on such things as: (a) the use of context clues as an aid in the identification of words; (b) silent reading for a purpose; (c) efforts by the teacher to stimulate students to think about and react to what they read in a variety of ways; (d) prepared oral reading by students to inform or entertain classmates in an audience setting.

Reading involves interaction between thought and language

We would be remiss if we did not mention one of the most recent developments with respect to definitions of reading; namely, that reading includes not only per-

---

1. John J. DeBoer and Martha Dallmann, *The Teaching of Reading,* 3rd ed., New York: Holt, Rinehart and Winston, 1970, p. 13. Reprinted by permission.

ception but the use of syntactic and semantic information. Goodman, one of the leading proponents of this position, puts reading into perspective as follows:

. . . reading is a selective process. It involves partial use of available minimal language cues selected from perceptual input on the basis of the reader's expectation. As this partial information is processed, tentative decisions are made to be confirmed, rejected, or refined as reading progresses. . . . More simply stated, reading is a psycholinguistic guessing game. It involves an interaction between thought and language. Efficient reading does not result from precise perception and identification of all elements, but from skill in selecting the fewest, most productive cues necessary to produce guesses which are right the first time.[2]

Goodman suggests that the redundancy and sequential constraints on language, which the reader reacts to, make predictions possible. He argues that skill in reading involves not greater precision, but more accurate first guesses based on better sampling techniques, greater control over language structure, broadened experiences, and increased conceptual development. Moreover, he suggests that readers use increasingly fewer graphic cues as they develop reading skill and speed.

What would be observed in a reading program guided by Goodman's definition would not be dissimilar from what would be seen in a classroom guided by the two-dimensional definition. There would undoubtedly be considerable emphasis on meaningful silent reading, with students being encouraged to predict outcomes ahead of their reading. The use of context clues, both semantic and syntactic, would be emphasized as the basic approach to word identification. Echoic reading, where the teacher reads a selection to students before they read it silently, would be used as an instructional strategy to help students to get a feel for the "melody of the language" and to aid them in making accurate "guesses." Finally, one would undoubtedly see a greater emphasis on relating writing, speaking, and listening to reading in such a program through a language experience approach.

Reading involves perceptual, cognitive, and affective responses

The definition presented below is our own creation and is the one upon which the remainder of the chapter is based:

Reading involves the visual perception of written symbols and the transformation of these symbols into their audible or inaudible oral counterparts. The audible or inaudible oral responses act as stimuli for thoughtful reactions on

---

2. Kenneth Goodman, "Reading: A Psycholinguistic Guessing Game," in *Theoretical Models and Processes of Reading*, 2d ed., edited by Harvey Singer and Robert B. Ruddell. Newark, Delaware: International Reading Association, 1976, p. 498. Reprinted with permission of Kenneth Goodman and the International Reading Association.

the part of the reader. The types or levels of thought induced by the stimuli are determined, in part, by the syntactic and semantic accuracy of the audible or inaudible oral responses; the general language sophistication, intent, and background of the reader; and the nature of the materials. In addition, the effort expended in the perceptual and intellectual acts is partially controlled by the reader's interest in a specific selection and by his or her attitude toward reading in general.

This definition is three-dimensional in nature. It recognizes word identification and comprehension as integral parts of the reading act and, in this respect, is similar in intent to the two preceding definitions. What sets it apart from the previously cited definitions, however, is its recognition that affective responses are involved in reading.

Support for including affect in the definition comes from two sources. First, teachers have observed and reported the influence interests and attitudes have on students' reading performances. For example, when a teacher reports that a boy who supposedly reads at third-grade level worked out words in and understood a football story written at seventh-grade difficulty, one can only surmise that his efforts were influenced by an interest in the topic and a glimmer of a developing appreciation for the value of reading. Second, such researchers as Schnayer (1969), Estes and Vaughan (1973), and Vaughan (1974) have noted the positive influence of interest on reading performance. Schnayer, for instance, studied the relationships between reading interests and reading comprehension for sixth graders. He concluded that interest may enable most students, particularly those with reading ability from two years below grade level to one year above grade level, to comprehend materials that would be considered too difficult for them. Vaughan, on the other hand, investigated the effect of interest on reading comprehension of good, average, and poor across grades four, six, eight, and eleven. He found that interest affected reading comprehension for all students across all grade levels, with poor readers being the most affected in all comparisons. Neither of these points of support, we must hasten to add, is intended to suggest that we believe that reading interests should be used to keep students constantly reading above their assessed reading level. Rather, they are intended to highlight the part affect, particularly interest, plays in the reading act.

A reading program designed to the specifications of the three-dimensional definition would, in some respects, resemble the programs based on the previously cited definitions. If one were to observe such a program, he or she would expect to see learning activities for the development of word identification skills as needed, efforts by the teacher to help students to think about and react to their reading in various ways, and activities which relate the other language arts to reading. However, the most striking feature one would see in such a program would be the attention given to the development of interests in, attitudes toward, and valuing of reading. The remainder of this chapter will be devoted to these affective behaviors and their involvement in and relation to reading.

The Affective Domain

There is no question in our minds that all programs must have an affective dimension. However, before we turn to classroom practices which focus on this dimension of reading, a deeper understanding of the affective domain in general is needed. Fortunately, Krathwohl *et al.* have provided an avenue for such an effort with their work *Taxonomy of Educational Objectives, The Classification of Educational Goals, Handbook II: Affective Domain (Taxonomy)*.

A Taxonomy of the affective domain

As a point of departure and a frame of reference for what will follow, Table 6.1 includes an outline of the Taxonomy, using category and subcategory titles as entries. To understand the contents of the table and to relate them to reading, one must understand two not readily apparent ideas which pervade the Taxonomy and help one to interpret it.

First, affective behavior emphasizes a feeling tone, an emotion, or a degree of acceptance or rejection. These behaviors are commonly labeled by such terms as interest, appreciation, attitudes/values, and adjustment and are implicit in various categories and subcategories of the Taxonomy presented in Table 6.1.

The second idea not readily apparent in Table 6.1, and one that is related to the first, is that the process or continuum of affective learning reflected in the hierarchy of categories in the Taxonomy is based on the process of internalization.

The process of internalization begins with an individual's simple awareness of a phenomenon, let's say jogging for the purposes of this discussion. Next the individual seeks out the opportunity to jog, gradually attaches emotional significance to it, and begins to value it. Third, jogging becomes a part of the individual's value system, which guides behavior. Finally, jogging is valued by the individual to the degree that he or she is characterized as a jogger.

The Taxonomy related to reading

With these general observations about the Taxonomy as a foundation, let us consider how interest in, attitudes toward, and valuing of *reading* might be related to the categories of the Taxonomy and the continuum of internalization which is the Taxonomy's organizing thread.

Reading and 1.0 Receiving
1.1 Awareness
1.2 Willingness to Receive
1.3 Controlled or Selective Attention

At the *awareness* level the student may simply be conscious of the fact that reading exists, which, as Darling (1967) suggests, may be more cognitive than affective. At the next stage of development the student will demonstrate a *willing-*

Table 6.1 Category and subcategory titles
in the Taxonomy of educational objectives—affective domain

Category	Subcategories
1.0 Receiving (attending)	1.1 Awareness 1.2 Willingness to receive 1.3 Controlled or selective attention
2.0 Responding	2.1 Acquiescence in responding 2.2 Willingness to respond 2.3 Satisfaction in response
3.0 Valuing	3.1 Acceptance of a value 3.2 Preference for a value 3.3 Commitment (conviction)
4.0 Organization	4.1 Conceptualization of a value 4.2 Organization of a value system
5.0 Characterization by a value or value complex	5.1 Generalized set 5.2 Characterization

Source: David R. Krathwohl, Benjamin S. Bloom, and Bertram B. Masia, *Taxonomy of Educational Objectives, Handbook II: Affective Domain,* New York: McKay, 1964, p. 35. Reprinted with permission.

ness to read on occasion, particularly if the reading material is interesting—an indication of *selective attention.* In the middle grades a reader at the *receiving* level of the continuum would probably need to be helped to see that reading can provide interesting possibilities.

Reading and 2.0 Responding
2.1 Acquiescence in Responding
2.2 Willingness to Respond
2.3 Satisfaction in Response

Acquiescence in responding will be demonstrated by a student who reads only at the request or under the direction of the teacher. The learner who reaches the *willingness to respond* level will be more inclined to read because of a positive attitude toward reading and an inner desire to do so. At this stage we would probably begin to see the reader make a greater effort to work out words and to understand what is read, particularly if it is of interest, and to search out reading materials dealing with topics of interest. Finally, at the *satisfaction of response* level, the reader will respond emotionally to reading because it is pleasurable. In other words, the reader will begin to seek out reading opportunities because emotional significance and value are attached to them.

Reading and 3.0 Valuing
3.1 Acceptance of a Value
3.2 Preference for a Value
3.3 Commitment

The student who has reached this point in the Taxonomy will demonstrate an increasing internalization of reading as a value. For example, a student who shows a liking for reading by working to improve skill through wide reading might be said to be *accepting the value of reading.* On the other hand, a learner (who frequently chooses reading when equally enticing activities are available) can be said to have acquired a *preference* for reading. The highest level of *valuing* behavior, *commitment,* would be demonstrated, as Darling suggests, by a student who frequently reads in spare moments and pursues, explores, or refines interests through independent reading. In general, a person who is *committed to reading* will show consistent behavior which reflects this value.

Reading and 4.0 Organization
4.1   Conceptualization of a Value
4.2   Organization of a Value System

Organization is the level in the Taxonomy where an individual personally incorporates reading and the other values he or she has acquired into a system which gives direction to her or his behavior. In order to do this, an individual must *conceptualize* reading as a value in such a form that it can be interrelated with other conceptualized values. Finally, reading is placed in the individual's proper hierarchical position within the individual's system. How much middle grade reading programs can contribute to this very personal and sophisticated activity is debatable; nevertheless, this brief discussion illustrates the fourth stage of internalization as reflected in the Taxonomy.

Reading and 5.0 Characterization by a Value or Value Complex
5.1   Generalized Set
5.2   Characterization

The ultimate in affective behavior suggested in the Taxonomy is demonstrated when the internalization and organization processes reach a point where the individual responds very obviously and consistently to various situations on the basis of his or her value system. Furthermore, an individual who reaches this level has a behavior pattern based on a value system which no longer involves emotion, except when that pattern is threatened or challenged. To put it yet another way, a person characterized as a reader will consistently show that reading, in and of itself, is a definite way of life. In fact, such individuals will feel uncomfortable if they cannot read at appropriate times. As we pointed out when we discussed Level 4, *organization*, it is rather difficult to see how middle grade reading programs may contribute or relate to *characterization* because of its personal and complex nature; nevertheless, it must be recognized as the high point on the internalization continuum in the Taxonomy.

The Taxonomy's implications for reading instruction

When reading is related to the five levels of the Taxonomy, as has just been done, one notices certain implications for instruction. First, it would seem that middle grade reading programs have a part to play in the development of interests in, attitudes toward, and valuing of reading as they relate to the *receiving, responding,* and *valuing* levels of the Taxonomy. Certainly, the Taxonomy can provide a useful way of evaluating students' development of affective behaviors involved in and related to reading. Second, the point along the internalization continuum which should be used as a goal to be worked toward by teachers of reading is *commitment,* which appears to be the pivotal point in the Taxonomy. In other words, if individual students can develop a commitment to reading as a result of the instructional opportunities provided and if the Taxonomy is valid as Mikulecky (1976) suggests, movement through the *organization* and *characterization* levels would be a personal matter for each individual to resolve.

Activities Related to the Affective Dimension of Reading

Up to this point in the chapter an attempt has been made (a) to highlight, both explicitly and implicitly, the importance of affective behaviors involved in and related to reading, and (b) to provide a way of viewing the development of such behaviors. In doing so it has been suggested that a definition of reading which includes an affective dimension calls for a reading program whose goals are the development of interests in, attitudes toward, and valuing of reading. In addition it has been suggested that a goal of middle grade reading programs should be to move students toward valuing and becoming committed to reading. We hasten to add, however, that Strickler (1977) and others remind us that attitudes and values take time to develop. A "one shot" program designed to develop commitment to reading on the part of students should not be expected to do it. With this in mind, let us turn to some things teachers can do to develop affective behaviors related to reading.

Developing interest in reading

Interests are powerful motivators and middle grade reading programs must develop and use them. To accomplish this objective, students must be made aware of and encouraged to respond to the many possibilities reading provides. Depending on where students are on the continuum of internalizing reading as a value, some or all of the following suggestions may be appropriate for use in the middle grades.

Oral reading by the teacher.   For years teachers have read out loud to students in order to expose them to good literature. Often, however, this practice, if used, has disintegrated into a time-filling device when nothing else is planned or when the end of the day is near. Even when teachers have read orally to their students for the right reason, it has sometimes been done in the wrong way; that is, teachers have attempted to read entire books to their students and have often been able to complete only two or three in a year's time. How, then, should teachers, particularly middle grade teachers, read to their students? Our answer is: selectively and widely. If the intent of oral reading by the teacher is to make students aware of the possibilities reading holds for them, the teacher should read from a variety of writings on a variety of topics. Also, only carefully selected excerpts should be read to stimulate and maintain the students' interest. By proceeding in this fashion, the teacher may be able to expose students to between 30 and 60 or even more different pieces of literature in a year.

Oral reading by students to one another.   In the middle grades the reading program should provide time for students to read orally to one another from books they are currently reading or have completed. The students can be grouped by interests or across interests, depending on the exposure desired. The activity could also be organized across grade levels so that older and younger students might interact and benefit from such an experience. In any event, students should be made aware that the intent for and approach to such reading is the same as when the teacher reads orally. They should be helped to see what makes a good excerpt for such a reading lesson and they should be encouraged to read the selection in a manner that will captivate and hold the interest of the listeners.

Using tapes and records to expose students to literature.   More and more "nonbook" media vie, or at least seem to vie with reading. Indeed, many teachers are using media such as tapes and records to expose students to literature and even to improve their reading skills. When tapes or records are used for this purpose, the students must be told that what they are hearing exists in print and is available to them in book form.

Many records, tapes, and cassettes are commercially available. One of the companies in this field is Miller-Brody Production, Inc., 342 Madison Avenue, New York, 10017. Included among its tape and record offerings which would appeal to middle graders are such titles as: *Pippi Longstockings* by Astrid Lindgren; *Stuart Little* by E. B. White; *The 13 Clocks* by James Thurber; *The Wind in the Willows* by Kenneth Grahame; *Call it Courage* by Armstrong Sperry; *King of the Wind* by Marguerite Henry; *The Trumpeter of Krakow* by Eric P. Kelly; *Sounder* by William H. Armstrong; *Amos Fortune, Freeman* by Elizabeth Yates; *Caddie Woodlawn* by Carol Ryrie Brink; *Invincible Louisa* by Cornelia Meigs; *Johnny Tremain* by Esther Forbes; *The Matchlock Gun* by Walter D. Edmonds; *Ann Frank The Diary of a Young Girl*. Other companies have equally good listings.

Of course, it is not necessary to use only commercial tapes and records. Many teachers and school districts have developed their literature-on-tape resources. An elaborate example of this was a Title 1 Story Tape Project in Madison, Wisconsin. Its purpose was to both stimulate interest and help students, third and fourth graders in this case, with their reading by encouraging them to read along with the recording. A unique feature of this project, aside from putting more than 30 pieces of literature on tape, was the fact that local radio and television announcers, as well as actors, volunteered their time to record the selections.

What can be done on the local level is also illustrated by an Iowa community which at last count had a collection of some 500 titles on tape, thanks to the American Association of University Women in that city who made the recording their project. Thus, if one believes that listening to literature will stimulate students' interest in reading and may even improve their reading skill if they read along, it will always be possible to find ways of developing appropriate resources on a noncommercial basis.

Using film strips and films to stimulate reading. The potential of visual media to stimulate interest in reading cannot be overlooked. Although cost and other matters have limited the number of titles available as films, film strips and video recordings, more and more are coming on the market. For example, Miller-Brody Productions have a number of the above-mentioned titles on sound film strips. Hollywood films and television productions are another important resource. Middle graders who see a production of *Sounder, Born Free, Tom Sawyer, Huckleberry Finn, Tom Brown's School Days, Pinocchio, Black Beauty, Lassie Come Home, Davy Crockett, Daniel Boone,* etc., may be stimulated to read the story or to read about the main character (nonfiction) when such material exists. Of course, for such follow-up reading to take place students must be informed that what they see on the screen is based on something in print which is available to them to read. That such follow-up reading does occur among middle grade students has been confirmed by many librarians whose shelves were literally swept clean of titles related to currently popular television and motion picture productions. The point is that visual media can be used to stimulate reading, not defeat it, provided students are aware that a written counterpart is available. Other companies also have fine listings.

Sharing literature. One of the commonly cited characteristics of the individualized approach to reading is that students share their reading with one another. Such sharing can be done through writing, reading, listening, speaking, dramatizing, and visual arts. Our concept of sharing, then, goes well beyond the traditional book report involving only the student and the teacher. In other words, sharing, as we see it, means that students should have the opportunity to communicate with one another about their reading, in the hope that a fellow student might become interested in it. Obviously, there are many ideas about ways to share literature. Some that seem appropriate for middle graders are:

- Telling fascinating incidents.
- Dramatizing stories read by two or more students.

- Illustrating stories with pictures and murals.
- Writing descriptions of favorite characters.
- Writing a monthly or bimonthly "Saturday Review."
- Showing action on the flannel board.
- Making puppet characters and dramatizing part of a story.
- Auctioning the book by giving hints of exciting plots.
- Exhibiting objects described in books.
- Making tape recorded summaries.

To reiterate, the point here is to suggest that middle grade students be exposed to the possibilities that reading holds for them. Hopefully, such exposure will create an interest on their part to read things for themselves. In terms of the Taxonomy, the teaching strategies suggested would help students to move from *awareness*, which is the lowest point in the *receiving* category, to the *willingness to respond* level in the *responding* category. One final comment must be made. Many children who are having reading difficulties in the middle grades may benefit greatly from being exposed to reading without having to read. Too often corrective or remedial instruction has focused on skills and drills. Although these activities may be necessary, it is hypothesized here that an affective approach to such teaching may be beneficial to many students.

Developing positive attitudes toward reading

Once students are responding—in other words, reading with guidance—there must be opportunities for them to strengthen their attitudes toward reading so that they move in the direction of internalizing reading as a value. Thus, as was suggested in Chapter 1, in our discussion of recreational reading, there must be time devoted to the type of learning activities that will promote this sort of affective development.

Self-selection. If students are to value reading, they must have an opportunity to select reading materials in which they have a personal interest. This rather innocent statement has several serious implications for reading instruction. First, teachers must believe that students should be given this opportunity as part of the reading program. All too often students are allowed to read what they want only when they have nothing else to do. Second, books must be readily available. Some kind of revolving classroom library is needed to provide students with access to books when the school library or materials center is not available to them. Although many teachers may find themselves in teaching situations which are not conducive to the creation of classroom libraries, those who believe that children should have access to books on short notice will build such a library. Finally, where there is a school library or a materials center, teachers and librarians will need to work together to keep the books readily available to students. If one believes in the principle of self-selection, and most librarians do, going to the school library once a week to take out two books is not enough. Frankly, most teachers who have incorporated a self-selection dimension into their programs have usually found the librarian to be a strong and helpful ally.

Students must have time to read their self-selected materials. If one believes that self-selection of materials will contribute to the development of affective behaviors involved in and related to reading, then it follows that one will believe in allotting time for reading self-selected materials. This is a roundabout way of saying that one of the most important commitments a middle grade teacher can make is to allocate blocks of time; for example, 45–60 minutes twice a week, to just plain reading.

To put it another way, a teacher who believes that a basic goal of the reading program should be to help students to come to value reading can no longer put forward the admonitions: "Read your library books when all your other work is completed," or "Take your library books home with you and read them there." When such admonitions are operating procedures they create obvious problems. First, they indicate to students, either explicitly or implicitly, that reading self-selected materials is not a very high priority in school. Second, such procedures will undoubtedly reduce or eliminate the opportunities for less able students to read the books they have selected in school. Very often the less able students are the ones who need all the help and support they can get to become personally involved in reading. And remember, if they cannot read to themselves for extended periods of time, have someone read to them.

Lyman Hunt (1967) has supported the inclusion of blocks of reading time, which he calls Uninterrupted Sustained Silent Reading (USSR), in reading programs for some time. He argues that when a teacher values USSR and transmits this value to the students, USSR can be the acme of all skill development activity. He feels that teachers must give effort and energy to establishing, developing, and expanding USSR so that students can develop a feeling for the benefits reading has to offer. Hunt also suggests that a brief evaluation period follow each session of USSR during which the teacher asks leading questions to guide students to evaluate what they have accomplished during the session. According to Hunt, discussion of the nature, quality, and quantity of reading accomplished during USSR will enable a teacher to help each student determine the kind of reader he or she is becoming.

An example of what can happen when a faculty is committed to the potential of USSR for developing affective behaviors involved in and related to reading is worth making here. In this instance, the entire school, which is an elementary school in a small community in the Middle West, participates in USSR for 30 minutes every day. Each person in the school, including the teachers, the principal, the custodian, the secretary, etc., reads something of his or her choice during the USSR period, which is set at the same time for everyone. Now, some people would say this is a waste of time. The faculty in this school obviously do not feel that USSR is a waste of time. Their position on this matter was captured some time ago by Darling:

The teacher projects a total image. If a teacher is committed to helping children come to cherish reading, it will be evident to her pupils. If a teacher is committed to teaching her pupils to read, even if it kills them, this attitude will come through. The constant din of the teaching of phonetics, syllabication, interpretation, comprehension, and the like stresses the importance of cognitive skills. Of course, one could not become committed to reading without mastery of the basic skills; but one can master all these skills and still not enjoy reading, be committed to reading, nor use reading for the purpose for which it is presumably taught—to enrich one's life. Some learners will come to enjoy reading regardless of what teachers do. But the goal is and must be to have all pupils become committed to reading—a goal requiring conscious effort. [3]

Pupil-teacher conferences. A final activity which can contribute to helping students value reading is the pupil-teacher conference. The objectives of conferences in this context are not the same as the objectives of conferences to help students improve their reading skills in individualized reading programs. The conferences we are proposing would not focus on the diagnosis of word identification skills or comprehension abilities. Rather, they would be concerned with how a student is feeling about the selection being read at the moment and about reading in general. Such conferences focus on the personal, humanistic aspects of reading. As such, they do not need to be rigidly structured or scheduled. In essence, the main objective for the type of conferences being proposed here is to permit a teacher and a pupil to have a private time to deal with reading as a personal enterprise, and if USSR is utilized in a classroom, individual conferences can be held in one corner of the room while the rest of the class is reading silently.

A Final Comment

The purpose of this chapter has been twofold. First, the position has been taken that affective behaviors—for example, interests, attitudes, and values—are involved in and related to reading. Implicit in this position is the idea that how and when students read is influenced by how they feel about what they are reading at the moment and about reading in general. Second, it has been suggested,

---

3. David W. Darling, "Evaluating the Affective Dimension of Reading," in *The Evaluation of Children's Reading Achievement,* edited by Thomas C. Barrett. Newark, Delaware: International Reading Association, 1967, pp. 134–135. Reprinted by permission of David W. Darling and the International Reading Association.

directly and indirectly, that a goal of any reading program should be to help students move in the direction of becoming committed to reading because of its value. Assuming these two positions are viable and acceptable, middle grade reading programs must be structured accordingly.

Something to Think and Talk About

Sally Tigue, a sixth-grade teacher, has been employing a three-group basal approach with her students without variations. She feels that what she has been doing is worthwhile, but she also feels that she needs to work more to help her students value reading as a leisure-time activity. One of the activities she wants to incorporate into her program to achieve this goal is the allocation of some class time for the reading of self-selected materials. However, she is afraid the parents of her students and her principal will not view the allocation of time for such an activity as true reading instruction. How should Sally proceed? (See Appendix 6 for Authors' Response to "Something to Think and Talk About.")

References

Bloomfield, Leonard, and Clarence L. Barnhart (1961). *Let's Read.* Detroit: Wayne State University Press.

Darling, David W. (1967). "Evaluating the Affective Dimension of Reading." In *The Evaluation of Children's Reading Achievement*, edited by Thomas C. Barrett. Newark, Delaware: International Reading Association, pp. 127–141.

DeBoer, John J., and Martha Dallmann (1970). *The Teaching of Reading*, 3rd ed. New York: Holt.

Estes, Thomas H., and Joseph L. Vaughan, Jr. (1973). "Reading Interests and Reading Comprehension: Implications." *The Reading Teacher* 27: 149–153.

Goodman, Kenneth S. (1976). "Reading: A Psycholinguistic Guessing Game." In *Theoretical Models and Processes of Reading*, 2d ed., edited by Harvey Singer and Robert B. Ruddell. Newark, Delaware: International Reading Association, 497–508.

Hunt, Lyman C., Jr. (1967). "Evaluation Through Teacher-Pupil Conferences." In *The Evaluation of Children's Reading Achievement*, edited by Thomas C. Barrett. Newark, Delaware: International Reading Association, pp. 111–126.

Mikulecky, Larry J. (1976). *The Developing, Field Testing, and Initial Norming of a Secondary/Adult Level Reading Attitude Measure That Is Behaviorally Oriented and Based on Krathwohl's Taxonomy of the Affective Domain.* An unpublished Doctoral Dissertation, University of Wisconsin—Madison.

Krathwohl, David R., Benjamin S. Bloom, and Bertram B. Masia (1964). *Taxonomy of Educational Objectives, Handbook II: Affective Domain.* New York: McKay.

Shanayer, Sidney W. (1969). "Relationships Between Reading Interest and Comprehension." In *Reading and Realism*, edited by J. Allen Figurel. Newark, Delaware: International Reading Association, pp. 680–702.

Strickler, Darryl J. (1977). "Planning the Affective Component." In *Classroom Practice in Reading,* edited by Richard A. Earle. Newark, Delaware: International Reading Association, pp. 3–9.

7

USING READING TO FOSTER CREATIVITY IN THE MIDDLE GRADES

A class of sixth graders had finished reading *The Yearling* (1938) by Marjorie Kinnan Rawlings and was discussing various aspects of the novel when the teacher asked the following question: "If you could give Jody any gift you wanted to at the beginning of the story, what would you give him and how might it change the action of the story?" The class recognized this as a "thinking" question, and the room became quiet. No hands were raised, but most of the students reached for paper, pencil, and their copy of the novel. Some students made unintelligible marks on their papers while they thought, others rapidly jotted down ideas as they occurred to them, and some just sat and leafed through the book. After approximately ten minutes of thinking, rereading, and making notes or doodling, the teacher announced that one minute of thinking time remained. When that minute had elapsed, the teacher divided the class into groups of four, and the talking started. The small-group discussions were lively, with some students talking and being questioned more than others and others "passing" their turn to talk for lack of an idea they wanted to share. The teacher moved from group to group, at times just listening interestedly and at other times asking a question or joining in the conversation. It was apparent from the teacher's manner that no formal evaluation was being carried on. Approximately fifteen minutes after the small-group conversations began, the teacher asked the students to terminate their discussions and called on a member from each group to share some of the ideas presented in his or her group with the entire class. The ideas ranged from giving Jody a new rifle with which he challenged all comers to "shooting matches," to giving him an older sister who was courted by and finally married to one of the Forrester boys. The experience with creative thinking was fun for most of the students and proved that a good story and a good question can send readers on a purposeful search for ideas that they didn't know existed.

Creativity might be defined according to the delineation by Bloom, *et al.* (1956) of the cognitive level of synthesis. At this level, thinking is the process of working with elements or parts and combining them in such a way as to constitute a pattern or structure not clearly there before. This necessitates a recombination of parts or all of a previous experience with new material, reconstructed into a new and integrated whole. Applied to reading, this means that ideas acquired from a reading selection are combined with ideas or information acquired elsewhere in a purposeful search for a new product, pattern, or structure. For instructional purposes, creative reading, then, is not completely free creative behavior, but rather creative behavior from a particular reading selection toward a prescribed goal. The rationale for this instructional procedure is succinctly stated by Torrance (1965), who says, "A good story, biography or other reading material is likely to evoke many ideas and questions which can send the reader far beyond what is read."

The Suitability of the Middle Grades for Fostering Creativity

Although reading may be used to foster creative behavior at all academic levels, the intermediate grades are particularly well suited to this kind of activity. Students in the intermediate grades have a greater wealth of background experiences than do those in primary grades, and they are not so inhibited in regard to divergent thinking as older students often become. Both of these characteristics are important to the success of reading-related activities designed to foster creativity. To be creative students must draw upon their repertoire of experiences and arrange them in a pattern that is different from any previous pattern in their thinking. To do this they must "dare to be different." The playful, yet purposeful behavior inherent in creativity lends itself well to the mind of the preadolescent.

Torrance reports that the general pattern of the developmental curve of most of the creative thinking abilities he assessed is as follows: "There is a steady increase from first through third grade. With one exception, there is a sharp decrease between the third and fourth grades followed by some recovery during the fifth and sixth grades. Another drop occurs between the sixth and seventh grades, after which there is growth until near the end of the high school years."[1] His observations of children between ten and twelve years of age are the following:

Children between ten and twelve delight in exploration, girls preferring to explore in books and in pretend play and boys through firsthand experiences.

1. E. Paul Torrance, *Guiding Creative Talent,* ©1962, p. 93. Reprinted by permission of Prentice-Hall, Inc., Englewood Cliffs, New Jersey.

It is a great age for reading. They have now become less restless and can read or think for long periods . . . The child at this state . . . is capable of deriving principles or generalizations or devising schemes to express sympathy, if challenged to do so. He seldom does so on his own initiative. [Torrance suggests] . . . that ten-to-twelves be given opportunities to explore, to build, to make and to read, as well as opportunities to communicate to others about his experiences . . . Children at this stage need to test out their ideas and skills.[2]

Creative reading experiences appear to be "a natural" for students in the intermediate grades. Curtis and Bidwell (1977) say,

The encouragement of creativity (and other learning attributes as well) is not solely the responsibility of the middle school. Yet, due to the plasticity of emerging adolescents, their ability to invent, explore, and try new modes is optimal at this stage. Considerable emphasis in elementary education is placed on acquiring basic skills and learnings where convergence is stressed. In the secondary school students are expected to show evidences of divergence and creativity. Although opinions differ and precise measures of creativity are of limited validity, it is generally agreed that divergence and creativity can be fostered by the formal and informal methods utilized within the learning situation. Children gradually learn to discriminate between fantasy and reality, yet retain their ability to "make believe" and to imagine if encouraged to do so. As children progress from concrete to abstract operational thinking they should be able to continue thinking in creative ways. Hence the school should attempt to foster and encourage creativity in as many areas as possible so that children will retain and develop their imaginations during the middle school years.[3]

Sample Instructional Activities

In the intermediate grades students can be taught that creative thinking tasks (1) have a focus and parameters, (2) ask for additions to the selection rather than a retelling or an interpretation of the author's meaning, (3) request the reader's personal ideas and feelings, and (4) cannot be evaluated as correct or incorrect. Unless brainstorming is the particular kind of creative activity solicited, students also need to know that most creative questions or tasks require more thinking time than noncreative questions or tasks.

Sometime in the intermediate grades most students study the human body in their science class. They read about the different systems of the body, how they

---

2. E. Paul Torrance, *Guiding Creative Talent,* ©1962, p. 97. Reprinted by permission of Prentice-Hall, Inc., Englewood Cliffs, New Jersey.

3. Thomas E. Curtis and Wilma W. Bidwell, *Curriculum and Instruction for Emerging Adolescents,* Reading, Massachusetts: Addison-Wesley, 1977. Reprinted with permission.

work together, and how to keep them healthy. Their textbooks are usually liberally illustrated with photographs and drawings to supplement the printed descriptions. All in all the students develop a good basic understanding of what the human body can and cannot do. An enterprising teacher can encourage some creative thinking relative to these factual texts by asking students as they read to speculate upon what products might be created to extend the ability of the body to do work, be more comfortable, or play games. For example, the teacher might say:

We have read about the human body and found that there are certain things we can and cannot do with our bodies. For example, we can reach just so high and no higher and hold just so many things in our bare hands at one time. Our tools, furniture, games, clothes, and machines have been developed to fit the shapes and movements of our bodies and to make our work easier and our lives more enjoyable. Baskets, for example, and other containers were invented to help us carry more things at one time than we could carry without them. If you were a brilliant inventor, what kinds of tools, machines, furniture, clothing, or games would you invent to make life easier? Would you make bookshelves for the library that move up and down when a button is pushed so that no book is ever out of easy reach? Look over this section in the book again and think about what might help the human body work, be comfortable, or have fun. If some possibilities occur to you as you are reading, jot your ideas down so we can talk about them later. Maybe you could make the custodian's life easier with some of your inventions. Don't worry about how to do it, just tell what you would do. How about a head holder for you people who quickly use up energy stored in your muscles when you read your science book?

After the students have read the assigned selection they might be placed in small groups to share their "creations" with their classmates. Some might even be encouraged to fashion a blueprint or draw a model of their invention. One fifth grader given the assignment above drew a model of an elaborate "pet exerciser" which amounted to a treadmill in a cage mounted on roller skates. The contraption permitted whoever was walking the dog to proceed at a leisurely pace while the dog ran as much as he wanted without tugging at a leash or disappearing from sight.

One teacher used the sports pages of the daily newspaper to get some sixth-grade boys to think creatively. All of the students involved in the exercise read the sports pages for several days for the purpose of finding stories for which they could create a dialogue that might be identified as taking place between two or more living persons without actually disclosing the names of the speakers. For example, one person discussing the need to "swallow" the football instead of throwing it when the pass receivers were covered could be identified as the coach of the Green Bay Packers chiding his quarterback for throwing so many interceptions in the Green Bay Packers-Detroit Lions game. Students worked together in teams of two to create their "guess who" dialogue and the members of the class had a good time trying to identify the speakers.

History books can be read creatively to give students a feeling for the personal element in historical happenings without distorting the facts. The teacher may ask the students to imagine and write behind-the-scenes conversations, set up courtroom scenes, and make posters advertising for soldiers to aid the colonies in their fight against the aggression of the crown. One imaginative teacher had students create scenes in which historical figures from the past met people who were currently prominent. Teams of students selected one name from a list of historical characters they had read about and one from their reading of current events. Some interesting dialogue resulted when Thomas Jefferson "met" George Wallace, Henry Ford met Ralph Nader, Abraham Lincoln faced Martin Luther King, and Benjamin Franklin was a guest on the Johnny Carson show.

Teachers could work with their classes to develop a mock court trial of an industry that was accused of polluting a community's natural resources, but was also supplying the community with jobs and tax revenues. Newspaper articles, brochures, textbooks, and magazines could be consulted for the purpose of creating a case for the prosecution and for the defense. The students would be getting the facts, but they would also be synthesizing them with other information they had about court trials and the working of a capitalistic society. They would be using reading as a base for doing something different. The final production might not be brilliant in its execution and it might resemble a lot of television dramas. But it would be original in that no one else had done exactly the same thing in the same way, and it would have been built upon reading experiences.

Some Guidelines for Designing Activities

An important aspect of reading-related activities that require creative thinking is their "goodness of fit" to the reading selections. Not all reading selections lend themselves to the development of related creative tasks without requiring some straining or without having a negative effect upon the reading experience. The teacher who asks students to rewrite the ending of the short story *The Lady or the Tiger* is asking students to destroy the essence of the story. Once the door is opened and either the lady or the tiger emerges, the story loses its charm. As a story it depends upon the unique ending created by its author. The teacher who asks students to redesign the human body may be soliciting, and may get, creative responses; but the assignment does not coordinate well with or build upon the objectives of the reading assignment that prompted·it.

Another aspect of reading-related creative activities that needs to be considered carefully is the degree of creativity necessary to complete the tasks assigned. Most intermediate grade students are not capable of redesigning the traffic patterns in a major city, writing a poem that expresses their feeling upon reading the *Declaration of Independence,* or composing music to provide a background for an oral reading of *The Raven*. Only some students are highly creative individuals, and so creative tasks should be broad enough to permit them to exercise their full powers without overwhelming classmates with less creative ability. The originality, fluency, and flexibility reflected in the new product that emerges from a creative task varies tremendously among students. The goal of the classroom teacher should be to provide opportunities for each student to grow in his or her individual ability to read creatively, not to make every child a highly creative person.

In line with the care that must be taken to construct tasks that are not too demanding of students, care should also be taken to construct tasks that permit students to get somewhere with their thinking. Telling students to "write a new ending" for some stories may result in a two-sentence response: "Instead of starting on his trip over the mountains to freedom and a new life, he decided to live happily ever after in Green Valley. So he did." A better task would be, "Project our hero five years into the future. Where might he be? What will he be doing? How will he feel about what happened five years ago? Use your imagination and add to the story any way you want to."

Writing letters that might have been sent from one character in a novel to another character is a good reading-related activity that stimulates creative thinking. Or the letter might be from one historical figure to another or from one scientist to another, or from someone in the current news to someone else. The possibilities are many. Another good reading-related creative writing task is to have students make diary entries for characters they meet in biographies or autobiographies. Imagine what Charles Lindbergh might have written while he was in flight or what Jonas Salk might have written after his successful development of the Salk vaccine.

Some fictional characters are developed well enough in a novel or short story to give students a feeling for what they might write in their diaries about a particular episode. A sensitive teacher will be able to tell whether or not students are likely to empathize with characters they read about sufficiently to enjoy writing what they think the character might have written.

Creative writing tasks relative to reading selections are probably most effective in fostering creative thinking if they are assigned prior to reading. If students are given a creative thinking "set," they will read for that creative purpose. Students who are told before they read a short story that they are going to make a play out of the story when they are finished will be creating dialogue, scenery, and sound effects in their minds as the narrative unfolds. The thinking processes they employ when they are reading for a creative purpose will be quite different from those they employ when they are reading to find a main idea, see cause-effect relationships, or note factual information.

The following format is helpful for getting students to read for a creative purpose or creative purposes. With modification the format may be used with newspaper or magazine articles, literature textbooks, or textbooks in other content areas. The procedure for creating the format is as follows:

1 Find a thought-provoking selection (one with ideas students are likely to be interested in).

2 Construct assignments that require students to make an addition to the selection (those in the illustrative format below are suitable for most selections).

3 Give students plenty of time to (a) make a tentative, prereading choice of the assignment they think they will want to answer after reading, (b) read the selection, (c) make a final assignment choice, (d) complete the assignment, and (e) share their completed assignments with other students. (Some recreational reading or other quiet work must be assigned to keep students who finish their assignments before other students profitably occupied.)

ILLUSTRATIVE FORMAT

Before you read the selection below, choose the assignment that you think you will most like to do after you finish reading. You may change your choice after you read the selection.

Assignment Choices (select one)

1 Create a title for this short selection and describe the audience you think it was written for.

2 Describe the person you think might have written this. Man or woman? Age? Hobbies? How does she or he dress? If the author is a man, does he wear suits, sports jackets, or sweaters? If the author is a woman, does she prefer pantsuits or dresses? What is the author's occupation?

3 Add one or two sentences (or a whole paragraph) to this selection. In other words, what do you think the author would say next?

4 Pretend that this is a speech you wrote, and you are going to deliver it to an audience. Prepare the first two paragraphs for your oral reading. Underline words you will emphasize, make slash marks to show where you will pause, draw a wavy line under the words you will speak rapidly and a heavy line under words you will speak slowly. Imagine yourself reading it aloud to your audience.

Now Read the Selection below.

Most of us don't take time to think about how difficult it would be to live in our society without the ability to read. Many of the good things in our society were built on the belief that everyone learns how to read. Newspapers, supermarkets, libraries, the postal service, greeting cards, and schools are only a few examples of the faith people have in the ability of other people to read. And that faith has paid off. Nearly everyone in our society does learn how to read.

So one reason reading is important is that almost everyone can read. Anyone who can't is handicapped. Imagine not being able to read a birthday card, or the sports page, or the labels on food containers, or street signs, or the questions on the driver's test, or a letter from a friend, or a school assignment. Reading is important in our society; and everyone wants to be able to do it because most people take it for granted that everyone can.

Another reason reading is important is that printed words are an excellent source of information. In spite of television, tape recorders, movies, filmstrips, and other technology the printed page survives as an information source. Why? For two reasons. First, so much more information is available in print. The New York City Library system is a good example of the immensity of the number of ideas stored in print. Even one atlas, encyclopedia, or textbook is a good example of the efficiency of print for collecting and storing information. Secondly, when getting information from print, the reader is always in control. The reader can decide when and where to read. The reader can decide to re-read a word, line, paragraph, page, or whole book. The reader can stop the flow of ideas coming off a page to think, question, memorize, or rest. With reading the information-getter, not the information-giver, is in control. And for learning information, that is where the control should be.

Finally, reading is important because reading brings so many people so much pleasure. Reading is on or near the top of the list of enjoyable activities for most good readers. Many people find relaxation and pleasure from reading a good book, the news, comics, magazines, or whatever they like to read. They simply would not let a day go by without reading something just for fun. They have a healthy addiction to reading.

Reading is important not only for people in our society, but also for our society itself. There are vast differences between a completely oral society and a society that uses print to store and transmit its culture. In an oral society storage and transmission of culture are limited to the memories and communication skills of the best memorizers and talkers in the group. There are no limits to the ideas and information a society that uses writing and reading can store and retrieve. Furthermore, societies that use writing and reading can communicate ideas and feelings with greater detail, greater precision, and greater complexity. Writers have an advantage over speakers. Writers can think, write, erase, re-write, think again, select just the right word or phrase, and polish their messages until they "sparkle." So, clearly, reading is important for people as individuals and for society in general.

Now Make Your Final Assignment Choice and Go to Work on It.

Suitable Material

Some stories allow students to write themselves in for a scene or two. Before they read the teacher might suggest that they watch for sections in the story where they would like to offer the main characters some advice or reprimand them. As they read, they can write down the counsel, admonition, or other verbalizations they would add. Class discussion of the story in terms of these creative insertions can be fun and sometimes show explicitly the wide range of feelings, judgments, and interpretations that readers bring to the same story.

Reading-related products that result from creative reading may range from a simple line of dialogue to an elaborate dramatic production. A poem can stimulate a response from students that can be manifested in art work, oral reading with a musical background, photographing natural scenes suggested by the poem, or other creative activities. Think of the possibilities for creating a title, writing a dramatic scene, describing the characters, making a list of emotion-packed words or phrases to add to those specified in the following poem, or speculating about the personal characteristics of the author.

The words were sharp and stung my ear.
What right had he to make me hear,
"You're old and mean. You're bad and dumb."
What cause to clench his fist on thumb?

A little stunned I stood and heard
My spirit sigh with each new word.
Such anger on a child's tongue.
Such anger in a head so young.

But then his voice was not alone.
The words he spoke were once my own.
Another voice, my own I heard,
Spitting, piling word on word.

The small boy's words which stung my ear
I once had made my father hear.
The words which now were such a bother
I once had said to my own father.
                    by Richard Smith

Consider also the excellent possibilities for reading beyond the lines in the following passages from William Cambell Gault's *Dirt Track Summer* (1968):

The flag flashed and bedlam reigned.
The lady seemed to leap as I bottomed her. To my right, Les Atwell
was staying with us, but to the left, Red Callahan was out of sight.
I had clearance and I cut toward the inner rail. Les was losing ground. (p.
168)

What is Les thinking? What is the loudspeaker blaring? What are the different sounds coming from the fans in the stands? What colors could be blended to illustrate the scene? If you were making a movie of this scene, what shots would you take? Would they be close-ups or distance shots?

The stage is set for motivating students to write short verses after they have read the short story "Herbert's Poem" by Hazel Wilson (1969). Students might enjoy trying to top some of the following attempts by Herbert who had to write a poem to satisfy a class assignment:

On a sunny day a boy's a fool
To stay shut up inside a school.

I'd be a sap
To wear a cap.

I'll go to beddy
When I'm ready. (p. 000)

The importance of suitable material cannot be overemphasized. Reading-related tasks that require divergent thinking fall flat if they are too contrived. Teachers should be on the alert for material that lends itself to creative thinking, but they should not expect any story, poem, or textbook chapter to suffice. Some material is excellent for convergent thinking but does not qualify for creative reading. Obviously, material from which students cannot gain a literal interpretation with relative ease is unlikely to evoke the kind of "free-wheeling" responses creative reading calls for.

The task itself, how it is structured, and how it is presented to students must be carefully thought out if it is to be the vehicle for moving students from printed material to the unique combinations produced by thinking at synthesis level. Teachers must take into consideration the previous experiences students have had with creativity, the present interests of the students, and the specific characteristics of a task that will (1) motivate students to do their best thinking, (2) relate clearly to the reading selection or selections, (3) give direction without stifling exploratory thinking, (4) permit students who are highly creative to "do their thing" and let students who are not highly creative use what creative ability they have. A task is probably most effective in teaching students to engage in creative thinking while they are reading if it is given to them before they begin their reading, and they are told that they are to complete the task when they finish reading. For example, the teacher might introduce a story in the following manner:

You are going to meet a character in this story named Stan. Stan lives on a
farm and has never really been to a large city like Detroit. As you read the
story, you will get to know a lot about Stan, what he likes, how he thinks.
You will also meet some of his friends. Because of what you learn about Stan
you might come to expect that Stan will leave the farm some day and move to
the city. If he does, he will need a job and a place to stay. After we have read

the story, we are going to write some Help Wanted newspaper advertisements and some Room for Rent advertisements that we think might be very appealing to Stan. So as you read, be thinking about where a fellow like Stan might like to work and stay if he moved to Detroit.

Training Students to Recognize Creative Tasks

Students need to be trained to recognize a question or a task that asks for creative thinking. The following distinctions have been helpful in showing intermediate grades students the major differences between noncreative and creative thinking tasks:

Noncreative tasks

1   Ask only for information that is in the selection.

2   Ask for responses that can usually be evaluated as correct or incorrect.

3   Focus the reader's attention upon the author's meaning.

Creative tasks

1   Ask for information not in the selection.

2   Ask for responses that are a reflection of the reader's background and experiences and therefore cannot be evaluated as correct or incorrect.

3   Focus the reader's attention upon his addition to the author's message.

Students need also to be told that responses to creative tasks usually require more thinking time. Studies of classroom interchanges show that most questions teachers ask are at the cognitive level of memory and can be answered quickly and straightforwardly. Consequently, students accustom themselves to giving quick responses to questions and assigned tasks. Teachers should make it clear that they expect some thinking time to go into responses to creative questions and tasks. Some teachers encourage their students to brainstorm on paper or just doodle to aid their thinking processes when they are working on a creative reading assignment.

The Importance of Teachers' Perceptions

Basic to teaching intermediate grade children to read creatively is the teacher's concept of reading and the teacher's understanding of the purpose of reading-related activities. Teachers who are uncomfortable if unable to evaluate responses as correct or incorrect or if confronted with long periods of silence while students think, or displeased by responses from their students that are very unlike the responses they would have given are unlikely to foster creativity through reading.

Kahlil Gibran (1965) in *The Prophet* writes that if a teacher, ". . . is indeed wise he does not bid you enter the house of his wisdom, but rather leads you to the threshold of your own mind." (p. 56) This is what creative reading is all about.

After their study of creativity and intelligence Getzels and Jackson (1962) concluded among other things that children learn to be noncreative. Classroom interaction studies and informal observation of the questions teachers ask and the assignments they give show that even if they are not expressly taught to be non-creative, students at all academic levels certainly are *not* taught to be creative. Perhaps there is still much truth in the related assertion of Getzels and Jackson that, "The problem . . . is that no one as yet knows how to educate for creativity." (p. 123) On the other hand, if creativity is defined as a synthesizing process in which parts or elements are combined in a way that gives rise to a structure or pattern new in the awareness of the creator, then teachers can "educate" for creativity. Good reading material and reading-related tasks that stimulate thinking at synthesis level are two vehicles for helping students exercise the creative ability they have.

Before instructional practices designed to help students read creatively can reach that goal certain conditions must be present. It is important for teachers to recognize that creativity in the classroom flourishes only in an atmosphere that encourages openness and is nonthreatening. Students soon learn that in certain classes it pays to "psych out" the teacher and think on his or her brain wave-length. If students are to stretch their minds to the cognitive level of synthesis, which means traveling in new territory, they must not be afraid of being arrested for trespassing. As a rule students in the middle grades are apprehensive about being different if being different means courting negative reactions, no matter how mild. Telling students that they will not be evaluated or embarrassed is not enough. To enter freely into reading-related creative activity, they must, over a period of time, experience ready acceptance of their creative products. Teachers who are inconsistent in their reactions to the creative responses they solicit teach students to be wary of expressing what they think and ultimately to be wary of thinking more than the author said.

Creativity is an elusive quality, difficult to define and difficult to evaluate, but an important phenomenon to the well-being of individuals and societies. All mature readers know the feeling of working with the author as they read—visualizing, predicting, wishing, adding some idea or feeling that wants expression. Schools must foster this dimension of reading just as consciously as they teach dimensions that are less difficult to define and easier to evaluate.

Something to Think and Talk About

A superintendent of schools addressing an assembly of all first-year teachers in the school district at a preschool orientation session:

This will be your first year of teaching, and we are pleased that you have chosen our school district for this important phase of your professional development. You are joining us in an age of accountability. If we want tax monies from the public, we must prove the monies are teaching children the things they need to know. We need hard data. We need improved scores on standardized tests. We must set behavioral objectives, teach to help students meet those objectives, and measure the effects of our instruction in terms of test scores. The public wants proof that students are learning a dollar's worth for every dollar spent.

This year we are focusing upon our middle school reading program. All students will be given a standardized reading achievement test in September and again in June. We want to be able to show that we have a good program by pointing to achievement gains on those tests. Reading is the most important subject we teach in our schools. We plan to prove that we're teaching reading well. This is a challenge I offer to all of you beginning teachers.

(See Appendix 7 for Authors' Response to "Something to Think and Talk About.")

References

Bloom, Benjamin, *et al.* (1956). Taxonomy of Educational Objectives. New York: McKay.

Curtis, Thomas E. and Wilma W. Bidwell (1977). *Curriculum and Instruction for Emerging Adolescents.* Reading, Mass.: Addison-Wesley.

Gault, William Campbell (1968). *Dirt Track Summer.* New York: Scholastic Book Services.

Getzels, Jacob W., and Philip W. Jackson (1962). *Creativity and Intelligence.* New York: Wiley.

Gibran, Kahlil (1965). *The Prophet.* New York: Knopf.

Rawlings, Marjorie Kinnan (1938). *The Yearling.* New York: Grosset and Dunlap.

Torrance, E. Paul (1965). "Guidelines for Creative Teaching," *The High School Journal* **XLVII**: 459–464.

Torrance, E. Paul (1962). *Guiding Creative Talent.* Englewood Cliffs, New Jersey: Prentice-Hall.

Wilson, Hazel (1969). *Great Stories for Young Readers.* Pleasantville, New York: The Reader's Digest Association.

DEVELOPING READING SKILLS IN THE MIDDLE GRADES WITH CONTENT AREA MATERIALS

One characteristic of a good reading program in the middle grades is that reading skills developed with materials constructed to teach children how to read pay off with materials written to transmit information, such as a science text, for example. The proof of the program, then, at least in part, lies in the students' growing ability to get the information they need from reading assignments in the content areas. Something is amiss with a program that has students performing well with basal readers, workbooks, games, and skill development kits but doing poorly with their social studies, language arts, science, and mathematics textbooks.

The Need for Transfer

The task of transferring reading skills from one kind of material to another is a critical one. Reading is a learning tool and, therefore, must not become an end unto itself. Teachers have often incorrectly assumed that students who appear to master reading skill development exercises and who score high on standardized reading achievement tests will have no trouble comprehending a description of a scientific procedure, an exposition of the causes and results of the Civil War, or the steps to be followed in finding how much longer it took C to paddle a canoe against the current than it took A and B. Such is not the case. Just as teachers strive to teach science, social studies, mathematics, and language arts so that the major concepts are relevant to one or another aspect of the students' daily lives, they must work consciously to help students *read* the particular materials used in the content area curriculums. Our observation has been that much more attention is given to making content relevant than is given to incorporating reading study skills instruction into the teaching of content in the various content area curriculums. One mark of good teachers is that they keep reading study skills development as clearly in focus as they keep other major curriculum objectives in the content areas.

The ideal, which seems to be a reasonable expectation in the middle grades, is for teachers to teach reading skills in reading classes, making a deliberate effort to show how these reading skills can be applied to content area materials and for teachers of content area classes to assign content area materials with instructions on how to read them. How much students learn from their social studies, science, mathematics, and literature reading assignments depends to a large extent on the kind of instruction their teachers of those subjects give them prior to and following their reading. Asking students to read something so that it can be discussed later often means that the teacher has to tell them later what they missed in their reading. Reading content area materials without direction amounts to traveling in unfamiliar territory without a map and with no knowledge of the points of interest along the way.

Teaching reading in the content areas should not be confused with the activity of the functional reading groups we discussed in Chapter 1. The basic difference is that the subject matter to be read in the content area curriculums is prescribed and usually follows some sequential pattern through the grades. Early United States History, for example, is usually given a particular slot in the total school social studies curriculum and is taught in relation to preceding and subsequent topics in that curriculum. The information-getting reading groups discussed in Chapter 1 are interest centered and follow no particular sequence or prescription for what should be learned through reading.

Perhaps an analogy will illustrate the need for, and the underlying concept of, teaching reading in the content areas. No coach would ever send the team on to the field of play without carefully scouting the opposing players and instructing the team in how best to encounter them. When the players meet, they know their opponents' plays, their own game plan, and the special obstacles to victory presented by each team they play. Unfortunately, too many content area teachers instruct their students after they have been beaten by a selection they were never prepared to encounter. The postreading activities should be enriching experiences that motivate students to read further in the subject—not replays of a defeat. Unfortunately, too many students lose too many games with content area materials and they quit trying to win.

Guidelines for Teachers

We present five guidelines for the teacher who wants to help middle grade students read content area materials successfully:

1   Whenever possible have materials relative to the topic being studied available at different levels of reading difficulty to accommodate the differing reading abilities of students in the class.

2 Make reading assignments short when the ideational content is difficult to understand or the writing style is difficult for young readers.

3 Know the reading strengths and weaknesses of the students well enough to anticipate difficulties with certain materials.

4 Read the material to be assigned carefully beforehand to become aware of ideational content, words, sentences, figurative language, or other aspects likely to present obstacles to comprehension.

5 Prepare students for the ideas they will encounter and for linguistic elements which are likely to give them trouble.

If these five steps are followed, postreading activities can indeed be used to reinforce and enrich reading experiences rather than to tell the students what they were supposed to have learned while they were reading.

The remainder of the present chapter is devoted to illustrating specifically how teachers may introduce and prepare students to read selections from content area materials used in grades four through eight. Unlike most discussions of teaching reading in the content areas, our presentation is not broken down into sections with each section devoted to one of the major curriculum areas in the middle grades. We are certainly aware of the fact that some material in particular content areas requires the application of special reading strategies. For example, we believe that teachers, if they inspect the material they assign carefully, will recognize the need for preparing students to read a particular math problem differently from the way they would prepare them to read a rainfall map of the tropic regions. However, we believe there is a good deal of overlap among the content areas in regard to the skills needed for good comprehension. And where substantial differences do exist, the differences are obvious.

Ultimately, teachers must be perceptive enough to know what characteristics of a reading selection may cause impediments to comprehension and prepare students for them. The variations *within* a collection of social studies materials or *within* a collection of science materials are sufficiently great to argue against compiling a list of specific suggestions for teaching students to read social studies and another, equally specialized list for teaching students to read science materials. As with most other aspects of teaching reading, the burden is upon the perceptiveness and resourcefulness of the teacher.

Our hope, then, is that the illustrations we present will make teachers more perceptive to the cues to meaning inherent in content area materials themselves and also give teachers a repertoire of instructional practices to draw upon when providing the needed help. An important point needs to be made here. The nine illustrative instructional practices that follow serve a two-fold purpose: (1) they help students learn important skills for reading content area materials and (2) they help students understand and retain the information they read. Teachers who incorporate the teaching of reading into their content area teaching not only teach reading skills, but also improve their teaching of the content itself.

Nine Illustrative Instructional Practices

1 Smith constructed a paragraph to illustrate the different mental processes
   students must employ to understand even a short *social studies* selection:

   At first *(1) government took a liberal position on the powers given them
   by the Constitution.* However, *(2) events soon proved that certain groups
   could interpret the Constitution to serve their own interests at the expense
   of other groups. Those in power enjoyed interpreting the Constitution so
   that their financial interests were helped.* Out of power *(3) these individuals found that* every coin has two sides. *(4) Some who had argued*
   vigorously *(5) for a liberal interpretation of the Constitution began to
   change their minds and ask for a narrower view of governmental powers*
   under *(6) the Constitution.*[1]

   Within this paragraph, students must (1) attend to words that tell them to
   hold an idea tentatively, (2) note the word that tells them how to relate a
   preceding and a following idea, (3) interpret a sentence that begins with
   an atypical syntactical pattern, (4) respond to figurative language, (5)
   know that a modifying word takes its meaning from the noun form from
   which it is derived, and (6) respond to the idiomatic use of the word
   "under." How students interpret this paragraph depends upon how well
   they think through the language employed by the author to express his or
   her ideas. Prereading instruction will maximize their interpretative powers
   and teach them how to respond to the same and similar language devices
   in other reading selections. Postreading activity may be used to clarify
   further or extend the meaning of the passage and again alert the students
   to the strategies employed by good readers when their purpose is to obtain
   as much information as possible from a selection.

   To teach reading in the content areas teachers must examine their
   materials carefully to find opportunities to focus students' attention upon
   a key word, a subtlety, an unusual sentence construction, a summarizing
   passage, a questionable assertion, an explanatory chart, a format clue, or
   other elements that bridge the gap between the ideas and intent of the
   author and the mind of the reader. There is no formula or check list that
   will do the job. The teacher must know the students' needs and the ideational and linguistic characteristics of the material. The task is a difficult
   one that requires careful planning for each assigned selection.

2 The following paragraph is taken from a fourth-grade *science* book:

   *In order to keep plants and animals alive in your classroom, you must try
   to provide the things they would have in their natural habitat. A frog in*

---

1. Richard J. Smith, "The Poor Reader in the Content Areas," *The National Elementary Principal* **LI**, 2 (Oct. 1971), pp. 55. Reprinted by permission.

your terrarium would need a small pan of water so that it could keep its skin moist. . . . Since cactus plants grow naturally in the desert, would they need much water?[2]

Prior to reading this paragraph students might be given the following instructions to make the passage more meaningful and to teach some specific reading skills:

a) Underline the last word in the first sentence. If you don't already know what it means, notice how the rest of this sentence and the following sentence tell you its meaning.

b) Do the same thing for the word "terrarium."

c) After you read the second sentence, pause and try to picture in your mind what is being described.

d) Think of another word that might be used in place of the first word in the last sentence without changing the question being asked.

e) The answer to the last sentence should be obvious. Add one more sentence to this paragraph that communicates the same idea as the last sentence.

Certainly teachers should *not* try to teach as many reading skills as possible with every paragraph they assign. Too much of a good thing is still too much. The number and nature of the tasks suggested for the paragraph above would be subject to the judgment of the teacher who would know the objectives of the science unit and the skills of the students. The specific tasks above are focused upon developing the following skills:

Task 1⎫ Getting the meaning of an unfamiliar word from the
Task 2⎭ surrounding context
Task 3   Forming visual images of descriptive passages
Task 4   Attending carefully to "signal" words that show relationships
Task 5   Extending the application of a concept by drawing upon background experience

3   The following excerpts are taken from a fifth-grade *social studies* text:

In June Richard Henry Lee of Virginia rose in the Continental Congress. He said, "These united colonies are, and ought to be, free and independent states." Congress talked about the idea. Then it decided that a committee should write a declaration of independence . . . Jefferson worked

---

2. Abraham S. Fischler, *et al., Modern Elementary Science,* New York: Holt, Rinehart and Winston, 1971, p. 8. Reprinted by permission.

*hard, writing, as he said, out of his heart and head . . . John Adams and
Ben Franklin made some changes.* [3]

In these few words teachers can find many opportunities to teach
important reading skills. For example, students might be given the following guidance by the teacher to make their reading experience maximally
productive:

Before reading:

a) How does the word "declaration" probably express the idea the colonists had in mind for letting England know their true feelings better
than any other word? What other words might have been used to
describe the colonies' message to their mother country? Would they
have been as effective?

b) The author tells us that this meeting of the Continental Congress was
in June. Is this an important fact to know?

c) When you read about how Jefferson describes how he wrote the
Declaration, pay careful attention to the exact words he used, and
think about what they mean. We are going to talk about these words
and what they mean when you finish reading the assignment.

d) Look at the fourth sentence. Underline the word "it." Pay careful
attention when you read this assignment to be sure you know what
the "it" refers to.

After reading:

a) Let's write a short statement that tells *who*, did *what*, *when*, *where*,
and for what reason (*why*). This will help us remember the facts in
this reading assignment.

b) How would you sum up what this reading assignment has added to
our knowledge of how Americans won their freedom?

c) What did Thomas Jefferson mean when he said he wrote the Declaration of Independence "out of his heart and head?"

d) How do you think John Adams and Ben Franklin told Thomas Jefferson that they made some changes in what he wrote? How do you
think Jefferson felt as he watched Congress making more changes?

e) Who will read Richard Henry Lee's challenge to the Continental Congress just the way you think he might have said it? Remember, he was
from Virginia.

---

3. Harold H. Eibling, *et al., Our Country,* Forest River, Illinois: Laidlow Brothers,
1965, p. 188. Reprinted by permission of Laidlow Brothers, a Division of Doubleday.

Within this short reading selection teachers are able, if they wish, to teach students:

a) shades of differences in meaning among words that appear to communicate the same idea;

b) that certain factual information included by the author may be used to gain a better general impression of a historical account;

c) to note, enjoy, and interpret figurative language;

d) to attend carefully to pronoun referents;

e) that answering the five "w's" will help clarify the facts presented in certain selections and aid retention of those facts;

f) that summing up information learned from a reading assignment and relating it to earlier assignment aid comprehension and retention;

g) that figurative language may be the best way to communicate certain ideas or feelings;

h) that history is made by people and an awareness of the personal element makes reading historical selections more interesting;

i) that readers must supply the intonation patterns and dialectal characteristics to gain the full impact of a speaker's words in print.

4 Reading *mathematics* is especially troublesome for students who have not learned to read slowly, analytically, and with pencil in hand. Since reading mathematics material requires such a high degree of concentration, teachers are wise to provide students with thinking games or puzzles as readiness activities before introducing reading assignments. Teachers are also wise to keep assignments short because of the heavy expenditure of intellectual energy necessary for most students to comprehend mathematics material. Another factor that interferes with students' understanding of mathematics material is anxiety. Some, perhaps many, students perceive themselves as poor mathematicians and consequently approach a reading assignment in math fearfully and with little confidence in their ability to learn what is in the book. Teachers must try to reduce this anxiety factor which interferes seriously with reading comprehension.

Although students have been given instruction on how to solve the problem presented in the following example taken from a book used in grade eight (Van Engen, *et al.,* 1969) they need to be told to (1) read it slowly, (2) draw a sketch of the problem, (3) reread it, concentrating on the question being asked, and (4) do the indicated calculations:

Boat X was 10 miles east of boat Y. Then boat X traveled directly north to shore. Boat Y traveled 26 miles directly to the same point on shore. Boat X's trip was how many miles shorter? (p. 173)

Specialized vocabulary used in mathematics material is sometimes difficult for students. For example, teachers need to be certain students understand the meaning of the mathematical terms underlined in the following explanation taken from a fifth-grade math text (Robert E. Eicholz and Phares G. O'Daffer, 1971):

You have seen that we write sums such as 23 + 8/10 more simply by writing a decimal point after 23. We agree that the digit placed to the right of the decimal point shows the number of tenths. The diagram below shows how we extend our "place-value" system in order to have a simple way to write sums such as . . . (p. 257)

Even if these terms have been explained and used previously in the book, teachers cannot assume that students understand them well enough to permit good comprehension of the heavily loaded paragraph above. The meaning of specialized terminology may need reteaching as it is encountered in new contexts.

5   *Poetry* is frequently interpreted with little understanding of the poet's message. Consequently any feeling for the poem is out of the question. Teachers often "teach" the poem after students have had an unproductive private reading. An *ex post facto* teaching frequently amounts to a eulogy at a funeral. The poem is not buried properly until the teacher heaps praise upon it. Prereading instruction might well save some poems from an untimely demise in the minds of student readers.

The delightful climax of *The Ballad of Father Gilligan* by William Butler Yeats is disclosed in the following words by the old priest:

"He who hath made the night of stars
For souls, who tire and bleed,
Sent one of His great angels down
To help me in my need."[4]

It may seem as though this stanza clearly indicated that God took pity on Peter Gilligan as he slept and in his stead sent an angel to minister to a dying man, thereby sparing the tired priest the feeling of guilt over a lost soul. However, before students encounter this explanatory stanza, they must read ten other stanzas containing figurative language, dialogue, and some rather profound concepts. Consequently, they often complete the ballad without quite knowing what happened. As a result of such unproductive reading experiences, their attitudes toward the poem and perhaps poetry in general may be more negative than positive. Somehow the joy

4. Robert Freier and Arnold Lazarus, eds., *Adventures in Modern Literature*, 4th ed., New York: Harcourt, Brace and Company, 1956, p. 346.

of discovering God's intervention in the life of Peter Gilligan is greater when the students discover it by themselves as they are reading. The teacher's explanation after the fact takes away some of the power of the poem and a little of the students' confidence in themselves as readers.

We have observed in our teaching and discovered in a research study (Smith and Burns, 1968) that having students place a mark next to that key stanza to remind them to attend carefully to the important idea in it improves their comprehension of the ballad. This simple prereading instruction consistently results in better understanding of the main idea of the selection and more positive attitudinal responses to it. It would seem that this technique would be generalizable to other poems that have similarly difficult key stanzas. In fact we have used the technique with other poems and found it to be as effective with them as it is with *The Ballad of Father Gilligan*.

Good poetry is around for many years and continues to find its way into anthologies and other materials long after it has been written. Often vocabulary which was used commonly during a poet's lifetime or which he chose from his large repertoire of words is unfamiliar to the language experience of the students who are assigned to read it. A cursory examination of poetry selected for middle grade students disclosed the following words and terms which might be totally unfamiliar to certain students and the meanings of which were not apparent from the context surrounding them.

taper	Duke
lulled	Duchess
bosom	brazen
lamp post	four-leaf-clover
lumbered	palfreys
tailboards	riders posting
hoary	ferny
kinship	wild abandon
watershed	cascades
twelve leagues ahead	crochet
fancy's wraith	

Some time spent discussing these words before reading the poem would make the reading of the poem more enjoyable and would enlarge the students' vocabularies. Some words might be explained briefly before the students came across them in the context of the poem, and discussed more thoroughly after reading. However, teachers must be extremely careful not to teach reading skills at the expense of the enjoyment students can get from the poem. Achieving the right balance must always be left to the judgment of the teacher.

6 Textbooks are intended to help students understand subject matter. Yet, in their attempts to be illuminating authors of textbooks frequently overload students' minds by writing in a manner that requires frequent shifting of mental processes. The following paragraph is taken from an eighth grade *language* book (Bernard, Tanner; Craig, Vittatoe; and Robert C. Shutes, 1968). Read it slowly, noticing the number of ideas contained in 45 words and the numerous ideational relationships the reader is required to make to comprehend an important concept.

The preceding paragraphs make clear how a modern biographer looks upon efforts to idealize the subject of biography or to invent dialogue or interesting but unrecorded facts. Some fictionalized "biography" can be quite entertaining as fiction, but it should not be looked upon as biography. (p. 61)

Although one might decry the style of writing frequently found in textbooks, the fact remains that students will be called upon often to learn ideas from books and other materials that are hard to read. Students can learn some strategies which will help them to comprehend and retain difficult material. For example, for the paragraph above, students might be asked to make a list of all of the important ideas in the passage. Then the lists prepared by different students could be compared, and with the teacher's help a permanent list compiled for their notebooks. The final list might contain the following items:

a) Some biographers fictionalize the characters or events they write about.

b) Fictionalized characterizations, dialogue, or descriptions of happenings may be interesting, but they are not biography.

c) Biographers must stick to recorded facts.

d) Some biographers deplore writers who claim to be biographers, but who in fact invent much of what they write about.

From this exercise students learn that breaking down and rearranging the sentences in a paragraph may help them extract the author's message. Teachers must cooperate with the students endeavoring to get information from difficult material by keeping assignments to read that kind of material short.

7 A number of important reading skills could be taught or reinforced in conjunction with teaching the content in the following selection from a *science* textbook:

As you may have guessed, the process described above happens very often in science: ask a question, make a hypothesis, test the hypothesis. You should not get the idea that these are the three steps in science. Scientific investigations don't always follow the pattern. However, the pattern does occur often enough that it will be worth your time to learn it.[5]

If the paragraph above is a key paragraph in the unit being studied and the teacher wants the students to learn the concepts presented via their reading, the teacher may help them by calling their attention to techniques that aid comprehension and retention. For example, the teacher might give the following prereading instruction:

The second paragraph on page 67 is very important, and I want you to read it slowly. Put a little mark in the margin next to that paragraph so you won't forget to read it carefully when you come to it. The information in that paragraph refers to a process that is described in the paragraphs preceding it. So before you begin reading the paragraph, pause and think back over what you have just been reading about. The first sentence in the paragraph will give you a precisely stated list of the steps in the process. The author lets you know they are coming by using a colored mark before them. You will need to know these steps in their exact order for the test tomorrow. Why don't you put a circle around the colored mark right now to remind yourself to get the three steps down in your notebook. Underline the word "not" in the second sentence. For our discussion after you read the page I've assigned, I would like you to be able to answer the questions on the board about that key paragraph:

a) How would you read the second sentence orally?

b) What are the key words in the third sentence?

c) What is another word you could use in place of the word "However" in the fourth sentence?

Any questions before you start reading on page 65?

If the students follow the teacher's instructions they will learn the content of the assignment better than they would if they do not, their postreading discussion will be better, and they will learn some important reading-study skills. The specific reading-study skills include the following:

a) pausing to reflect upon reading done prior to reading a summary paragraph,

b) reading difficult or important material slowly,

c) using punctuation clues,

d) noting sequence of steps in a scientific process,

---

5. Frederick A. Rasmussen, *et al., Man and the Environment,* Boston: Houghton Mifflin, 1971, p. 67. Reprinted by permission.

e) writing down key items,

f) attending carefully to key words,

g) noting the intonation clues indicated by words in italics,

h) attending carefully to words that show relationships between or among ideas.

It is unlikely that most middle grade students would apply these skills if specific instructions to do so did not accompany the assignment.

Postreading discussions are often more revealing of how much students without prereading instruction did *not* learn than they are indicative of how much they did learn. The fact of the matter is that content area materials are so heavily loaded with concepts, specialized vocabulary, facts, and other important data that unless students read them slowly and thoughtfully they miss a good deal. We recommend strongly that teachers give much shorter reading assignments than they typically do in order to get more mileage—in terms of subject matter mastery and study skills development—out of the materials students do read. Generally, teachers assign too much reading and force students to read superficially material that requires and deserves slow, thoughtful reading. In the following short description of how snakes move, note the vocabulary, visual images, and factual information to be dealt with (Carr, 1963).

Generally they are able to accomplish this in a familiar wavy, or "serpentine," fashion of thrusting sideways with the body, much as a fish swims, with the plates or scales on their undersides finding a purchase against irregularities on the ground (if there are no such rough spots, as on a pane of glass, they cannot move at all). (p. 100)

There is no point in moving one's eyes across this passage unless the mind accompanies them. This is excellent descriptive material that can teach students much if they think as they are moving their eyes and holding the book. The joy of reading and learning will be lost if passages such as this are hurried through to get to the next assignment. Teachers who want to incorporate the teaching of reading into their content teaching must be selective about the materials they assign to be read; they must assign parts of chapters or parts of books with accompanying instructions on how to read them. Students would learn most of the content that is typically assigned to be read better by listening to the teacher tell about it. Unfortunately, too many teachers present in class the same material they assigned students to read the night before. When this happens, students learn to be haphazard readers because "The teacher will tell us what's important anyway." Material which is read should be discussed, not retold.

8 The following illustration is still another example of how content area materials can be used to help students become better readers. The material is taken from a *social studies* book for the middle grades (Patterson, *et al.,* 1963, pp. 111–114). The six reading development objectives, the material, and the instruction given to students for each are specified below.

a) *Helping Students Set Purposes for Reading*

Subsection title: "The Apaches: Swift Arrow's Test"

Suggested instruction to students: Having read the title, what do you think this part of Chapter 11 is about? How do you interpret the picture at the bottom of the page?

b) *Helping Students Attend to Format Clues*

Format clues (subheads within the subsection): "Warrior Raiders," "Wickiups and Wanderers," "Waiting and Wondering," "The Test."

Suggested instruction to students: Leaf through the pages, noticing the subheadings in bold print and the pictures on each page. Now tell me what you think we will learn about in this subsection.

c) *Helping Students Enlarge Their Vocabulary*

Key words: wickiup, mesquite

Suggested instruction to students: You will meet two new words for your vocabulary notebook. They are on the board. Find them in the second column on page 111 and underline them. See how much you can tell me about them in our discussion of this subsection after we have finished reading it.

d) *Helping Students Use Visual Imagery*

Key passage: " . . . he could see the bright new moon. It was like a strand of silver hanging in the sky."

Suggested instruction to students: Put a little "x" next to the last paragraph in the first column on page 111. When you read that paragraph, imagine that you are Swift Arrow and see if you can see the moon as he saw it on his bed of grass and leaves. Those of you who have been camping may recall similar experiences of your own.

e) *Helping Students Make Predictions*

Key sentence: "He did not know what it would be, but he was ready."

Suggested instruction to students: Before you turn to page 114 predict what Swift Arrow's test will be. Write your prediction on a piece of paper and we'll compare our predictions in our discussion of this chapter.

f) *Helping Students Summarize Ideas*

Final sentence: "Swift Arrow had passed the test."

Suggested instruction to students: When you finish reading this subsection, make a list of the five aspects of the Apache culture you think are most important to remember. Compare this list with the list you made after we read about the Hopis. We'll compare our individual lists as part of our discussion. Then I'll read you what the encyclopedia has to say about the Apaches.

9 A final illustration of how to use content area materials to develop students' reading skills and to help them learn and remember the information in the materials is given below. The model is especially useful for material that is important enough to be studied carefully for thorough understanding. It is unlikely that teachers would use the technique with every assignment.

To illustrate the model we have selected the first four chapters from a *social studies* book designed for middle grades students. What appears below is the assignment itself. It is a model of what the students actually see and work through.

Reading Assignment for Beginning Chapter II

Your assignment is to read the first four paragraphs of this chapter, then choose one of the questions below and answer it. Before you read, mark the question you think you will probably choose to answer. You may change your mind after you have read the paragraphs.

1 Create a different title for this chapter. Compare yours with the author's title and decide which one you like better and why.

2 Tell which of the men mentioned in the paragraphs you admire most and why.

3 Write out one question for the author of this chapter. Ask about something you wish you knew more about and that you think the author could answer.

4 Pretend that this chapter is a speech you wrote. Prepare the first two paragraphs for your presentation. Underline the words you will emphasize, put slash marks where you will pause, draw an arrow under the words you would speak slowly. Imagine yourself reading it aloud to your audience.

5 Tell why you think studying about this period in American history does or does not interest you.

Now read the first four paragraphs of this chapter.

Chapter II

Liberty or death! Fighting begins

Because of the Tea Party, Parliament passed three new laws to punish the people of Boston. The laws were so harsh that the colonists called them the

Intolerable Acts. The first law said that the people could no longer hold their town meetings. The second ordered the colonists to shelter the British soldiers in Boston. The third closed the port of Boston until the tea was paid for. No ships were allowed to come to Boston harbor. This meant that the people of Boston would soon be without food.

Samuel Adams wanted the other colonies to know about these laws. He started the Committees of Correspondence. One committee sent letters to the other colonies telling them what was taking place in Massachusetts. The other colonies set up their own committees. When the letters were received, each committee would write to others they knew in the thirteen colonies. In this way, the colonists began to work together to resist the Intolerable Acts. Food and money were sent to help the people of Boston.

The Massachusetts Colony called a meeting of the leaders of all the colonies in 1774. All of the colonies except Georgia sent representatives. This meeting of the First Continental Congress was held in Philadelphia. Samuel Adams, George Washington, and Patrick Henry were some of the important men present. The members of the Congress stated again the rights they had won over the years. They asked Parliament to repeal the unjust trade laws and to be willing to settle disputes peacefully. They drew up a list of actions by the king which denied their rights. They also agreed not to buy English goods until these differences with the mother country were settled.

Patrick Henry made another speech before the Virginia House of Burgesses defending the First Continental Congress. It was a very powerful speech. Here it is, in part: "There is no longer any room for hope. If we wish to be free . . . we must fight! I repeat it, sir, we must fight! . . . Gentlemen may cry peace, peace—but there is no peace. The war has already begun! . . . Why stand we here idle? What is it that gentlemen wish? What would they have? Is life so dear, or peace so sweet, as to be purchased at the price of chains and slavery? Forbid it, Almighty God! I know not what course others may take; but as for me, give me liberty or give me death!"[6]

Now make a final selection from among the questions you read before you read the first paragraphs and answer it. Be prepared to share your answer with the class.

A good procedure is to give the students ample time to answer the questions they chose (the faster students might do some recreational reading while they are waiting for slower students to finish) then assign them to discussion groups and have them do the following:

1 tell whether they did or did not change their tentative choice of which question to answer and why they did or did not,

2 share the answers they gave for the choices they made, and

3 suggest answers for the questions no one in the group chose.

---

6. Melvin Schwartz and John R. O'Connor, *The New Exploring American History,* New York: Globe Book Co., Inc., 1974, p. 127. Reprinted by permission.

The teacher might then lead a discussion with the entire class regarding the answers to various questions.

Teachers who want to get even more mileage out of the reading selection might form postreading groups and assign or let the groups select one of the following illustrative activities to do as a group and share with the whole class.

Some Postreading, Small-Group Activities

1   Write a letter from a Committee of Correspondence in Boston to the colony of Virginia.

2   Read Patrick Henry's speech at least two different ways and analyze the differences in meaning when different words are emphasized and different pauses are used.

3   Pretend that one of the members of the Virginia House of Burgesses who is opposed to war rises to speak when Patrick Henry sits down. What does he say?

4   Sketch a cartoon that might have appeared in a colonial newspaper either supporting or opposing the meeting of the First Continental Congress.

5   Create a dramatic scene in which a newspaper reporter interviews George Washington after the first day of the First Continental Congress.

6   What are the arguments for and against going to war with England that a wealthy Boston Merchant would probably consider?

The steps for teachers to follow, then, in preparing a content area reading assignment according to our model are the following:

1   Identify a piece of reading that warrants careful study by students and that lends itself to the kinds of questions and activities in the illustration above.

2   Construct thought provoking questions that do not elicit answers that can be evaluated as correct or incorrect for students to study before reading the selection. The questions in our model lend themselves well or can be adapted to fit most reading assignments in most content areas, especially questions 1, 3, 4, and 5.

3   Have students make tentative choices of questions before reading. This alerts students to the variety of learning possibilities within the selection and gives them a specific reason to read carefully.

4   Permit each student to select whichever question appeals most to her or him. This individualizes the reading assignment and requires some thinking about all of the questions.

5   Have students share their responses, first in small groups, then as a whole class. This gets students thinking and talking about the content and allows the teacher to pull it all together and make additions and clarify anything that might need clarification.

6 Construct postreading activities to assign or to let students select if more postreading activity is desirable. The activities work best if they require some creativity.

Obviously, this model could be, and indeed should be, adapted to be suitable for needs of particular classes or for particular curriculum objectives. For example, for some classes three or even two prereading questions for students to choose from might be better than five.

The Importance of Teachers' Attitudes

Deciding to do the job is the first step for content area teachers to take. Our readers may enjoy assessing the likelihood of their making that decision by responding to the attitude inventory developed by Vaughan (1977) to measure teachers' attitudes toward teaching reading in content classrooms. Respond to each of the following items with one of the following responses:

Strongly Agree
Tend to Agree
Neutral
Tend to Disagree
Disagree
Strongly Disagree

1 *A content area teacher is obliged to help students improve their reading ability.*

2 *Technical vocabulary should be introduced to students in content classes before they meet those terms in a reading passage.*

3 *The primary responsibility of a content teacher should be to impart subject matter knowledge.*

4 *Few students can learn all they need to know about how to read in six years of schooling.*

5 *The sole responsibility for teaching students how to study should lie with reading teachers.*

6 *Knowing how to teach reading in content areas should be required for secondary teaching certification.*

7 *Only English teachers should be responsible for teaching reading in secondary schools.*

8 *A teacher who wants to improve students' interest in reading should show them that he or she likes to read.*

9   *Content teachers should teach content and leave reading instruction to reading teachers.*

10 *A content area teacher should be responsible for helping students think on an interpretive level as well as a literal level when they read.*

11 *Content area teachers should feel a greater responsibility to the content they teach than to any reading instruction they may be able to provide.*

12 *Content area teachers should help students learn to set purposes for reading.*

13 *Every content area teacher should teach students how to read material in his or her content specialty.*

14 *Reading instruction in secondary schools is a waste of time.*

15 *Content area teachers should be familiar with theoretical concepts of the reading process.* [7]

Score all positive items (1, 2, 4, 6, 8, 10, 12, 13, 15) as follows:

Strongly Agree 7
Agree 6
Tend to Agree 5
Neutral 4
Tend to Disagree 3
Disagree 2
Strongly Disagree 1

Reverse the scores (1, 2, 3, 4, 5, 6, 7) for all negative items (3, 5, 7, 9, 11, 14). According to Vaughan a total score of 91 or higher indicates a high attitude toward teaching reading in content curriculum areas; 81-90, Above Average; 71-80, Average; 61-70, Below Average and 60 or lower, Low.

A Plan for Individualizing Instruction

A continuing problem in content area teaching has been providing for the wide range of reading ability among the students in any one class. Even within classes that are grouped to keep students of similar ability together there are substantial differences in reading achievement.

Materials, organizational plans, and teachers' training have all contributed to the individualization of instruction in the reading curriculum. However, individualization in the content areas is more difficult to achieve. Content area

---

7. Joseph L. Vaughan, Jr., "A Scale to Measure Attitudes Toward Teaching Reading in Content Classrooms," *Journal of Reading* **20**, 7 (April 1977), pp. 605-609. Reprinted by permission of Joseph L. Vaughan, Jr., and the International Reading Association.

teachers have a prescribed body of knowledge to transmit and often only one textbook to use as a printed resource. Furthermore, content area teachers have spent more time learning the content of their subject than learning how to teach it. They are usually not taught how to individualize instruction and not impressed with the importance of individualization. Nonetheless, content area teachers can accomplish some degree of individualization by using the plan described below, if not for all units of study, at least for some.

Before presenting the plan we want to point out that it is not the kind of plan that most teachers can implement on more than a limited scale without identifying and collecting the materials needed over a period of several years. Time and effort are needed for most curriculum changes that really make a difference in the quality of instruction students receive, and this curriculum plan is no exception. Over a period of three or four years teachers who are interested in the plan should be able to collect the materials needed and develop the teaching skills needed to implement the plan for many, if not all, units of study in their classes.

Five steps in preparing to implement the plan

Before our plan for individualization of instruction in content areas can be implemented some important preparatory steps must be taken. They are as follows:

1 Teachers must discover their students' approximate reading abilities. Either standardized reading achievement test scores or informal reading assessments (See Chapter 11) will provide these.

2 Teachers must learn how to apply a readability formula to find the difficulty levels of materials they collect for particular units of study. The graph shown in Fig. 8.1, taken from Fry (1977) is one of the simplest to use.

3 Teachers must organize their courses or parts of their courses into thematic units of study (for example, The Civil War, Early Human Growth, Food Preservation).

4 Teachers must identify, collect, and store materials at different levels of difficulty and relevant to the units of study.

5 Teachers must prepare specific assignments (for example, study guides to fill in, questions to answer, projects to complete) for the various materials.

Seven steps in implementing the plan

Step 1: Teacher introduces the unit (motivates, gives some background information, explains the objectives of the unit in terms of student learn-

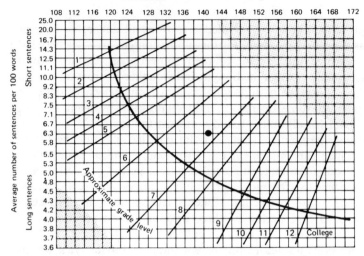

Average number of syllables per 100 words

Directions:

Randomly select three 100-word passages from a book or an article. Plot average number of syllables and average number of sentences per 100 words on graph to determine the grade level of the
material. Choose more passages per book if great variability is observed and conclude that the book
has uneven readability. Few books will fall into the gray area, but when they do grade level scores
are invalid.

Example:

	Syllables	Sentences
First hundred words	124	6.6
Second hundred words	141	5.5
Third hundred words	158	6.8
Average	141	6.3

Readability 7th grade (see dot plotted on graph)

Additional Directions for Working Readability Graph

1. Randomly select three sample passages and count exactly 100 words beginning with a beginning of a sentence. Don't count numbers. Do count proper nouns.

2. Count the number of sentences in the hundred words, estimating length of the fraction of
   the last sentence to the nearest 1/10th.

3. Count the total number of syllables in the 100-word passage. If you don't have a hand counter
   available, an easy way is to simply put a mark above every syllable over one in each word, then,
   when you get to the end of the passage, count the number of marks and add 100.

4. Enter graph with average sentence length and number of syllables; plot dot where the two lines
   intersect. Area where dot is plotted will give you the approximate grade level.

5. If a great deal of variability is found, putting more sample counts into the average is desirable.

Fig. 8.1 *Graph for estimating readability. (From* Elementary Reading Instruction *by Edward B. Fry, p. 217. Copyright 1977. Used with permission of McGraw-Hill Book Company.)*

ing, and explains the procedures that will be used to implement the plan).

Step 2: Teacher makes different reading assignments (materials and purposes) to different students or student groups. We advise dividing a typical class into three or four groups according to reading ability and distributing sets of materials so that six or seven eighth graders might be reading the same selection at a third-grade level of difficulty or whatever difficulty level is appropriate.

Step 3: Teacher acts as a resource person for individual students needing help to complete their reading assignments. Students who or groups which finish early should spend their time re-reading the assignment or reading self-selected material, perhaps from a table of supplementary course readings somewhere in the classroom.

Step 4: Individuals and/or groups present the information they learned to the class (oral reports, panel discussions, drawings, debates, dramatizations). A definite time limit should be set and adhered to for the presentations. Five to ten minutes is sufficient for most presentations and straightforward oral reporting from notes is most efficient.

Step 5: Teacher "pulls together" information from the presentations (for example, "These are important pieces of information to remember from the first group's report: . . . from Maria's presentation: . . . .

Step 6: Teacher contributes what he or she wants the class to know (lecture, discussion, film, demonstration).

Step 7: Teacher evaluates (unit test that holds students accountable for information presented by students and by the teacher).

Sources of materials

For Poor Readers (nonreaders to fourth-grade level of ability)

- audio tapes
- films, filmstrips, video tapes
- selections from elementary school textbooks and/or magazines (Weekly Reader)
- selections from basal readers
- selections from kits, books, magazines, workbooks designed and marketed to teach reading skills to low achievers.

For Average Readers (fifth-grade to seventh-grade difficulty level)

- selections from elementary school textbooks
- magazine articles
- newspaper articles

- pamphlets or brochures from service agencies
- selections from basal readers
- selections from kits, books, magazines, workbooks designed and marketed to teach reading skills

For Good Readers (eighth-grade level +)

- regular textbook
- magazine articles
- newspaper articles
- any desired options for poor and average readers

A Final Word

No two reading selections are exactly alike. Each presents different challenges to the student reader and different opportunities to the teacher of reading skills. Although certain reading skills (for example, visual imagery, reading maps, sequencing ideas, noting cause-effect relationships, getting the meaning of words from context, finding main ideas, studying graphs) are used more in some content areas than in others, considerable overlap among the content areas exists. Therefore, there is no substitute for careful teacher analysis of each assigned reading selection if teaching reading in the content areas is to be effectively accomplished.

We hope that the discussion in the present chapter will give teachers a reasonably good understanding of some of the many reading skills that can be taught in the content areas. We have presented a variety of instructional practices that might be used in conjunction with selections from specific reading materials, in order to illustrate specifically how the various skills might be taught. However, the theme we have emphasized in other chapters is also basic to this chapter: there is no substitute for a perceptive, skillful teacher. The examples we chose for our discussion are only illustrative. Teachers must draw upon their knowledge and resourcefulness each time they assign a reading selection in the content areas and decide to incorporate reading instruction into the teaching of the subject matter.

Something to Think and Talk About

Principal to teacher after observing a sixth-grade science class: "Your class discussion wasn't very lively or enlightening. I was surprised that some of our best students and I assume also our best readers either couldn't or were not able to take off on the questions you asked them about Chapter 5. We paid a lot of money for those books. What's wrong?"

Teacher: "The kids say the books are boring. But I don't think they really read the assignments I give them. Too much TV at home. I give them one chapter to read overnight and they moan and groan about how hard it is. They can read the stuff O.K. I know because I've had some of them read a paragraph or two orally and they do pretty well."

Principal: "I guess it's the same old story. School work always comes last. I can't understand kids' lack of interest in science with all that's happening in the field of science today. Science was always my favorite subject. How are they doing in social studies? We bought new books for that subject too."

(See Appendix 8 for Authors' Response to "Something to Think and Talk About.")

References

Carr, Archie, and the Editors of *Life* (1963). *The Reptiles,* Life Nature Library. New York: Time Incorporated.

Eibling, Harold H., *et al.* (1965). *Our Country.* River Forest, Illinois: Laidlow Bros., 1965.

Eicholz, Robert E., and Phares G. O'Daffer (1971). *School Mathematics, Book 5.* Menlo Park, California: Addison-Wesley, 1971.

Fischler, Abraham S., *et al.* (1971). *Modern Elementary Science.* New York: Holt.

Fry, Edward B. (1977). *Elementary Reading Instruction.* New York: McGraw-Hill.

Patterson, Franklin, Jessany Patterson, C. W. Hunnicutt, Jean D. Grambs, and James A. Smith (1963). *Man Changes His World.* Chicago: L. W. Singer Co.

Rasmussen, Frederick A., Paul Holobinko, and Victor M. Showalter (1971). *Man and the Environment.* Boston: Houghton Mifflin.

Schwartz, Melvin, and John R. O'Connor (1974). *The New Exploring American History.* New York: Globe Book Co.

Smith, Richard J. (1971). "The Poor Reader in the Content Areas," *The National Elementary Principal* **LI**, 2: 54–58.

Tanner, Bernard, Craig Vittetoe, and Robert Shutes (1968). *English 8.* Menlo Park, California: Addison-Wesley, 1968.

Van Engen, Henry, *et al.* (1969). *Mathematics Concepts Application.* Glenview, Illinois: Scott, Foresman, 1969.

Vaughan, Joseph L., Jr. (1977). "A Scale to Measure Attitudes Toward Teaching Reading in Content Classrooms," *Journal of Reading* **20** (7): 605–609.

PROVIDING READING-RELATED ACTIVITIES IN THE MIDDLE GRADES

If there is one characteristic common to most middle graders it is their need for learning-related activity. They are not satisfied to learn for learning's sake. They want to test their knowledge and exercise their skills. Generalizations are always dangerous, but teachers of grades four through eight generally agree that "these kids need to be kept busy." Therefore, we have devoted this chapter to discussing reading-related activities in the middle grades. The intent is to help teachers "keep the kids busy" with activities that improve reading skills without causing students to develop negative attitudes toward reading.

It is perhaps because print is perceived as the basic learning medium in our society and because students with good reading skills are considered the mark of a successful school program that reading is often taught as if it were a subject in itself. This is unfortunate, because to teach reading as an end in itself distorts the true nature of reading, which is a communication process. The reference from Moffett (1968) cited in Chapter 1 is also germane to the major theme of this chapter: "Symbol systems are not primarily about themselves; they are about other subjects. When a student 'learns' one of these systems, he learns how to operate it. The main point is to think and talk about other things by means of this system.''(p. 6) Teachers need to be wary of becoming so engrossed with developmental exercises and standardized test scores that the result is only more developmental exercises and more standardized tests. Reading should be a launching pad to reflection, writing, talking, artwork, and other personally satisfying pursuits. The reading program in the middle grades should reflect a deliberate effort to involve students in reading-related activities that enrich their lives.

The reading program should enable students to:

feel sorry for a character in a book,
laugh at jokes and comics,
get information from school textbooks,
use the school and public library with confidence,
match wits with the detective in a mystery story,
learn about personal greatness by reading biographies,
be secure on a trip with a road map,
take comfort in a poem or religious material,
relax with a novel,
learn about places that are too expensive or too far to visit,
become angry enough while reading the newspaper to write a letter to the editor,
study political issues thoroughly enough to do something about them,
discover social injustice through the eyes of a novelist,
compare the book with the movie,
read the Declaration of Independence,
improve at a sport or hobby by reading about it,
form a mental picture of a scene described on a page,
share a sense of pride or humility with a character,
discover the greatness of the mind of the person who wrote a particular essay,
share the depth of feeling of the person who wrote a particular poem,
find,
discover,
learn,
feel,
know,
relax,
get . . .   by reading!

Reading is a language art that can be used to promote listening, speaking, writing, and other activities that foster maturity in using language which ultimately results in greater total personal maturity. The key to this kind of development is meaningful personal interaction. Keeping the kids busy is not sufficient. The kind of business they are put to is vital to their reading-skills growth and their attitudes toward reading. Jennings warns against the debilitating effect on students' perceptions of reading when faced with the impersonal, uninteresting activities so frequently suggested in textbooks and teachers' manuals:

The effect upon children is nowhere more painfully demonstrated than in the Language Arts books. In the upper grades the "reader" becomes an anthol-

ogy, often euphemistically labeled "Adventures in Something" or "Treasury of Something" or "Something about Living." There is a lot of good writing between these covers, along with the usual leaven of "stupid stuff." If the child should by any chance find enjoyment in what he reads he is disabused when he turns the last page of the story to find "Something to Think About," "Something to Do," etc., and usually the teacher wants him to think and do what the book says. Even if she didn't, that page of contrition would be there warning him to suffer for his joy. [1]

Too many teachers have supplanted rather than supplemented their own resourcefulness in creating worthwhile and enjoyable learning experiences with the suggestions of authors of instructional materials. There is no substitute for a teacher who knows his or her students' abilities and interests when planning and implementing reading-related activities. It is distressing to find teachers assigning students to "Do numbers 1 and 5 on page 41 when you have finished reading, and then we'll discuss your answers." A little bit of resourcefulness on the teacher's part can prevent a reading selection from being a "real drag" and result instead in getting more "mileage" out of a good selection. The burden, then, for designing and implementing reading-related activities rests with the teacher who must: (1) choose selections that permit extended activity and match students' abilities and interests; (2) read the selections carefully to discover the kinds of activities that are logical outgrowths of the reading; and (3) make decisions about the structure of the activities in terms of the students' cognitive and affective needs. Teachers who want their instruction to have a lasting, positive effect on students' reading will be careful not to neglect the affective domain in their structuring of activities. Krathwohl *et al.* (1964) opine that, ". . . under some conditions the development of cognitive behaviors may actually destroy certain desired affective behaviors and that, instead of a positive relation between growth in cognitive and affective behavior, it is conceivable that there may be an inverse relation between growth in the two domains." (p. 20)

Although the task of planning reading-related activities rests with each individual teacher, illustrations of activities that other teachers have found workable and profitable to students' reading growth may be useful. However, what works well with one teacher and a particular group of students may be ineffective in another setting, so teachers are cautioned to modify the illustrations given here to fit their particular needs and situations. As a matter of fact, we would hope that our readers will use the illustrations we offer only as aids to stimulate their own resourcefulness and will feel free to subtract from them, add to them, and reject any that don't fit.

---

1. Frank Jennings, *This is Reading*, New York: Bureau of Publications, Teachers College, Columbia University, 1965, p. 62. Reprinted by permission.

Reading and Conversation

One of the most pleasant reading-related activities available to middle grade teachers and their students is conversation. We have chosen to use the word "conversation" because it connotes an unstructured oral exchange of ideas and feelings that middle grade students are capable of having relative to their reading experiences. Conversation is exploratory in nature rather than focused on problem solving or some kind of task completion. Therefore, it is a suitable activity for students in a curriculum that emphasizes exploration rather than basic-skills development or subject-matter mastery.

Students need training to be good conversationalists in school. Overemphasis on finding the right answers, completing study guides, or finishing projects can cause students to become inept or uncomfortable about unstructured talk. Teachers have reported that until students have sufficient opportunities to become comfortable in conversation groups, they are often silly, quarrelsome, bored, or fearful that they are wasting valuable time. Unfortunately, teachers often experience the same fear of wasting time and abandon their attempts at establishing conversation groups before the groups have had a proper chance to succeed. Yet most educators agree that small-group activities can be highly productive in improving students' language skills. Moffett says, "Group discussion is a fundamental activity that should be a staple learning process from kindergarten through college. It is an activity to be learned both for its own sake and for the sake of learning other things by means of it. It is a major source of that discourse which the student will transform internally into thought." (p. 94)

Groups that are formed solely for the purpose of conversing about reading experiences usually function best when they are comprised of four or five students. The students should be heterogeneous in their reading ability and general verbal ability. Putting all "nontalkers" or all "talkers" in one group is not a good procedure. If students are to learn from one another, they must work with students who have different things to offer to a group. To expect equal amounts of listening and talk from all students is unrealistic, and forming groups to attain this level of competition or noncompetition is self-defeating. Some people talk more than others, and if the groups are changed frequently, students will have opportunities to participate according to their natural inclinations. Students who are offensively dominating or abnormally withdrawn are usually restrained or drawn out by other members of the group. When certain students habitually exhibit abnormal behavior, some intervention by the teacher is needed. Often, the teacher can join a group and do some gentle shaping of the group process. For certain students, professional counseling may be needed to help them develop more acceptable behavior in groups.

If students are expected to converse freely and enthusiastically about their reading, they should be allowed to select their own reading materials. Magazines, newspapers, paperback and hardback books, catalogs, brochures, and other interesting materials should be readily accessible. Students should know that no grade or testing is involved in the reading they do for conversational purposes, and therefore, they may, if they so desire, read material that interests them, even if they don't know all of the words and can't get all of the ideas. Hunt has commented on reading material that is considered to be at the frustration level (see Chapter 9) as follows:

One phenomenon which contradicts the validity of the reading levels theory is readily observed. It is the case of the high-interest book and the low-powered reader. Every observant teacher has seen the highly motivated reader engrossed in a book which for him is obviously of considerable difficulty. But because interest and involvement are high, he persists in the pursuit of ideas and he gets some.

He adds:

Given the opportunity, then, the reader who finds a really good book for him, the book that has ideas he truly wants to learn about, frequently will outdo his own instructional level of performance. When the criteria of complete comprehension and perfect oral reading are used, then the power of the interest factor is markedly reduced. By contrast, when the classroom atmosphere encourages self-selections, usual reading level performances become less meaningful.[2]

Students who get personally satisfying experiences from reading will want to share their thoughts and feelings with others. Teachers need only give students enough time to get into a selection (less than a half hour is usually not enough time to stimulate good conversation) and give the signal to stop reading and begin talking. Many teachers have found that conversation is more natural and more enthusiastic when the group that talks together also reads together. Tables and chairs are excellent for grouping four or five students for a reading-and-talking session, but desks arranged in a circle serve the purpose as well. As a rule, students need to be told only to "tell each other what you were reading about," and the group process takes over. After students have learned to feel at ease in small groups and confident that no grades are being given, conversation often becomes harder to stop than to start. Often, a conversation involving the whole class is a natural outgrowth of the small group sessions. The teacher may tell the whole class about something he or she has been reading, or the conversational topic of an especially spirited group may be shared with the entire class.

The role of the teacher while the small groups are reading is clear. Like the students, the teacher should be reading something of interest (not grading papers)

2. Lyman C. Hunt, "The Effect of Self-Selection, Interest and Motivation upon Independent Instructional and Frustrational Levels," *The Reading Teacher* **24**, 2 (Nov. 1970), p. 147. Reprinted with permission of Lyman C. Hunt and the International Reading Association.

in full view of the students, perhaps in the circle of one of the small groups. Johnson and Kress (1969) suggest that "Much in the way of recognition of the importance of reading could be gained by the child's seeing his teachers and parents absorbed in reading which had nothing to do with school work, father's business, or the running of the house."(p. 594) Petre (1971) reports the favorable results of a daily 35-minute "reading break" on a school-wide basis. Prior to instituting this program, one high school surveyed its students and found that only two percent could remember seeing a teacher practicing the art of reading. Since the advent of the program, students have learned their teachers' reading preferences and request teachers to read certain books so they can talk about them together. Students have made two requests: (1) more time to read, and (2) opportunities to discuss their reading with others.

The role of the teacher while the small groups are engaged in their postreading conversations varies. The teacher may move quietly among the groups, listening and becoming more sensitive to students' interests and their academic and social needs. The teacher may sit in with a group for a short period and either listen or join in the conversation. A teacher may also make some helpful suggestions to a group that has bogged down in silence or become embroiled in a controversy going nowhere. The teacher should not carry a clipboard or notebook and assume the role of an evaluator. Reading-related conversations should not be subject to formalized evaluation.

Reading and Directed Oral Expression

Reading is a good stimulus for oral expression that is more structured and goal-directed than conversation. The full impact of a reading selection may not be realized until an individual's interpretation of the selection has been verbalized and the verbalization receives a reaction from an interested listener or audience. As the ideas encountered in reading are being utilized for some specific purpose, both the ideas themselves and their relationships to other ideas become clearer. Certainly, not all reading selections lend themselves to debate, dramatization, and other related oral activities. Teachers should be careful not to try to get more out of a selection than it has to offer. On the other hand, many selections are not as enhanced by directed oral expression as they could, and perhaps should, be. The fourth-grade students who made up their own dialogue and acted out the meeting of John Adams, Benjamin Franklin, and Thomas Jefferson to discuss the Declaration of Independence were spared the experience of perceiving history as dull reading.

Dramatization

The dramatization of stories, historical events, customs of a different culture, and other aspects of life that are read about can be highly entertaining and educational. The following illustrations show how reading selections can be enriched by involving students in dramatizations relative to the selections.

Illustration 1: Scenes from a novel. A class of eighth graders had read *The Yearling* by Marjorie Kinnan Rawlings. The teacher divided the class into eight groups and assigned each group a section from the novel to be presented as a dramatic scene (the students had previously studied drama and play production). Each group was made up of the correct number of students to allow every student to be a character. After some planning and after talking the scene through once or twice in their groups, the students turned the front of the room into a stage and presented their scenes, giving their roles their personal interpretations. Although the teacher did not allow much time for the creation of special effects, one group played a tape recording of *Sonata Pathetique* to provide the proper background to intensify the mood of their scene.

Illustration 2: Characterizing historical figures. A class of fourth graders was reading about the writing of the Declaration of Independence in their social studies class. The author of their textbook mentioned that Jefferson had written the first draft of the Declaration "out of his heart and head" and that Adams and Franklin had later made some changes. After some discussion the teacher divided the boys in the class into groups of three and asked them to portray Jefferson, Adams, and Franklin discussing the changes the latter two wanted made. The characterizations which the boys presented differed greatly among the groups. In some groups Jefferson was angry, while in others he was thankful and even apologetic. The characterizations of Adams and Franklin differed also. Afterward, the girls in the class gave their reactions to the dramatizations.

Illustration 3: Tape recording a play. The teacher of a class of sixth graders organized the class into three "production companies" to produce a tape recording of a play based on the tale of Paul Bunyan and his blue ox. The play (included in the sixth-grade reader of a popular basal series) called for six characters and a narrator. Each group of students was given a tape recorder, a phonograph, several phonograph records of classical music to provide background, and a record of sound effects. The three groups, with the help of the teacher, organized, practiced, and recorded their productions. Students without speaking parts directed the productions, selected the sound effects, and ran the machines. The final recordings were made in separate rooms. When the recordings were completed, the whole class listened to the three products. The tapes were then played for other classes in the building.

Choral reading: Prose and poetry

Choral reading is good fun for middle graders, and most basal readers are filled with poems and short prose selections that can be read in unison, either in entirety or in part. Teachers need only find selections that lend themselves to choral reading and experiment. The poem "Night" by Sara Teasdale is an example of a short poem that can be read with one effect by three or four girls and with a quite different effect by three or four boys. The poem can be read by different groups, and the different effects can be discussed to give students insights into literary interpretation and what is meant by "my kind of poem." The following illustrations show how choral reading can be used effectively with middle grade students.

Illustration 1: Recording a choral reading. "The Walrus and the Carpenter" by Lewis Carroll became a delightful experience for a class of sixth graders who read it chorally and tape recorded their best effort. Some students were given solo parts, only girls read some passages, only boys read other passages, and the entire class read some parts. The teacher and the class experimented with different combinations until they got an effect that they felt was good enough to record and play for a class of younger students.

Illustration 2: Biography for choral reading. A book titled *American Biographies* by Eva Knox Witte (New York: Holt, Rinehart and Winston, 1968) contains a short biography of Frederick Douglass. The biography is written in a style conducive to choral reading by fifth graders. For example, the biography begins, "The boy herded the cows home from pasture. He was barefoot. All he wore was a rough shirt that reached to his knees. The April evening was chilly, and he was hungry." An enterprising teacher could delete some sections, assign solo parts, perhaps add some lighting effects, and produce an effective choral presentation that would add to the students' understanding and enjoyment of the biography.

Debate

Students in the upper middle grades (grades six, seven, and eight) enjoy debating the issues that emerge from reading selections if the debate is controlled but not too tightly structured. Teachers and students together can usually arrive at satisfactory guidelines for the order of speakers, the time allotted to each speaker, and the purpose of each presentation. If teachers are watching for opportunities to get students more involved with reading selections, even a science textbook can become a source of controversy and debate. After reading about some discovery, students might debate its value to humanity as compared with other discoveries. For example, the ultimate value of the scientific experimentation that led to our exploration of the moon might be legitimately questioned by students. It could then be stated as a proposition and debated by volunteer or selected class members, with other class members acting as judges. Another source of a good debate might be the relative values of scientific inquiry in the field of medicine and some technological field. The debates do not need to settle the issues. In themselves they are enjoyable and make the reading of factual materials more relevant. Perhaps best of all, they motivate students to read more widely in order to get information to support different positions.

Illustration 1: Freedom vs. discrimination. *Canalboat to Freedom,* a novel by Thomas Fall, is a favorite of many young readers. It can be used to focus their attention on the contradiction between the philosophy of a country which claims to be the "Land of the Free" and its actual practice of racial discrimination. A number of debatable issues might emerge as the book is read and discussed. For example, "Resolved: The black race in America should receive special considerations from the government because of the unfair treatment they had to endure in the early history of our country." Another example could be, "Resolved: The Underground Railroad should be given an entire chapter in all United States history books because it exemplifies the true spirit of all democratic nations." Debates such as these help students to gain a deeper understanding of words like "spirit," verbalize the feelings that accompany the reading of a good book, and get excited about the ideas implanted in their minds by an author's storytelling skill.

Illustration 2: Revolution and heroes. *Johnny Tremain* by Esther Forbes is a novel about a young boy working with the patriots in Boston just before the American Revolution. Seventh and eighth graders are easily moved to take opposing sides regarding revolutions and heroes, because of their personal involvement with the story. For example, "Resolved: In a democracy schools should deliberately teach students to be revolutionary in their thinking," or "Resolved: All students in American schools should be required to read *Johnny Tremain* or some other similar novel that shows the greatness of our founding fathers."

Discussion focused on an issue

Many times a class or small groups of students can be assigned to discuss an issue arising out of a reading selection without a structure as formal as a debate but with more direction than conversation. These discussions focus the students' attention on specific aspects of a reading selection that are thought-provoking. The idea of the discussion is not to argue competitively on both sides of the issue, as is the case when debating, but rather to explore together such things as the merit or lack of merit in a character's action, the truth of the moral of a story, or the wisdom behind a historical decision. Discussing the issues that emerge from reading experiences trains students to read more critically and with more personal involvement. This is an important objective at a time when overloaded curriculums and hectic life styles conspire to create superficial readers. Jennings' comment is pertinent:

In a world where no thing is certain, where all things change, change is sometimes frightening. Man must devise some way of holding things still long enough to permit examination and the growth of understanding. . . . When things are written down they are in fact pinned down. It is the written record, the printed page that holds things still long enough for them to be examined.[3]

Teachers who do not give students opportunities to reflect upon life through books and discussion are remiss in their duties.

Illustration 1: Are lies ever justified? The short story "Judge" by Walter Edmonds describes the trials of the oldest son of a fatherless family. The son is lied to by a respected member of the community, the judge, who tells him that his father died in debt. The boy works hard and undergoes mental as well as physical anguish to repay the debt. In the process, and perhaps because of his sense of duty, the boy becomes a good man and takes his place in the community. At the conclusion of the story the boy is told of the judge's hoax, and the money he worked so hard to repay is returned to him. The judge's motivation is clear, but students might question the means he uses to train the boy. The whole question of whether or not the end justifies the means might be the topic of discussion for students in the upper middle grades. A good procedure would be to divide the class into groups of four or five students and ask each group, after some discussion, to write a letter to the judge either praising him for his wisdom or censuring him for his deceitfulness. Each group's letter could be read to the entire class.

Illustration 2: Biographies raise issues. Biographies and autobiographies are often good sources of ideas to think and talk about. Fifth or sixth graders are able to discuss with clarity and insight, the following questions relative to biographical and autobiographical selections.

1   Lincoln Steffens, *I Get a Colt to Break In:* Do children and young animals who need training respond better to praise or punishment?
2   Mae Blacker Freeman, *Welcome Genius,* a biographical sketch of Albert Einstein: How can we protect people who have creative minds and challenge existing institutions from governments that disagree with their ideas and want to silence them?
3   Murray Sussman, *Henry Ford:* If Henry Ford had known the problems as well as the advantages his automobile and gasoline engine would give the world, would he have invented it anyway? Should he have?

Illustration 3: Poetry as a source of ideas. Poetry is another good source of thought-provoking ideas for students to discuss. Too often, students feel that

3. Frank Jennings, *This is Reading,* New York: Bureau of Publications, Teachers College, Columbia University, 1965, pp. 66. Reprinted by permission.

poetry is "pretty," but has little to offer to the world of ideas. "Primer Lesson" by Carl Sandburg cautions against using "proud words" because it is not easy to call them back. Students from fourth grade through high school can discuss for enjoyment and intellectual growth such questions as "What are 'proud words'?" "Why do some people use 'proud words' when there is no need to?" "What should one do when hearing a friend using 'proud words'?"

Illustration 4: Creative ideas from science. Students often tend to think of science textbooks as factual and thus containing little material for discussion. However, fifth graders are intellectually able to discuss whether they would rather live without magnets or without gravity after reading about both. Small groups might prepare lists of conveniences they would have to live without if magnets were not available, and lists of devices that would be needed if the pull of gravity were to diminish. Enterprising students might like to design "weight belts" or "earth fasteners" as a creative exercise growing out of the group discussions.

Illustration 5: Identity and cartoons. Charlie Brown remains a favorite cartoon character for all age groups. He is especially good for middle graders to identify with because they often feel like "Charlie Brown." The Charlie Brown cartoons are good to laugh at, but they can also be used to stimulate some good thinking and discussion. The characters and situations created by Charles M. Schulz (New York: Holt, Rinehart and Winston, Inc.) raise such discussion topics as, "How much is our success in life determined by how we feel about ourselves?" or "How does our behavior toward other people influence their behavior?"

Illustration 6: Catalog shopping. Going on shopping trips in catalogs or classified advertisement sections of newspapers is a favorite activity of students in the middle grades and teaches them the skill of reading for details. Students can be divided into groups, given a certain amount of money, some catalogs, and newspaper advertisements, and told to furnish a living room, outfit a camping expedition, find a good used car, clothe a family of four, or carry out some other project that they will enjoy working on in a group. At the end each group can be asked to submit a report to the class on their purchases and the reasons for spending their money as they did.

Reading and Listening

Of all the language arts, listening is probably the most poorly provided for in school curriculums. After a review of the literature concerning the attention given to listening in the school curriculum, Dixon (1964) concluded that "From the appearance of the first research on listening in 1917 to the present, the record of the place of listening among the language arts is a chronicle of neglect." (p. 285)

Because we have already discussed the possibilities reading presents as a stimulus for oral discourse and because it is obvious that speakers require listeners, we shall not devote space here to specific illustrations of the reading-speaking-listening relationship. We do, however, feel that several points should be explicated.

First, listening to speakers who use language well has a direct positive influence on the speaking and writing of students who use language poorly. Therefore, when good speakers communicate the ideas they have gained from silent reading or when they read orally, they are serving as good communication models for other students. Consequently, teachers should not feel that students are being educated only when they are reading or talking. They also learn when they are listening. The most effective way to improve children's use of language is to expose them frequently to good models and motivate them to interact with them.

Second, students are motivated to read materials they have heard other students talk about. Students in the middle grades have a great need to feel like one of the gang. They want to use the same language, see the same movies, listen to the same music, and read the same books. Therefore, listening to a peer talk about something he or she has read and enjoyed is powerful motivation for others to read the same thing.

Third, students learn from one another what to look for and what to expect from reading experiences. The same selection may be interpreted differently by different readers. The same ideas that may command the careful attention of one reader may be given only cursory attention by another. A particular phrase that catches the fancy of one reader may be overlooked entirely by another. If students are to become mature readers, they need to learn the great variety of purposes for which reading can be utilized. Students also profit by hearing the manifestation of specific skills other students have used while reading, such as noting cause-effect relationships, finding main ideas, or getting the meaning of a word from context.

Finally, listening to readers talk enthusiastically about their reading establishes the concept of reading as a meaningful personal process. This is important when self-correcting instructional materials are so plentiful and most curriculums so overloaded that teachers are tempted to overuse the approach of "read a paragraph, pick the correct response choice for each question, and check your answers on the answer card."

Reading and Writing

Much has been written about the close relationship between reading and writing. If the writing of a selection, the resultant selection, and the reading of that selection were expressed in a paradigm frequently used in communications theory, the interrelationship might be expressed as

sender ———→ message ———→ receiver.

Whether or not writing is an activity that has a direct effect on the improvement of specific reading skills is questionable. Certain students handle the mechanics of reading well, but have difficulty with determining an author's bias or understanding the concept of writing for a particular audience. For such students the act of writing a paper with a specific point of view for a particular audience may be helpful. To receive the readers' responses to it may also be helpful. However, poor readers are usually poorer writers, and trying to teach basic reading skills through writing activities is usually poor practice.

Writing frequently serves to impress upon students that reading is a highly personal activity which cannot take place outside the personality system of the author as sender of the message and that of the reader as receiver of the message. Teaching this concept is a worthy objective for the middle grades where we want students to read critically and creatively. In addition, having to write about a reading selection may motivate students to be more careful readers and to interpret ideas in print with greater insight. It is one thing for a student to know that he has read about something. It is quite another thing for him to have read about it carefully enough to verbalize it. Pauk (1968) says, "An idea encountered in a book does not become a part of our intellectual framework until we have had time to reconstruct it and to rethink it in terms of our own personal language." (p. 507) Writing is sometimes better for this purpose than is oral expression.

Perhaps Pooley (1961) has best expressed the relationship between reading and writing which we wish to establish in the present chapter: "So far as possible, artificial barriers between the two types of activities should be removed, allowing the child to advance and mature in the conviction that what is written is meant to be read and what is read becomes the substance or point of departure for writing." (p. 48) We would add that only writing activities which enrich the reading experience without detracting from the overall satisfaction received from the selection should be assigned. Krathwohl, *et al.* caution against teaching practices that improve cognitive behavior but at the same time develop negative attitudes toward the learning process and the object of the learning, in this case reading:

There are some instances where the cognitive route to affective achievement has resulted in learning just the opposite of that intended. Thus the infamous example of the careful and detailed study of "good" English classics, which was intended to imbue us with a love of deathless prose, has in many instances alienated us from it instead. Emphasis on very high mastery of one domain may in some instances be gained at the expense of the other.[4]

This caution is especially pertinent in a discussion of the use of writing as a reading-related activity. For most students, a written composition is a difficult process, albeit satisfying and instructive. Therefore, teachers need to know their stu-

---

4. David Krathwohl, *et al., Taxonomy of Educational Objectives, Handbook II: Affective Domain,* New York: David McKay, 1964, p. 56. Reprinted by permission.

dents well and construct reading-related writing assignments carefully to ensure that they appeal to the students *and* are within their ability levels.

The following illustrations are descriptions of reading-writing activities that have been successfully implemented in the middle grades.

Illustration 1: Extending a story. A class of fourth graders read a story of a boy whose friends played tricks on him because they thought he was stupid. However, he managed to gain some personal advantage out of each goose chase on which he was sent. For example, he once found a precious stone and another time saw a rewarding spectacle. At the conclusion of the story the boy was no longer considered stupid, but had in fact won the admiration of his peers. The class enjoyed the story and accepted with enthusiasm the opportunity to elaborate on it. Each student was assigned to write an extension to the story by telling what happened to the boy as he grew up. The students then read their stories to one another in small groups. A few of the extensions were read to the entire class, rewritten, and placed on the bulletin board. Some students were highly imaginative in their writing while others came up with short and uninteresting creations. However, each student was given the opportunity to write about the story, and since no grades were assigned, the activity was a successful experience for everyone.

Illustration 2: Describing hometown. A fifth-grade geography class in a rural area of Wisconsin read a short description of New York City with its many huge buildings and teeming population. The teacher suggested that they write a description of their small city and the advantages it offered. In preparation, the students read other descriptions of cities and noted important aspects of descriptive writing. In time, teacher and students took photographs and colored slides of the locations and scenes described by the students. The class chose the best of the students' descriptions for tape-recording. Some of the best descriptions were read by students who were better oral readers than were the authors. Thus, what could have been just another chapter in a geography book became an integrated language arts-geography activity.

Illustration 3: An hour with Edgar Allan Poe. An accelerated class of eighth graders read and discussed several short stories and poems by Edgar Allan Poe. To illustrate the full effect of certain passages, the teacher asked students to read them aloud, and then suggested that the class write and tape record "An Hour with Poe." Groups were formed and assigned selections for which they were to write introductory paragraphs and transitions. Some students found suitable music to be played in the background during the reading of certain passages. One group of students wrote the introductory and concluding statements for the entire program. In writing their descriptions and narratives, the students improved their composition skills and gained a greater appreciation for the imagery in Poe's writing.

Illustration 4: Letters to the editor. After reading in their social studies books and supplementary materials about community problems caused by overpopulation, citizen apathy, suburban sprawl, and other factors, a group of seventh graders wrote letters to the editor of one of the local papers outlining the problems as they saw them and calling for remedial action. Some of the letters were printed in the newspaper.

Illustration 5: Letters to authors. The teacher of a class of sixth graders reading self-selected books asked his students to write letters of appreciation, inquiry, or disapproval to the authors of the books. The students expressed their enjoyment of a character, asked how the author got the idea for the plot, or offered their personal suggestions for improving the book. The letters were mailed; to the delight of the students, nearly 60 percent of the authors responded. The students then organized their letters and the responses they received, wrote short descriptions of the books they had read, and compiled a little booklet that was duplicated and given to other students to read.

Illustration 6: Adapting short stories for play reading. Writing a play based on a short story provides opportunities for related speaking and listening activities as well as for a more thorough understanding of fictional characters and the problems that are part of the human condition. A class of eighth graders was divided into groups of four or five for a small-group reading experience. Each group was assigned a different short story to read and adapt for presentation as a play-reading exercise. The students had previously discussed stories which they had read and also seen in movie or television versions. The students were permitted to "take liberties" with the stories, but were asked to keep the basic characterizations and plots intact. Ring Lardner, O'Henry, and Jesse Stuart were three of the authors whose stories were written as plays and read before the class. Each group had a narrator who introduced the play, provided transitions, and described settings as they changed. The actors and actresses wrote their own lines with guidance from the rest of their group. Only the actual lines each spoke were written out completely. However, the final three words of each preceding speech were also written to provide necessary cues for the actors.

Illustration 7: Writing a magazine. After a unit in mass communications during which a class of sixth graders studied popular magazines, among other things, the teacher and the class decided to write their own magazine. The class compiled a list of articles, illustrations, and advertisements to be included in the magazine. An editor was elected, and the students volunteered to take on assignments from the list. The project required approximately three weeks of language arts class time, and much of the reading class time for three weeks was devoted to reading magazines carefully for ideas. Considerable reading and writing were also done at home by the students with major assignments. The finished product was duplicated, and then sold throughout the school and to parents to defray the cost of materials. Letters to the editor were solicited, received, and read with interest by the student production staff.

Illustration 8: Reading and creating advertisements. A fifth-grade teacher discovered that although her students were spending a lot of time watching television commercials, they were largely unaware of newspaper and magazine advertising, perhaps because they rarely read newspapers and magazines. As an introduction to reading and writing advertisements, the teacher asked the students to identify products, ideas, or feelings they would most like their parents, friends, political leaders, or other groups of people to know about. The class was then given ample time to examine magazines and newspapers in order to discover how professionals advertise their products and ideas. Eventually, each student designed and wrote an advertisement reflecting his or her own experience and thinking. The advertisements ranged from a glowing account of the excitement provided by a new recording of a pop rock group to an appeal for better understanding between black and white students.

Integrating Reading, Writing, Speaking, and Listening

In some of the preceding illustrations reading was combined with more than one of the other language arts, and some incorporated artwork and music as well. However, none of the activities described thus far has involved the integration of as many of the language arts as will the activities described in this section.

Illustration 1: Simulating court trials. Simulated court trials are usually eagerly entered into by all students at grade levels four through eight. Most students have observed courtroom procedures many times on TV and at the movies. Students enjoy performing the very roles which they watch professional actors play on almost any night of the week. With a little moving of furniture, most classrooms can be arranged to look something like a courtroom. The jury box can be set up on one side of the room near the places established for the prosecuting attorneys and the defense attorneys. The teacher's desk makes a fine "bench" for the judge, and the spectators can stay in their regular places. The accused may be a fictional or historical character. The scientists who developed the atomic bomb, patriots from the American Revolution, pacifists who refused to serve in the military, politicians who did not support legislation favored by local ecologists, fictional characters who mistreated animals or manipulated their friends are possible candidates found in novels, newspapers, biographies, textbooks, and other reading matter. Organizing, implementing, and evaluating a simulated courtroom drama may take as long as three or four weeks of the time allocated for one or more curriculum areas. However, the benefits derived by the students in terms of interest, creative thinking, reading, writing, speaking, and listening are manifold.

Illustration 2: Radio or TV interviews. Students in the middle grades benefit from and enjoy writing and tape recording a "Face the Critics" radio show. The author of a novel, a short story, an essay, a poem, an editorial, a textbook, or other reading material is chosen as the target of student reviewers in a simulated interview. A narrator is often assigned to introduce the show and the participants. Commercial messages may be prepared and some "lead-in" and "sign-off" music selected. Students usually acquire a deeper understanding of the reading selection being discussed and this deeper understanding reinforces the concept of a reading selection as a message from an author to a reader, each of whom is a unique personality with individual perceptions of the world.

Illustration 3: Planning historical tours. One of the best reading-related activities we have observed was produced by a teacher and her sixth-grade class. The project could be equally successful with younger or older students. After learning about different places of historical interest, the class decided to arrange for trips to historical sites that were especially appealing. Although it was unlikely that the trips would actually take place, the students selected their favorite sites and wrote to Chambers of Commerce and other institutions and sources for information regarding tours, hotel accommodations, eating places, and anything else that would aid in planning a trip. Bus, train, and airplane schedules and prices were obtained, and automobile routes were studied on maps. As the information arrived, the student groups read it and planned their itineraries. Obviously, some groups received relatively little information, but atlases, geography books, magazines, and other sources were always available to supplement what was received. Ultimately, each group discussed its planned visit to the place of interest with the rest of the class. Tables were prepared, with the information each group had assembled being prominently displayed. An original travel poster above each pile of brochures, pictures, maps, books, etc., helped students find the information they were most interested in.

Illustration 4: Matching descriptions with pictures. The teacher of a class of low-ability eighth graders wanted to help his students discover the beauty of literature. For the most part these students perceived reading as a chore and were unable to enjoy the visual imagery of poetry or descriptive prose. The teacher began the reading-related activity by collecting and distributing pictures from magazines and calendars of outdoor scenes during the four seasons of the year. The students looked at the pictures, discussed the seasons they liked best, and told about times when they had particularly noticed the beauty of a morning, evening, or night. The teacher then read some stanzas from selected poems and descriptions from short stories, essays, and novels. The students tried to match the pictures which had been hung up around the room with the passages read by the teacher. Next, the teacher darkened the room, projected a colored slide of the sunrise over the Grand Canyon, and turned on the "Sunrise" movement from the

Grand Canyon Suite. Then, the teacher projected several other slides of natural beauty and played musical selections that enhanced the feeling. To conclude the presentation, the teacher showed several slides that were accompanied by background music and read some descriptive passages that matched the music and the picture. The students were highly appreciative of the presentation and agreed to bring in as many colored slides as they could find to supplement those of the teacher. When the slides were brought in, they were viewed by the class. Then, musical selections furnished by the teacher were listened to. After that, the students were referred to their literature books and to the library to find poems or writing of any kind that could be matched with the music they had heard and the slides they had seen. Ultimately, the students produced a synchronized program of slides, music, and descriptive passages which were practiced, read orally, and tape recorded by the students themselves. The theme of the presentation was *The Seasons of the Year in Music, Pictures, and Words.*

A Final Word

A powerful aid to reading for comprehension is reading for purpose. The essence of reading maturity is knowing what is wanted from a reading selection, and then varying the rate and thinking strategies accordingly. Too often, teachers have "sprung" comprehension tests or other reading-related activities on students after they have read for different purposes or no particular purpose at all. Obviously, some activities should be introduced after reading. However, many times the reading experiences themselves and the related activities are of a better quality when the students know both what to look for in their reading and what they will do with what they find.

Something to Think and Talk About

Conversation in the teachers' lounge:

Teacher A: I would like to get my fifth graders involved in some kind of activity stemming from their reading because I know a lot of them don't like reading very much, and I think they don't understand a lot of things I have them read. But honestly, those projects take so much class time and besides, I'm not very creative and neither are my students.

Teacher B: I know just what you mean. These kids just don't bring much with them from home. They watch TV all the time.

Teacher A: I heard that next year we can adopt a new basal series. I hope we can find one that has a lot of good things for the kids to do without taking up too much time.

Teacher B: I hear that instructional reading materials are really getting a lot better. The suggestions in the manual for the books we're using now are lousy. Besides, the workbooks we have now take up so much time.

Teacher A: Time sure flies. Do you realize that it's almost February, and I'm not even half way through our social studies book?

(See Appendix 9 for Authors' Response to "Something to Think and Talk About.")

References

Dixon, Norman R. (1964). "Listening: Most Neglected of the Language Arts," *Elementary English* **41**: 285–288.

Hunt, Lyman C. (1970). "The Effect of Self-Selection, Interest and Motivation upon Independent, Instructional and Frustrational Levels," *The Reading Teacher* **24**, 2: 146–151, 158.

Jennings, Frank (1965). *This Is Reading*. New York: Bureau of Publications, Teachers College, Columbia University.

Johnson, Marjorie S. and Roy Kress (1969). "Readers and Reading," *The Reading Teacher* **22**, 7: 594.

Krathwohl, David R., Benjamin S. Bloom, and Bertram B. Masia (1964). *Taxonomy of Educational Objectives, The Classification of Educational Goals, Handbook II: Affective Domain*. New York: David McKay.

Moffett, James (1968). *Teaching the Universe of Discourse*. Boston: Houghton Mifflin.

Pauk, Walter (1968). "Beyond Nuts and Bolts," *Journal of Reading* **11**: 507.

Petre, Richard M. (1971). "Reading Breaks Make It in Maryland," *Journal of Reading* **15** (3): 191–194.

Pooley, Robert C. (1961). "Reading and the Language Arts," *Development In and Through Reading*. Chicago: University of Chicago Press.

10

THE POOR READER
IN THE MIDDLE GRADES

Poor readers probably become most keenly aware of their handicap during the middle grades. For it is in these grades that the emphasis in the curriculum changes from the development of basic reading skills to the utilization of those skills for academic purposes. Their inaccurate word recognition skills, their faulty comprehension, and their slow rate of reading combine to reinforce their lack of confidence in themselves as readers and to make reading a frustrating way for them to learn. In addition, they are often painfully aware of the fact that they cannot share in the world of recreational reading that many of their peers are discovering with great personal satisfaction. Like the policeman in the Gilbert and Sullivan song from the *Pirates of Penzance*, a poor reader's lot is not a happy one.

At some time prior to or during their middle grade school experience, many, if not most, poor readers have been identified and given special instruction without being substantially helped by teachers, pediatricians, psychologists, neurologists, speech therapists, ophthalmologists, their parents, and others concerned about their welfare. Consequently, they are extremely sensitive to their problem and understandably fearful that because it has not yet been solved, it will never be solved. Unfortunately, for some this fear is well founded because of the complexity of their problem and the uncertainty of the results of remedial instruction with the limited availability and techniques of diagnostic and remedial programs.

Although we would have it otherwise, it appears that poor readers will be a major concern of teachers at all academic levels for a long time to come. Therefore, it is incumbent upon all teachers to accept poor readers as worthy school citizens and to work to improve their reading ability without denying them the information they need and without damaging their self-concepts. The key to

179

meeting the poor reader's needs in the middle grades turns on (1) understanding the nature and causes of reading retardation, (2) setting realistic expectations, and (3) providing corrective instruction.

The Nature of Reading Retardation

For some people, the development of the reading process is affected more adversely by negative factors than for others. What would be generally regarded as a stressful home environment appears to have no harmful effect on the reading growth of some students, while a similarly stressful home situation has a very debilitating effect on the reading growth of others. For no apparent reason some students may respond very poorly to a particular instructional approach while most of their classmates prosper. Some students miss a good deal of school because of illness or other reasons and manage to keep up with their classmates. Other students, however, never seem to catch up after a prolonged absence. A teacher's "no-nonsense" approach may result in good achievement for most students, but may seriously interfere with the learning of others. Some students who score only average or slightly below average on intelligence tests learn to read quite satisfactorily, while students who score well above average may become disabled readers. Studies that investigate the nature and causes of reading retardation usually conclude that growth in reading is a highly individual phenomenon and that difficulty in learning to read is usually the result of several factors which interact to lower a particular individual's reading ability.

Very simply (and for classroom purposes), retarded readers may be described as those students who are unable to extract meaning from print with enough facility to use the reading materials most of their classmates use for informational and recreational purposes. Whether students are or are not retarded readers should be determined by their ability to read silently. Their oral reading may be characterized by omissions, substitutions, mispronunciations, lack of expression, and other faults; but if they can get the meaning they need from silent reading experiences, they are "readers" in the most important sense of the word. It is unfortunate that some students are categorized as poor readers and come to perceive themselves as such because they make mistakes when they read aloud. Although students who read poorly when they read for an audience may also be poor silent readers, the two different abilities should be considered separately, with the greatest importance being given to silent reading comprehension.

Poor reading ability manifests itself in different ways. Two manifestations, however, are exhibited by many poor readers and are important for classroom teachers to know about. Most poor readers are emotionally upset because of their disability. The emotional disturbance may be shown by feigned indifference, defensiveness, hostility, withdrawal, showing off, or other undesirable behavior. Teachers who recognize the undesirable behavior as symptomatic of anxiety and insecurity will react to the behavior with understanding and kindness and will resist the temptation to attribute the reading problem to the negative attitude of a nasty kid.

The second characteristic exhibited by most poor readers is a confused notion of what reading is and what they are supposed to get from reading. This confusion about the nature and purpose of reading is understandable if we consider that poor readers have rarely, if ever, experienced reading as a flow of ideas between authors and themselves. Their reading performances have for the most part been halting, inaccurate, interrupted by distractions, and distorted by anxiety interference. As poor readers become more aware of their problem, they resort to guessing, avoidance of reading activities, absorption in distracting maneuvers, and other behaviors that lead them even further away from experiencing reading as a communication process. Therefore, when they reach the middle grades their perception of reading is very different from that of good readers. Teachers must be careful not to interpret their confusion, poor motivation to read, and avoidance of reading as stupidity or obstinacy. Poor readers have not had productive, satisfying reading experiences and consequently have not learned what good readers do and what benefits they receive from reading.

Causes of Reading Failure

Teachers who are themselves good readers, who never had trouble learning to read, and who have not had much experience diagnosing disabled readers may be unable to understand how some disabled readers could spend three or more years in school and read no better than first or second graders. The causes for a particular student's reading disability are sometimes difficult to pinpoint, but a number of factors appear to be major contributors in many cases.

The instructional program

Most students probably learn equally well regardless of the particular approach that is used to teach them. Studies have shown that there are more differences within an approach, probably because of the teacher variable, than among approaches. For most children, then, a phonics approach, a linguistic approach, a language experience approach, a typical basal approach, or a modified alphabet approach for initial reading instruction will produce satisfactory results. However, certain children may not do well with a given approach because it demands too much in the way of aptitudes they lack. Children with poorly developed auditory discrimination may, for example, do poorly if their initial reading experience is based on an approach that relies heavily on hearing sounds and blending them into words. Children with poor visual memories may have trouble with an approach that stresses the development of a sight vocabulary before introducing phonics. Unfortunately, it is difficult to predict whether any given child will do well or poorly with a particular approach, and so some children may get off to a bad start because the instructional program chosen for them makes too heavy demands on abilities they do not possess to the extent required by the program. And when children get off to a bad start, it is often difficult to get them on the right track.

The poor reading ability of some middle graders may be traced to the introduction of formal reading instruction before they were ready for it. The individual differences in children should be as carefully considered in initiating reading instruction as they are in continuing instruction. Reading ability simply cannot be developed until oral language, experiential background, visual and auditory discrimination, and other factors that contribute to reading development are in a state of readiness to respond to formal reading instruction.

Teacher ineptness is another factor that may contribute to reading retardation. The kinds of questions teachers ask, how they group students for reading instruction, whether or not they teach phonic elements and generalizations inductively, how well they help students set purposes for reading, how they pace their instruction, and other aspects of their teaching are all factors in the reading growth of their pupils. Some children are more negatively affected by poor teaching than other children are. When compiling the case history of a disabled reader, a diagnostician will frequently hear from the parents that the child had a poor personal relationship with, or received poor instruction from, one or more of his or her primary grade teachers. In a number of cases this complaint appears to have some validity.

In addition to the quality of a child's reading instruction, the amount and pacing of instruction he or she receives are also factors affecting achievement. Some children require more of the teacher's attention, more skill development exercises, and more practice reading than do other children. Time is a precious element in the elementary school curriculum, and some children don't receive as much reading instruction as they need to master the basic reading skills. Illness may also cut into a child's school attendance, and consequently the child may be deprived of the instructional time needed to become a good reader.

Physical well-being

A student's reading growth may indeed be adversely affected by his or her physiological condition. However, it is likely that relatively few reading problems are the result of physical causes. Certainly, most physical ailments that might interfere with development in reading can be corrected or controlled if medical treatment is obtained.

Acuity, both visual and auditory, is especially important to reading achievement. Children cannot be taught to perceive visual and auditory likenesses and differences in letters and words if they cannot bring form configurations into focus or clearly hear the range of sounds used by speakers of their language. On the other hand, some highly motivated people have learned to read in spite of substantial losses of sight and hearing. Middle grade students should have their vision and hearing checked at regular intervals to be certain that their progress in school is not being jeopardized by deteriorations in their seeing and hearing ability.

The communicable diseases that afflict most children during their elementary school years do not in and of themselves cause reading problems, nor do other more serious ailments, unless they result in brain damage. Absence from school because of illness is, however, a definite factor in the poor reading development of children who have a history of illnesses throughout their schooling.

General debility resulting in decreased motivation to learn and inability to concentrate during instruction are probably the most prevalent physiological causes of reading retardation. Children handicapped by improper diets, substandard housing, inadequate clothing, and other conditions that contribute to generally poor health are prime candidates for disabled readers. Many times the reading problems of these children cannot be successfully corrected until their general state of health has been improved. Students with perpetually runny noses, low-grade fevers, persistent coughs, rashes, decayed teeth, or other symptoms of chronic illness should be referred to whatever health services are available. Until they get the medical attention they need, the reading instruction they receive will not be maximally productive.

Emotional factors

Learning to read demands concentration. Children who are emotionally distressed cannot be expected to concentrate on finding the main idea in a paragraph, recalling facts in the sequence in which they were presented, or setting purposes for reading. Children with too much hostility to accept help or who are insecure, anxious, or depressed are often listless or haphazard readers. Their reading performance, like much of their other behavior, is erratic and unpredictable. Until they are made more comfortable emotionally, the best instruction schools can offer may not be maximally effective. However, successful reading experiences and a comfortable school setting can sometimes give the child enough emotional security to permit the development of good skills and attitudes.

Environmental factors

Both the home and the school environments contribute to success in reading, in part because of their effects on the student's physical and emotional health. Parents and siblings who provide motivation to read, intellectual stimulation, and a rich background of experiences to bring to the printed page are positive influences. Schools that give children a feeling of warmth, security, quiet, and structured freedom are also positive factors. In contrast, homes and schools devoid of these elements adversely affect the reading growth of the child.

Intellectual ability

The entire area of intelligence and measuring intellectual potential is filled with controversy. Nevertheless, there is a high positive correlation between students' achievement on measures of verbal intelligence and their ultimate reading achievement. Certainly, a low level of general verbal intelligence is a factor in reading retardation. However, many students with below-normal performances on intelligence tests learn to read well enough to get the information they need and the recreation they want from printed material. Therefore, teachers should be extremely wary of assuming that students who have intelligence scores in the 80s will never be functional readers. This assumption is especially invalid if it is based on scores on intelligence tests that were group-administered.

Neurological deficits

More questions than answers surround the role of neurological dysfunction in reading retardation. There is no doubt that damage to certain areas of the brain can result in mild to severe disability. However, relatively few reading problems can be traced to brain damage from a blow, a prolonged high fever, or some malady involving the central nervous system. The concept of neurological maturational lag has been suggested as a cause for reading retardation, but the assumptions underlying that concept are difficult to prove with our present lack of knowledge about neurological development and its effect on reading ability. All in all, the most sensible position regarding neurological deficits and their effect on reading appears to be that they play a minor role in the overall problems of reading retardation in our society.

Setting Realistic Expectations

An understanding of the many factors in an individual's life that can singly or in combination result in poor reading achievement should help middle grade teachers be more tolerant of poor readers and more realistic in the expectations they set for them. Certainly, poor readers should not be abandoned as hopeless victims of irreversible forces. On the other hand, they should not be expected to get as much from reading as their more fortunate classmates. Finally, they should not be trundled off to a remedial reading teacher with the expectation that they will come prancing back after a short while, ready to hold their own with students for whom reading has never been a problem.

Out-of-class remedial instruction is necessary for many students to make any progress at all in reading. Some students do indeed make great strides in their reading growth because of good remedial instruction. However, most students profit only moderately from remedial help unless it is complemented by an adapted classroom program which includes corrective reading instruction. Classroom teachers do need to recognize the limitations of remedial teaching and coordinate their teaching with the remedial instruction being given. As a team, the classroom teacher and the remedial specialist can do more for disabled readers than either can do alone. One or the other should take the initiative in establishing and maintaining the desired cooperative working relationship.

In the middle grades, students with reading problems frequently become pessimistic about their ability to improve their reading. As they see the gap between themselves and their more able classmates widen, they become discouraged and often give up. Teachers who give the impression that reading is the only way to learn or who suggest that schools exist only for good readers in effect encourage poor readers to withdraw from the learning process. Middle grade teachers will find that a healthy attitude toward, and realistic expectations with respect to, poor readers are essential to the continued (albeit slower) reading development of these children.

Corrective Instruction

Broadly conceived, corrective reading instruction includes all of the accommodations a classroom teacher can make to instruct poor readers at their present level of reading achievement and to improve their reading ability at the same time. An important, though sometimes overlooked, dimension of corrective teaching is that poor readers need information which, if they can't read, must be given to them through media other than print. Another important dimension is the improvement of specific reading skills which help them become increasingly able to get meaning from print. Finally, their attitude toward reading must not become so negative that they refuse to use the reading skills they do have.

The following suggestions will help middle grade teachers practice corrective reading measures. They should not be implemented as a personal concession to students who have no right to special treatment, but rather as a major responsibility teachers have for accepting the reality of poor readers and giving them the corrective instruction they need at all academic levels.

1 *Discover each poor reader's reading strengths and weaknesses.*
Standardized reading achievement test scores available to most teachers in grades four to eight help to provide a general impression of the level of the class as a whole and to discover striking individual differences within the class. However, standardized achievement tests do not provide teachers with the specific information they need to do some corrective teaching. We recommend that middle grade teachers construct an inventory of materials at different levels of difficulty whose subject-matter content is comparable to that they will be assigning or will have available for students' voluntary reading. Selections from basal readers, textbooks, multilevel kits, or graded skill-development books can be compiled readily. The teacher should use these materials in a private 15- to 30-minute conference with each poor reader to make an informal diagnosis to determine: (1) just how difficult it is for the student to read orally; (2) how well he or she responds to questions based on a silent reading passage of 100–200 words; and (3) how well he or she can discuss a 100–200-word selection with no questions or other prompts after having read it silently. (We discuss this more thoroughly in Chapter 11.)

The informally administered inventory we recommend is a rough diagnostic survey at best and should be considered a minimum assessment. However, we believe that classroom teachers should not be expected to conduct highly sophisticated and time-consuming diagnoses of the poor readers in their classes and indeed do not require the kind of information obtained in a thorough diagnosis to give some corrective instruction. The remainder of our suggestions for poor readers, we believe, can be implemented at the classroom level so long as the teacher has at least a cursory knowledge of their oral and silent reading performance obtained in a private setting with informational and recreational materials. However, cursory knowledge is at least a minimum requirement.

2 *Give poor readers encouragement and opportunities to read materials of their own choosing, with no comprehension checks or other penalties to pay after reading.*

One reason poor readers do not develop good reading skills is that they do not spend enough time reading to get the practice they need. When they enter the middle grades most poor readers have the ability to read at some level, and they should be given opportunities to use the abilities they do have for interesting and purposeful reading. The temptation in the middle grades is to work poor readers harder and harder with developmental exercises to "catch them up" before they reach senior high school. This narrow approach can be deadly in the middle grades, when students need to get the feel of reading for meaning if they understand only 10 percent of what they read. Ten percent of something they want is better than 80 percent of something that turns them away from reading or 100 percent of nothing. Hunt (1970) comments as follows:

Every observant teacher has seen the highly motivated reader engrossed in a book which for him is obviously of considerable difficulty. But because interest and involvement are high, he persists in the pursuit of ideas and he gets some. Certainly in such instances the reader does not get all the ideas, not even all important ideas, but he does get enough to sustain his interest. [1]

All middle grade teachers, whether they teach in self-contained classrooms or in departmentalized schools, should be on the alert for opportunities to put attractive materials at a reasonable level of difficulty into the hands of poor readers. Story books, biographies, how-to-do-it books, magazines, newspaper articles, sporting equipment catalogs, and other materials should be within easy grasp of every teacher to pass on to "might-be-interested" poor readers who may be complimented enough by the teacher's perception of them as readers that they will try them. All schools should provide free reading periods and easy access to materials to peruse and perhaps check out. Many middle graders are involved in

---

1. Lyman C. Hunt, "The Effect of Self-selection, Interest, and Motivation upon Independent, Instructional, Frustration Levels," *The Reading Teacher* **24**, 2 (Nov. 1970), p. 148. Reprinted by permission.

extracurricular activities or have jobs or family responsibilities and cannot, or at any rate will not, read or investigate reading materials unless schools schedule reading time into the curriculum.

Poor readers should not be subjected to comprehension tests after every reading experience. Hunt gives 13 questions for teachers to ask of students to assess their growth as readers and to emphasize that reading is a meaning-getting process:

1 *Did you have a good reading period today? Did you read well? Did you get a lot done?*

2 *Did you read better today than yesterday?*

3 *Were you able to concentrate today on your silent reading?*

4 *Did the ideas in the book hold your attention? Did you have the feeling of moving right along with them?*

5 *Did you have the feeling of wanting to go ahead faster to find out what happened? Were you constantly moving ahead to get to the next good part?*

6 *Was it hard for you to keep your mind on what you were reading today?*

7 *Were you bothered by others or by outside noises?*

8 *Could you keep the ideas in your book straight in your mind?*

9 *Did you get mixed up in any place? Did you have to go back and straighten yourself out?*

10 *Were there words you did not know? How did you figure them out?*

11 *What did you do when you got to the good parts? Did you read faster or slower?*

12 *Were you always counting to see how many pages you had to go? Were you wondering how long it would take you to finish?*

13 *Were you kind of hoping that the book would go on and on—that it would not really end?*[2]

These questions and other informal measures will help poor readers gain an understanding of what good readers do when they read, without subjecting them to the unsuccessful and unproductive experience they would be likely to have with the typical multiple-choice comprehension test. Teachers who like the concept underlying Hunt's questions, but who would prefer questions that ask for more than "yes" or "no" responses may wish to modify Hunt's questions as follows:

1 What was good about your reading period today? How much did you accomplish?

2 What evidence do you have that you have improved?

2. *Ibid.*

3   On what phase of your reading were you able to concentrate best?

4   What ideas in the book held your attention? At what points did you have the feeling of moving right along?

5   Where did you have the feeling of wanting to go ahead faster to find out what happened?

6   What interferences, if any, made it hard for you to keep your mind on your reading?

7   What outside noises bothered you?

8   What helped you keep the ideas straight in your mind? At what points did you find it difficult?

9   At what points did you get mixed up and have to go back and straighten yourself out?

10   What words gave you difficulty? How did you figure them out?

11   How did the good parts of the story affect your speed of reading?

12   At what point, if any, did you check to see how many more pages you had to read? Why?

13   How did you feel at the end of the story?

3 *Teach poor readers to rely heavily on context clues to get the meaning of unfamiliar words.*

A major reason for the poor reading ability of many poor readers is that they failed to learn to use phonetic analysis to attack unfamiliar words. For one reason or another the strategies employed in sounding words out were difficult for them to master. Many times the special attention given them was aimed at improving their phonetic-analysis skills. Consequently, they became convinced that good readers had to be good at sounding out words, and they were not. Furthermore, as they concentrated more on sounding out individual words, they attended less to the context surrounding the unrecognized words and to the meaning being communicated by the author. Informal observation has shown us that poor readers will often struggle unsuccessfully to sound out words whose meaning is perfectly obvious from the surrounding context. The last word in the following sentence is a good example of such a word: "On the Fourth of July the sky was red with the glow of pyrotechnics."

Perhaps the most revealing example of the relief poor readers experience when they discover that the first letter or letters of an unrecognized word plus the context around it will frequently prompt the word is provided by a sixth grader named Sam. After two weeks of specific training in contextual analysis, he remarked, "I don't have to sound words out to know what they mean." Interestingly enough, having discovered that he didn't have to do it was the beginning of his learning to do it. Eventually, he learned to use both contextual and phonetic-analysis skills, but he had to be convinced he could do the former before he could relax enough to learn the latter.

Seven types of context clues teachers should be aware of so that they can help poor readers develop work-attack skills that may be effective and at the same time less difficult for them to learn than phonetic-analysis skills are the following:

1 *Definition.* (The unknown word is defined within the passage.)

2 *Background experience.* (The unknown word can be determined from the student's general awareness or knowledge of the situation being discussed.)

3 *Comparison or contrast.* (The unknown is compared or contrasted with something the student is familiar with.)

4 *Synonym.* (A synonym is given for the unknown word.)

5 *Familiar expression.* (The student is required to recognize common expressions heard every day. For example, "He got himself into a *pack of trouble.*")

6 *Summary.* (The unknown word summarizes information that has preceded it.)

7 *Reflection of a mood or situation.* (The context describes a situation or establishes a mood or tone. The unknown word reflects that kind of situation or that kind of mood.)

These types of clues should not be taught to poor readers deductively. Rather, teachers should be alert to the possibilities of unlocking the meaning of a word through context clues and call students' attention to the specific clues as they are present in material the students are reading. Over a period of time students will inductively learn the different types of clues and strategies available to them for getting the meaning of a word from context.

    4 *Before poor readers begin reading a selection, alert them to specific linguistic structures and devices likely to cause interpretation difficulties* (for example, figurative language, unusual or long sentence structures, specialized vocabulary, punctuation).

Too many teachers fail to carefully read in advance the material they assign to poor readers. Consequently, they are unable to prepare such readers for potential "trouble spots" in the linguistic structure of the material. Students should be told to pay attention to key words, specialized vocabulary should be defined, words showing important relationships should be identified and marked, topic sentences might be underlined, and figurative language likely to be misinterpreted should be discussed. Preparations of this kind are extremely important for poor readers, who often do not give sufficient attention to important linguistic elements in an author's writing.

5 *Provide poor readers with information that relates to the ideational content of their reading material.*
Poor readers frequently possess meager experiential backgrounds. They are unable to gain much from print because they bring little to it. Time spent discussing concepts, viewing a film, or looking at pictures that can provide a cognitive framework into which the ideas in a reading selection fit is time well spent. For example, before reading a story about a character who made an unwise decision and suffered the consequences, teachers might discuss with poor readers the necessity for all people to make decisions daily, talk about the importance of carefully considering all factors before making major decisions, and share personal experiences related to decisions.

With certain material, poor readers require "guideposts" to lead them through a selection and give them feedback that tells them that they are being successful as they progress through the selection. For example, teachers might tell students, "You are going to read a story about a boy who discovered he had a friend with a problem. He had to make a decision as to whether or not he would get involved with his friend's problem. You will read about how he struggled with his decision. Then you will find out why he made the decision he made, and finally you will learn the consequences of his decision." As students reach the guideposts that have been given them, they in effect get positive, reinforcing feedback that sends them off to search for the next guidepost.

6 *Teach poor readers to pause periodically in their reading to reflect on what they have just read and make some predictions about what they will read next.*
Ideas encountered in print need to be sorted out, reflected upon, and fitted into the existing information in the reader's mind before they can be comprehended and retained. It is characteristic of poor readers never to pause, collect their thoughts, and speculate on what the author will say next. As a result their minds are overpowered with the input of ideas which they don't organize and consequently comprehend only vaguely, if at all. Retention of ideas which are not organized and reflected upon in the personal language of the reader is practically nil.

Poor readers need special aids to do what good readers do; namely, organize ideas into an existing cognitive framework. Teachers can ask poor readers to mark places in a passage that are good for reflection and prediction. A slanted pencil line after a summary statement can serve as a signal for reflection, and a dash or straight line after a transition sentence can serve as a signal to predict what the author will say next. The point is that poor readers have not learned to reflect and predict while they are reading and have to be taught repeatedly in a straightforward way.

7 *Do not require poor readers to read orally in front of their classmates.*
Reading ability is not improved by a poor reading performance before one's peers. Therefore, poor readers should be required to read orally only in private, for diagnostic or corrective purposes. Many students with reading problems are

better silent readers than they are oral readers, and an embarrassing display of their greatest weakness is a degrading experience of no instructional value.

Although more prevalent in the primary grades than in the intermediate grades, some poor readers continually volunteer to read orally before the class. In most cases this is probably an attention-getting device or a way of not feeling left out. Teachers report that these students are difficult to cope with. The temptation is to call on them and give them their moment, even though little is to be gained for themselves or the class. Perhaps the most sensible approach to this dilemma is to hold a private conference with each of these students, stressing that there is no need for everyone to read orally in class since all members of the class may learn more by listening to the students who read best for audiences. However, if these students wish, they may have an opportunity to prepare a particular selection that is scheduled for oral reading, and they will be called upon if they volunteer to read that particular selection. They will be called upon to read orally, then, only if they prepare beforehand to ensure a reasonably good performance in front of the class. As a matter of fact, this is good procedure for all audience-type reading experiences. While one student is reading, the rest of the class should close their books and listen, not try to follow along.

8   *Give poor readers opportunities to be successful with tasks or projects that do not require reading.*

Many middle grade students who are poor readers have other abilities that are well enough developed to let them engage successfully in oral discussions, artistic endeavors, the operation of mechanical equipment, or other activities which contribute to the class but do not require reading. For example, a good reader may read the directions for setting up a science experiment to a poor reader, who could do the actual setting up. Or, poor readers could record the efforts of a play-reading group. The important thing is to find tasks for poor readers that keep them involved in class activities despite their reading deficiencies. Some, perhaps most, poor readers in the middle grades will never turn into good readers and must discover and develop other abilities if they are to preserve their self-concepts and learn to become useful citizens.

9   *Assemble a library of audio tapes, filmstrips, phonograph records, and films to help poor readers get the information they need without reading.*

Certainly, some information can best be obtained by reading. However, reading is only one way for students to get much of the information they need in order to satisfy school objectives. Units of study can be taught so that some students read, some view a filmstrip, some listen to a tape, or learn from other media that do not require reading. Later, the students may be brought together to share, organize, and extend what they have learned.

Some teachers have discovered that senior high school English classes, speech classes, drama groups, and various community groups are likely to have good oral readers among their members and hence are excellent resources to draw upon. Individuals from these groups are generally pleased to tape-record a particularly important chapter from a textbook, a math problem, a poem, or other material that is especially important for students to learn. The availability of tape recorders and headsets allows poor readers to have important material read to them by good readers while good readers read the material for themselves. Over a period of years teachers can assemble for poor readers a fine library of materials that do not require reading. These materials might be catalogued and kept in the central library, or in the instructional materials center in the school, or in the classroom, depending on the school's facilities and policies.

10 *Poor readers should, whenever possible, be provided with content area-related reading materials at easy readability levels instead of the materials good readers use.*

A search of newspapers, magazines, multilevel reading kits, and books designed for reading-skills development will disclose selections dealing with school subjects that are much easier to read than most of the textbooks written for middle graders. Enterprising teachers will be able to collect science, social studies, and literary materials written from a first-grade difficulty level on up. Material at the third-grade level can be read by most poor readers in the middle grades, and some poor readers in the upper middle grades can handle selections at fifth- and sixth-grade level. Teachers should not insist that all students read the same selections. Class discussions are often more interesting and meaningful when they bring out the students' different reading experiences relative to a broad, common topic.

11 *Give poor readers many opportunities to discuss reading experiences with better readers in small groups.*

Segregating good readers from poor readers in the middle grades deprives the latter of the models they need if they are to learn what good readers do when they read and what they get from their reading experiences. This point of view was set forth in Chapter 1 in the discussion about the formation of information-gathering and recreational-reading groups. Suffice it to say here that poor readers need frequent contact with good readers under conditions that encourage the kind of discussion that keeps the nature of reading as a meaning-getting process in clear focus.

12 *Guard against assignment overload for students who read slowly, reluctantly, and inaccurately.*

Some teachers are inclined to give the same assignments to poor readers and good readers. Although this may seem to be the only fair approach when students are competing for grades, it quickly discourages poor readers. The fact of individual differences in reading ability demands differentiation of reading assignments. We are aware of the difficulties differentiated assignments create in schools where students and parents perceive assignments as a kind of penalty that must be paid to attain a satisfactory grade on a report card. Why should two students' work be considered satisfactory when one was required to read more than the other?

The only solution to this dilemma lies in a different perception of the objectives and rewards of reading assignments. Students and parents must be helped to understand that the goal of education is not to satisfy a group penalty imposed by society, but rather to help each individual attain the best our culture has to offer, given his or her personal resources. Teachers must learn that reading assignments need to be given to help students achieve specific objectives that are recognized as valuable by the students as well as by the teachers. The task is not an easy one and will perhaps require some basic changes in educational philosophy and curriculum development. Nonetheless, poor readers cannot realistically be given and expected to complete the same reading assignments as good readers.

13 *Refer seriously disabled readers to remedial instruction and coordinate classroom programs with remedial programs.*
Remedial reading instruction is a difficult process with no guarantee of success. The work of the remedial specialist is essentially the same as that of the classroom teacher: to teach the student with learning problems how to read. Unfortunately, many classroom teachers regard remedial reading as an esoteric enterprise. Some feel it is beyond the understanding of teachers who are not specialized in the field; others feel it is work relegated to teachers who couldn't make it in the classroom. It is unfortunate that remedial reading teachers are often perceived as being either superior or inferior to good teachers. Teachers must understand that for most students, remedial reading is essentially the reapplication of good developmental instruction to children who have experienced reading as a series of failures.

A fault in many remedial reading programs is that they are not coordinated with the students' classroom programs. Too often, the remedial reading teacher and the classroom teacher are not aware of each other's efforts to improve the child's reading ability. Hence, opportunities to share insights, adjust curriculum, and reinforce skills are lost. The remedial reading teacher should seek the assistance of the classroom teacher in diagnosing reading problems and in planning suitable remediation. The classroom teacher should seek the assistance of the remedial teacher in adjusting the disabled student's classroom program so that it is consistent with the student's ability and so that it reinforces the skills, attitudes, and habits being taught by the remedial teacher. Frequent conferences between the remedial teacher and the classroom teacher are essential if the ultimate objective of remediation, returning the child to the regular classroom program, is to be attained.

Other Resources for Poor Readers

The two first-line resources available to most middle grades students with reading problems are classroom teachers (for students whose reading can be improved at the classroom level using the corrective measures described above) and remedial reading teachers (for students whose problems are so severe they need highly specialized and individualized diagnosis and teaching). Other resources which middle grades teachers and administrators may want to consider using or urging parents to consider using are listed below. We have included some editorial comments based on our personal experiences with each of the resources.

Reading consultants

Reading consultants can be of great help to classroom teachers who have students with reading problems. Consultants are trained to diagnose students' reading strengths and weaknesses, search for underlying causes of reading problems, refer students to other specialists when needed, and advise classroom teachers about poor readers' instructional programs. They can help classroom teachers find suitable materials, plan units of study, make assignments, construct and administer informal reading inventories (see Chapter 11), prepare reading assignments, and effect other curriculum adjustments that improve the working relationships between teachers and poor readers. Most schools have access to reading consultants who are regular staff members or who can be secured on a temporary basis from state departments of public instruction or nearby colleges or universities. Obviously, the greatest help to classroom teachers will come from consultants who are full-time staff members of a school and who can work with classroom teachers on curriculum development for poor readers on an ongoing basis.

School principals

As a group, school principals are no more knowledgeable about teaching students with reading problems than classroom teachers. Principals are helpful in (1) arranging for special classes or teachers for children with serious reading problems, (2) securing special instructional materials, (3) referring children to specialists for diagnostic evaluation, and (4) persuading the board of education to employ reading consultants to help classroom teachers if consultants are not readily available.

Learning disabilities teachers

Learning disabilities (L.D.) teachers may or may not be helpful in regard to helping students with reading problems. Many L.D. teachers have very little training in the field of reading. Often they are better equipped to work with mentally retarded or emotionally disturbed children than with children with reading problems. However, some L.D. teachers have taken considerable course work in the field of reading and may be as competent as remedial reading teachers. Rarely, however, are they competent to work with classroom teachers as reading consultants.

Pediatricians

Pediatricians are trained to care for the health of infants, children, and young adults. They are important for finding and eliminating any physical problems that may be contributing to reading problems. As a rule, it is wise to have a child with a serious reading problem given a complete physical examination. Pediatricians, however, generally are not trained to diagnose, treat, or prescribe for reading problems.

Neurologists

Neurologists are specialists in diagnosing and treating brain disorders. Neurological examinations may be indicated for children who are very seriously disabled and for whom brain dysfunction is suspected. However, neurological examinations rarely uncover the cause of the reading problem, and they never indicate the kind of corrective or remedial teaching a child needs. Neurologists are not generally trained to diagnose, treat, or prescribe treatment for specific reading problems. They may prescribe medicine to help control hyperactivity or some other behavior that appears to result from a brain dysfunction and that may be contributing to the reading problem, but they are not familiar enough with school settings to become involved with curriculum matters.

Tutors

Before teachers recommend or employ a particular tutor, they should ask for the tutor's qualifications for teaching middle grades students with reading problems. A qualified tutor (1) has teaching experience; (2) has taken course work in the diagnosis and treatment of reading problems; and (3) has the personal qualities of patience, enthusiasm, and warmth. Retired classroom teachers or college students may or may not be good remedial reading teachers. Middle graders with reading problems have other personal and social needs with which tutors must be familiar. Unless tutors and tutees can establish good personal relationships the tutoring is likely to be wasted and perhaps even harmful. Peer tutoring for middle graders should be approached with extreme caution. University students doing graduate work in the area of reading are often excellent tutors if they have had some classroom teaching experience in the middle grades. Whether tutors should be of the same or a different sex for their tutees seems to be purely a matter of individual tutee preference, and in our experience tutees often have a special preference.

Clinics

Students living in larger communities may have access to a reading disability clinic. These clinics are often connected with a hospital. The clinics usually have medical specialists and one or more remedial reading specialists on staff. In most cases reading disabilities clinics are more important for students who have physical and/or emotional problems contributing to the reading problem than for students who do not. The effectiveness of clinic programs for poor readers depends heavily upon the academic and personal qualifications of the clinic teachers and how well the clinic program can be coordinated with the student's regular school program.

Short-term programs

Summer school, summer camps, units of study, and other short-term (less than a year) programs are generally not effective in making a lasting impact on serious reading problems. They are generally more effective in helping good readers read better and in correcting very minor reading problems. In fact, they may be more detrimental than helpful to a child with serious reading problems because they get a commitment from the child, but they don't produce noticeable improvement. Teachers, administrators, and parents should campaign for long-term help for their students with reading problems in school districts where only short-term programs are available.

Psychologists

Psychologists may be helpful in giving IQ tests and other tests that help determine a child's potential for learning to read. Their tests may also be helpful in discovering the causes of emotional problems that may be contributing to the reading problem. School psychologists have also been very helpful in making the powers that control the purse strings aware of the need to provide reading teachers and reading consultants for students and teachers who need them.

Child psychiatrists

Child psychiatrists are trained to care for the mental health of children. Occasionally middle grades students have such severe mental health problems that they cannot concentrate on learning to read. Sometimes the mental health problem must be attended to before remedial teaching can be effective. Other times, the psychiatrist and the remedial teacher work together, tackling the mental health problem and the reading problem at the same time.

Vision specialists

Some vision specialists have been known to prescribe remedial reading programs or exercises to improve reading ability. However, this is rarely within their sphere of expertise. They are most helpful in diagnosing any vision problems that might be contributing to the reading problem. The diagnosis and treatment of reading problems themselves are best left to specialists in remedial reading.

Commercial schools

A number of people have gone into the business of diagnosing and/or teaching children with reading problems. Some of these businesses (which are called "schools," "institutes," "clinics," "centers," and other names) have good teachers, use good materials, and have good programs. Others have better advertising programs than instructional programs. Before teachers recommend or parents enroll students in a commercial school they should do the following:

1   Obtain a description of the diagnostic procedures that are used.
2   Obtain a list of the instructional materials that are used.
3   Find out how the commercial school coordinates its program with the programs in students' regular schools.
4   Find out the general philosophy of the school regarding the cause or causes of reading problems.
5   Ask for the credentials of the people who will be doing the diagnostic work and the remedial teaching.
6   Obtain a list of fees for services.

This information should be taken to a state certified or university certified reading specialist for appraisal. Public schools, state departments of public instruction, colleges and universities (departments of education) are good places to find reading specialists who can evaluate the programs offered by commercial schools. Teachers who recommend enrollment and parents who enroll students with reading problems in a commercial school on the basis of an appealing advertisement with a list of impressive sounding names and degrees may be doing the students a disservice and putting an unwarranted strain on the family budget.

A Summary Statement

Helping middle grades students with reading problems improve their reading usually requires the combined efforts of administrators, classroom teachers, specialists in diagnosing and teaching children with reading problems, and parents. In some cases the assistance of professionals other than educators is needed. Teachers need to know that eliminating reading problems is not a simple process. They should also know that most students with reading problems can be helped. The key to helping poor readers improve their reading lies in bringing the best knowledge and efforts of teachers, parents, and other professionals together in a coordinated program. The role each should play varies from student to student because reading problems and the conditions which cause them are so varied. For that reason alone, teachers should be highly skeptical of programs or instructional materials that promise help for all students with reading problems.

Something to Think and Talk About

The educational problems presented by poor readers will decrease and perhaps disappear entirely as media that do not require reading to gain information and recreation are developed, gain respectability, and possibly supplant books and other printed material. As a matter of fact, "reading-free" curriculums are presently possible and should probably be developed using a part of the resources that are being expended to make readers of the entire population, an objective that seems increasingly unrealistic.

Learning to read well enough to use print functionally is a goal apparently beyond the grasp of many people in our society. To subject these people to years of struggling and failure seems unkind and almost inhumane. How much better it would be to let those who learn to read easily, as many do, read; and those who cannot readily master the process turn to other media. Of course, nonreaders must be considered just as valuable citizens as readers are. Indeed in the future, nonreaders are likely to become better citizens in every way because they will no longer be forced to suffer the stigma and burdens presently placed on them by a school system which clings to the myth that educated people must know how to read. (See Appendix 10 for Authors' Response to "Something to Think and Talk About.")

References

Hunt, Lyman C., Jr. (1970). "The Effect of Self-selection, Interest and Motivation upon Independent, Instructional and Frustrational Levels," *The Reading Teacher* **24** (2): 146–151, 158.

11

EVALUATING READING GROWTH IN THE MIDDLE GRADES

A number of studies have found that students who are not "readers" before they reach senior high school are unlikely ever to develop the reading habit. The importance, then, of carefully evaluating students' reading growth throughout the middle grades cannot be overemphasized. The evaluation, however, should be concerned with the effect of reading instruction on students' attitudes toward reading and on their reading habits as well as their skills development. Students who are good exercise doers, score well on standardized reading tests, but never use reading unless they are assigned to do so, or who cannot get information from content area textbooks are manifestations of a reading program that has stopped short of its ultimate goal.

Standardized Reading Achievement Tests

The value of standardized reading achievement tests has been a major concern of reading specialists, classroom teachers, and administrators. The complexity of the reading act is such that trying to measure it objectively is analogous to evaluating teaching ability. There is a difference in the performances of a good reader and a poor reader, just as there's a difference in the performances of a good teacher and a poor teacher. However, in trying to measure that difference we run the risk of changing the performance of those being measured, or of measuring some behavior that is only a small part of the total performance. The standardized reading achievement tests in common use are no more than gross measures of reading ability. An individual's score on a particular test is, at best, only an indication of where that individual stands in relation to the norm group for the particular test. There is no assurance that the reading behaviors sampled by the test reflect the reading demands encountered most often by that individual or that he or she might not have performed quite differently had other behaviors been sampled. At worst, an individual's score may reflect nothing more than rapid but lucky guessing or an inability to cope with the constraints and demands imposed by the test and/or the testing situation.

A study by Kretschmer (1972) addressed itself to the content of the selections included in tests. He analyzed 16 standardized reading achievement tests to determine the types of subject matter used for passages in reading-comprehension subtests. The analysis showed that for the 16 subtests:

1   Passage content was unevenly distributed, since it was weighted in favor of animals in the primarily level, animals and school subjects in the intermediate levels, and science and school subjects in the advanced levels.

2   The most popular and relevant subject areas such as social problems, humor, fantasy, adventure, poetry, and city life were absent or underrepresented.

3   Passages were frequently biased in favor of middle-class culture.

Although there is good reason to be skeptical about the results obtained from standardized reading achievement tests, they do provide some indication of how one student or more students compare with other students on tasks that require the mental processing of printed material. As long as teachers recognize that the reading behavior required by the test cannot be generalized to all and perhaps most nontest reading tasks, the test results can be kept in proper perspective. The truth is that in spite of their limitations, reading achievement tests probably do a good job of identifying students who have well-developed basic reading skills. This identification would seem to be valuable in making decisions about adjusting the instructional program to meet the different needs of different students and in getting some evidence about the effectiveness of the reading program. Perhaps the greatest danger in interpreting the results of reading achievement tests is the tendency to assume that students who do well on the short selections and multiple-choice questions which typically comprise these tests, also do well with longer selections and more sophisticated reading-related tasks. That assumption is not valid. The best procedure is always to view the results of reading achievement tests in the light of other measures of reading achievement for students who score high as well as for students who score low.

The number of different reading achievement tests on the market is large. Buros (1972) provides a valuable service by periodically soliciting reviews of the various tests from reading specialists and including them in a collection of reviews of mental measurement instruments. A study of the latest collection of reviews of reading tests would be good supplementary reading for this chapter. We have chosen not to recommend or even describe specific tests that are available commercially. First, the number of tests is too large to permit us to do an adequate job. Second, the tests are revised at different intervals, and so recommendations and descriptions are often outdated before they appear in print. Finally, the selection of reading achievement tests is usually not the prerogative of individual classroom teachers, but is more often an administrative decision made in cooperation with classroom teachers. Therefore, the most helpful information for classroom teachers regarding reading achievement tests would seem to be not a strong bias for one or two tests, but rather some criteria for evaluating tests. A list of questions that have been helpful to teachers and administrators follows:

1 Are the students who were used to gather normative data similar to our students and, therefore, likely to provide helpful comparisons?

2 Are the reading passages on the test good representations of the kind of reading material students must learn to read?

3 Are the tasks students are asked to perform good representations of what good readers do when they are getting meaning from print?

4 Are the comprehension questions asked of students carefully constructed to measure different levels of thinking about significant aspects of the content of the material?

5 What are the strengths and weaknesses of one particular test in regard to the strengths and weaknesses of other available tests? The reviews provided by Buros are especially helpful in this regard.

6 Is reading rate always measured as rate of comprehension? A rate-of-reading score that does not take comprehension into consideration is meaningless.

Certainly, there exist more sophisticated criteria, and it is hoped that a resource person with considerable experience in reading-test construction will be available to the classroom teacher to help select reading tests for particular purposes. However, the teacher who has relatively little background in educational measurement will find that the questions listed above will provide considerable guidance in making a proper test choice.

Diagnostic Reading Measures

Diagnostic testing differs from achievement testing in that it focuses on discovering the strengths and weaknesses among the abilities of one individual, whereas achievement testing attempts to discover differences in abilities among individuals or groups (testing for differences among groups is a more valid procedure). For example, for diagnostic purposes a teacher may wish to determine whether a particular fourth grader has more difficulty learning the meaning of a word from the context surrounding it than he has sounding words out. He may be good at phonic analysis but very poor at contextual analysis. Or, a teacher may want to find out if a particular seventh grader is able to recall facts after reading a selection even though she is unable to make an inference or see a unifying idea.

The purpose of diagnostic testing is to obtain information about students' reading in order to develop an instructional reading program that corrects their weaknesses within the context of successful reading experiences. Stated simply, teachers must give students opportunities to do what they are good at, while they are also working to become more proficient in areas in which they are weak. This is an especially important concept for middle grade teachers because of the weak ego characteristic of many students between the primary grades and secondary school. Middle grade pupils who come to perceive themselves as failures in reading are likely to be like the little engine that thought it couldn't—indeed it couldn't. A positive concept of oneself as a reader is a requisite for reading growth.

Information obtained from diagnostic assessment that does not suggest which instructional materials and practices to use for teaching purposes is without value. Therefore, reading diagnosticians should utilize materials and tasks that lead to reading program development.

Standardized diagnostic tests

A test which we urge middle grade teachers to examine as an example of standardized diagnostic reading tests is the *Stanford Diagnostic Reading Test, Brown Level* (The Psychological Corporation, 1976). This test is designed for group testing, and the accompanying manual contains information which gives good insights into the nature and purpose of diagnostic testing. The test is especially relevant to the discussion in this book, because Brown Level is recommended for use in grades 4.5–9.5.

Some evaluation specialists prefer "criterion-referenced" tests for diagnosing the strengths and weaknesses of students' reading skills in a way that does lead straightforwardly to instruction. Criterion-referenced tests judge a student's performance against a specified criterion score without reference, or comparison, to the scores of other students. *The Wisconsin Design for Reading Skill Development* (Otto and Askov, 1970) is an example of a system of assessment exercises that attempts to measure, or identify, the adequacy of students' performance on criterion-referenced reading tasks. Objectives that define basic skills in terms of observable behaviors (for example, given a paragraph in which a main idea is implicit but not stated, the student is able to state an appropriate, literal main idea) make possible the assessment of individual skill development status through the use of formal paper-and-pencil tests or informal observation of relevant behaviors. The tasks are constructed at different levels of difficulty and attempt to elicit information about students' abilities in six areas: word attack, comprehension, study skills, self-directed reading, interpretive reading, and creative reading. Since the tasks require actual reading behaviors, teachers learn specifically which abilities a student has acquired and the level at which he or she has acquired them. Once this is known, teachers may select from the available array of instructional materials and practices those that seem to be most appropriate for a given student. Smith, Otto, and Hansen (1978, Chapter 7) discuss criterion-referenced testing and give a complete list of behaviorally stated objectives for testing reading-skill development in the appendix. We have chosen not to discuss individually administered diagnostic reading tests in this chapter because classroom teachers rarely have the time or training needed to administer, score, and interpret them. For readers who want a thorough discussion of these tests we recommend Spache (1976, Chapter 7).

Instructional materials

Instructional materials may be used effectively to evaluate students' reading ability. A student's performance with materials constructed to teach specific skills at a specific level of difficulty may provide good insights into that student's reading development in regard to those skills. However, teachers using instructional materials to evaluate reading ability must remember to look carefully not only at the number of errors a student makes on a given number of responses but also at the kinds of errors that are made. Many instructional materials for middle graders have been designed to allow for ease of response and self-correction. Consequently, teachers and students tend to think in terms of "How many right?" instead of "Why were the responses incorrect?" or "Why were different ones correct?"

The *Reading for Understanding* laboratory (Chicago, Illinois: Science Research Associates, Inc.) can be quite effective in diagnosing comprehension ability. However, teachers must note not only that the student erred but also why he or she made the particular error. For example, the student who selects "A" as the correct response in the following example must be cautioned against hasty reading which results in word associations which have quite a different relationship in one context than in another (from card 31 in the General RFU laboratory).

The soil of China is so rich and her climate so
favorable that for centuries one of her most important industries
has been

A. Raising Silkworms   B. Ancient
C. Agriculture   D. Transportation

The student who selects "D" as the correct response has probably focused heavily on the word "industries." Incorrect responses on this item indicate a need for instruction in seeing relationships between ideas. Or, they may indicate the student's lack of familiarity with the word "agriculture." Beginning the statement with the word "Because" and eliminating the word "that" might be an instructional practice that could help the student learn how to relate the ideas in the item. Another instructional practice derived directly from the diagnostic finding would be to ask the student to state the conditions mentioned in the statement which support the selection of agriculture as the most important industry of

China. If the problem appears to be one of lack of familiarity with the word "agriculture," the teacher might start the student on a vocabulary-building program.

Among other instructional materials well suited to diagnosing reading abilities are the *Specific Skill Series* books (New York: Barnell Loft, Ltd.). The eight books in this series which are best suited to classroom diagnosis of middle graders reading skills needs are "Detecting the Sequence," "Using the Context," "Working with Sounds," "Following Directions," "Locating the Answer," "Getting the Facts," "Drawing Conclusions," and "Getting the Main Idea." For six of these skills, there exist books at six different difficulty levels, and for two, there are books at seven different levels of difficulty. Teachers can find out in which of the eight skills each student needs instruction and at which level of difficulty the student begins to falter. The best approach is to use the various books with students individually or in small groups to get an idea of their abilities in each skill area. It is not unusual to find that one or the other of these skills has been neglected. In one school, for example, nearly all the students were good at working with sounds, but did rather poorly in using the context. Apparently, phonics instruction had been given almost exclusive attention in developing word analysis skills.

Nearly any type of developmental material can be used for evaluation purposes if teachers choose to use it that way. The point is that careful analysis of students' performances with developmental materials focused on the development of specific abilities at various difficulty levels is a good way to measure the effectiveness of the total reading program in regard to those specific skills. Obviously, when instructional materials are used diagnostically, the information obtained can be easily translated into individualized instructional activities.

Teacher-constructed informal reading inventories

Informal reading inventories have become increasingly important in the evaluation of students' reading achievement as teachers' and administrators' faith in standardized achievement tests has diminished. Professional journals, especially *The Reading Teacher*, have reported the research findings and opinions of a number of researchers and teachers who have become interested in the informal reading inventory as an approach to reading evaluation. Farr (1969) says, "The use of informal reading inventories (IRI's) for determining students' functional reading levels and diagnosing reading skills is a fairly well-established practice."[1]

Teachers constructing IRI's may use whatever reading material they feel is most appropriate to their testing purposes. Farr says,

---

1. Roger Farr, *Reading: What Can Be Measured?* Newark, Delaware: International Reading Association, 1969, p. 99. Reprinted with permission of Roger Farr and the International Reading Association.

. . . when they are used to plan instruction, informal measurement procedures have more validity than standardized reading tests. In using informal assessments of students' reading in daily classroom situations, the teacher can evaluate the students' ability to apply their reading skills to various learning tasks. [2]

Informal inventories may be used merely to find the level of difficulty at which a particular student reads productively, or they may be used to discover particular skill strengths and weaknesses. One characteristic of an IRI which should be highly appealing to teachers is that the evaluation is conducted with the same (or similar) material as that which the students are using for instructional purposes. When the evaluation is concluded, teachers know at which level within graded materials the students will be able to read with no help, at which level they can read with assistance, and at which level they cease to get meaning regardless of a reasonable amount of help. In addition, in the evaluation process teachers are able to observe areas of strength and weakness. These observations may then be used in planning the kind of instruction to be given at the level of difficulty at which the students can read with assistance.

An IRI is a collection of short reading selections at various grade levels. The range of difficulty levels should comprise about as many years as the grade of the students with whom the inventory is used. For example, the IRI for seventh graders should contain selections at levels ranging in difficulty from about fourth grade through tenth grade. For middle graders each selection should be 200–250 words long. Three excellent sources for graded selections are basal readers (from the same series), *Science Research Associates Laboratories* (Chicago, Illinois: Science Research Associates, Inc.), and *Reader's Digest Skill Builders* (Pleasantville, New York: The Reader's Digest Association, Inc.).

At least two selections are needed at each difficulty level: one to evaluate oral reading ability and the other to evaluate silent reading ability. Teachers who want to do a more thorough evaluation with an IRI may wish to have four selections at each difficulty level: one for unprepared oral reading, one for oral reading after preparation, one to test unaided silent recall, and one to test aided silent recall. Differences in student performance among these four reading tasks may be substantial and may indicate strengths and weaknesses that would not be apparent if the four were not used.

Guidelines for determining whether a student is able to read material at a particular difficulty level without assistance (independent level of difficulty) or whether he or she needs assistance (instructional level of difficulty) have become somewhat standardized in regard to IRI testing. The standards (established somewhat arbitrarily) are:

---

2. *Ibid.,* p. 98.

Oral reading 99 percent accuracy (misses only one word in one hundred): independent level

95 percent accuracy: instructional level

Silent reading 90–100 percent accuracy: independent level

75–80 percent accuracy: instructional level

Obviously, the number of questions asked following the silent reading is a factor in determining the percentage considered to be acceptable for a judgment of accuracy. The degree of differentiation is clear, however. Performances below those standards supposedly indicate that the material is at the student's frustration level of difficulty and cannot be read productively even with teacher assistance.

Since the construction and administration of IRI's rest heavily on the teacher's judgment, we recommend that teachers also use their judgment in interpreting a student's performance at the time of test administration. Therefore, we are more comfortable when teachers regard the percentages above as only approximations. We believe that the final determination of whether or not a student can productively read material at a particular difficulty level rests squarely with the teacher. Among other things, there is such a variation among materials written at a particular difficulty level according to a readability formula that hard and fast criteria are impossible to defend.

Unprepared oral reading. Having students read a selection orally with no pre-reading help provides information as to how they can be expected to perform with a selection at a particular difficulty level when they are asked to read it "cold." We have found that under such conditions most students turn in their poorest oral reading performances. Whether or not unprepared oral reading is a good indication of how students perform when they read silently is questionable. We tend to believe that many poor readers comprehend material they read orally better than they comprehend material they read silently. The vocalization is helpful to their understanding. However, there is probably considerable variation in this regard among students.

Two kinds of information obtained from unprepared oral reading are valuable. First, if the students read with good expression in spite of some inaccuracies (omissions, substitutions, insertions, mispronunications, reversals), they probably have a good concept of reading for meaning and are aware of intonation cues as signals to meaning. Second, if the students' inaccuracies are such that they do not interfere with the essential communication of the selection, of if they correct errors that do interfere with the essential communication of the selection or that produce nonsense, they are reading for meaning. Certainly, a student who strives to get meaning from reading is preferable to a word caller and needs different instructional emphases.

Prepared oral reading. Prepared oral reading provides an indication of students' oral reading performance after they have had an opportunity to survey a selection and get help with words they don't recognize, sentences they aren't sure they can say with good intonation, and ideas they don't understand well enough to communicate to a listener. In fact, prepared oral reading is a good measure of how students can read for an audience when they have had the advantage of a teacher's guidance. Certainly, the audience-type reading which middle graders do should be preceded by instruction so that the reading performance is a successful experience for both reader and listeners.

Unaided silent recall. An evaluation of a student's unaided silent recall is probably the most useful measure to be obtained from an IRI. After all, it is the ability to discuss a reading experience without any prompting which comes closest to what we want of students in their information-getting and recreational-reading experiences. It is indeed important for teachers to know how well their students can talk about a selection after they have completed reading it. Some students are quite good at answering specific questions they are asked about a reading selection, but do very poorly without question prompts. Many widely used developmental reading materials reward students for good aided recall. Students learn what kinds of questions to expect and how to respond to simple questions about short reading selections. This is why there are so many middle graders who do well when they are asked specific questions about a short selection (especially when the questions are true-false or multiple-choice) but who do poorly when they are not prompted. Unaided silent recall seems to us to be the best test of a student's reading ability.

One variation of an unaided oral summary of a silent reading experience is to ask for a written summary of the text. Probably the one best test of middle graders' reading achievement is their ability to write, given all the time they need, a summary statement of a 200–250-word reading selection.

Aided silent recall. Three kinds of questions are important in testing aided silent-reading recall on an IRI:

1 Questions that ask for the recall of specific facts, for example:
   What was the boy's name?
   When did the event occur?
   How many horses were there?

2 Questions that ask for recall of sequential happenings:
   What happened first?
   Then what happened?
   What next?

3   Questions that ask for main ideas:
    In your own words, what are the important or main points in this
    selection?

Teachers may find considerable variation in a given student's ability to respond
intelligently to questions with these three different focuses. Knowing the variation is useful in planning an instructional program which gives students extra
training in the areas that need strengthening.

Most teachers find that it is desirable to modify the questions they originally
constructed for testing aided silent-reading recall. What in theory appears to be a
good question for evaluating a student's ability to recall sequential happenings,
for example, may, in practice, prove to be ambiguous or too simple. Therefore,
teachers should be prepared to make improvements in the questions or tasks they
plan for IRI's as they receive feedback from their students. The same may be said
for the choice of selections. A good IRI and its skillful administration are developed over time and with cumulative experience.

Two commercial informal inventories

Two commercially available informal reading inventories are described briefly
below because we have found them to be useful diagnostic instruments for middle
grades teachers and reading specialists. We think teachers and specialists who are
looking for published informal reading inventories would do well to examine *The
Reading Miscue Inventory* (Goodman and Burke, 1971) and the *Classroom
Inventory* (Silvaroli, 1973).

The Reading Miscue Inventory is designed to help teachers analyze the
mistakes or miscues students make while reading orally in terms of how those
miscues affect the sense of the printed message. The underlying assumption of
this qualitative analysis is that reading miscues are not all of equal import and,
therefore, they should be analyzed rather than merely quantified. The *RMI*
includes a series of questions which help the teacher to focus on the effect each
miscue has on the meaning of what is being read. The procedure used for gather-
ing the necessary information for the *RMI* consists of five steps: (1) The child
reads a selection orally. This reading is taped; the teacher provides no assistance
but does mark the reader's miscues. After the oral reading the child is asked to
retell the story. (2) The teacher reevaluates the miscues using the tape recording
and assigns a score to the retelling of the story. (3) The teacher analyzes the miscues using the questions provided in the RMI. (4) The *RMI* reader profile is
prepared. (5) The reading program is planned using the results of the profile. The
RMI not only allows the teacher to see the problems a reader has, it also gives
insight into the reader's strengths. The *RMI* is also useful for assessing growth in
reading proficiency as well as for analyzing reading material to determine suitability for student use.

The *Classroom Reading Inventory* is a diagnostic tool designed to be used by classroom teachers in grades two through ten. The inventory has three forms each composed of two main parts: Part I of the inventory tests word recognition skills; Part II consists of paragraphs for oral reading accompanied by questions to test comprehension. Parts I and II are intended for use with the individual child who needs testing beyond a group administered test. According to the information provided with the inventory, this individual testing takes about 15 minutes. Part III (spelling survey) is included to provide additional data on the child's ability to integrate and express letter-form, letter-sound skills. Part III may be administered to the total class group. The inventory provides the teacher with information concerning the child's independent, instructional, and frustration reading levels and hearing-capacity level. It helps the teacher to identify the reading level of the child and to assess specific word recognition and comprehension abilities. The information from the inventory is intended to be helpful to a classroom teacher in planning reading programs for particular children.

The same note of caution given for all tests must also be given for the *RMI* and the *Classroom Reading Inventory:* The results obtained are only an indication of a student's reading behavior. A good amount of subjectivity enters into the administration and scoring of these tests. When teachers make decisions about a student's reading strengths and weaknesses, they are wise to make those decisions on the results from more than one instrument or procedure and over a period of time long enough to give a good picture of a student's true ability.

Cloze Testing

The cloze technique has been used to evaluate students' ability to comprehend certain materials, and as one among several measures it has merit. However, as was pointed out in Chapter 4, comprehension is a difficult concept to define. Consequently, techniques to measure it are never completely satisfactory.

The cloze procedure is essentially a matter of deleting every fifth word from a reading selection and asking students to fill in the blanks:

The cloze procedure is _____ a matter of deleting _____
fifth word from a _____ selection and asking students
_____ fill in the _____.

For middle grade students a selection should be at least 250 words long if it is to provide a good notion of how well students are "tuned in" to the story line.

We believe teachers who use the cloze procedure should accept reasonable replacements for the actual words that were deleted. Since cloze is only one kind of measure and is in our opinion only a rough estimation of comprehension ability, final judgment on a student's reading ability should not rest on his or her scores on cloze exercises.

A good and much more thorough discussion of the history and use of the cloze procedure can be found in Ekwall (1976, pp. 286–290). Suffice it to say here that we recommend teacher judgment to determine students' reading comprehension on the basis of the words they supply for deletions. In our judgment the cloze procedure is most helpful to classroom teachers for diagnostic purposes when it is used informally. We would recommend that middle grades teachers give their students a cloze test on the material they are assigning once a month or more. The results of the cloze test will help teachers know their students' changing reading strengths and weaknesses and will keep them aware of how well their students can comprehend the material they assign.

Measuring Attitudes

Like comprehension, attitudes are difficult to measure. Nonetheless, the students' affective response to reading selections is critical to their becoming readers. Therefore, some kind of test measuring the middle graders' attitudes toward their reading experiences is an important aspect of the total evaluation process in a middle grade reading program. If in the process of learning to read students learn to be bored with or even hate reading, the educational process is harmful rather than helpful to their growth in reading. Measuring an attitude toward "reading" is difficult since reading takes so many forms and means so many different things to different students. For example, a student might enjoy reading the sports page or the comics of a local newspaper, but be completely miserable reading a library book to complete an English assignment. Whether or not students like "reading," then, depends on what they are reading and for what purpose.

Therefore, the most valid measures of students' attitudes toward reading would seem to be their responses to individual selections. Since we know that people tend to repeat pleasurable experiences and avoid unpleasant ones, we can assume that students who have more pleasurable than unpleasant individual reading experiences are probably learning to regard reading as a life-enrichment experience.

The following scale has been useful in measuring middle grade students' attitudes toward reading selections:

1 I enjoyed reading this selection.

_____ Strongly Agree
_____ Agree
_____ Uncertain
_____ Disagree
_____ Strongly Disagree

2 This selection was boring.

_____ Strongly Agree
_____ Agree
_____ Uncertain
_____ Disagree
_____ Strongly Disagree

3 This selection held my attention.

_____ Strongly Agree
_____ Agree
_____ Uncertain
_____ Disagree
_____ Strongly Disagree

4 I disliked reading this selection.

_____ Strongly Agree
_____ Agree
_____ Uncertain
_____ Disagree
_____ Strongly Disagree

If the response choices are scored 5, 4, 3, 2, 1 for the positively stated items (numbers 1 and 3) and 1, 2, 3, 4, 5 for the negatively stated items (numbers 2 and 4), then a score of 20 would indicate the highest possible attitude; a score of 4, the lowest possible attitude. Numbers 1 and 3 can be checked against numbers 2 and 4 to determine the degree of consistency in the students' responses.

Students should not be expected to respond positively to all their reading experiences, but if the majority of their responses indicate negative attitudes toward reading selections, something is amiss. One would hope that students would respond positively to most of the selections they read. If they do not, then the reading program needs review.

Administering the attitude scale after each reading experience would probably be too much of a good thing. Therefore, we recommend that the scale be used to spot-check students' attitudes, and that for all students a profile of all their scores be kept as an ongoing evaluation of their attitude toward reading.

General Observations

If students are checking books out of the library and reading them, and if they are giving evidence that they are reading newspapers and magazines regularly, it is likely that their reading program is a good one. The ultimate test of a reading program is whether it leads students toward or away from reading.

The evaluation measures discussed in this chapter are all useful in helping teachers and administrators monitor the reading growth of the middle grade student. However, they should be used selectively, depending on the information the teacher intends to obtain, and they should always be considered against the background of the general observations made regarding the reading habits of a school's student population.

How well students perform the reading-related activities described in Chapter 7 is one of the best indications of their reading growth. Exercises that have been completed correctly and standardized test scores are only one way of assessing reading achievement. Teachers and administrators are urged to employ many different evaluation measures, always with the intent to utilize the findings to improve the instructional program.

Something to Think and Talk About

As a fifth-grade teacher I am confused. My principal tells me I must be accountable for my students' reading growth, and my reading methods professor impresses me with the lack of validity of reading-achievement tests. Parents want to know what grade level their children are reading at, and I know the answer depends on what they're reading. But how do you explain that to parents? I'm not sure I understand why myself. I know I should do a better job of evaluating my students' reading growth, but I need all the time I have for teaching. I wish someone would straighten this whole mess out. Why doesn't some reading expert construct a test that we can administer easily and that we can believe in? (See Appendix 11 for Authors' Response to "Something to Think and Talk About.")

References

Buros, Oscar, ed. (1972). *Mental Measurement Yearbook*, 7th ed., 2. Highland Park, New Jersey: The Gryphon Press, 1068–1215.

Ekwall, Eldon (1976). *Diagnosis and Remediation of the Disabled Reader*. Boston: Allyn and Bacon.

Farr, Roger. *Reading: What Can Be Measured?* Newark, Delaware: International Reading Association, 1969.

Goodman, Y. M., and C. L. Burke (1971). *Reading Miscue Inventory*. New York: Macmillan.

Kretschmer, Joseph C. (1972). "Subject Matter As A Factor in Testing Comprehension." *Reading World* 21 (4): 275–285.

Otto, Wayne, and Eunice Askov (1970). *The Wisconsin Design for Reading Skill Development: Rationale and Guidelines*. Minneapolis, Minnesota: National Computer Systems.

Silvaroli, N. J. (1973). *Classroom Reading Inventory*. Dubuque, Iowa: Wm. C. Brown.

Smith, Richard J., Wayne Otto, and Lee Hansen (1978). *The School Reading Program: A Handbook for Teachers, Supervisors and Specialists*. Boston: Houghton Mifflin.

Spache, George D. (1976). *Diagnosing and Correcting Reading Disabilities*. Boston: Allyn and Bacon.

APPENDIXES

Authors' Response to "Something to Think and Talk About"

Apparently, there is some confusion in this principal's mind about organizational plans. What he refers to as team teaching is in actuality a modified Joplin Plan which even broadly considered is not team teaching. Evidently he is relying heavily upon the 45-minute daily planning session to help his teachers work as a unit. It is difficult, however, to see the advantage of getting information about a child's reading from another teacher over getting it firsthand. One must wonder whether these 45-minute sessions would not be more profitably spent by having the teachers give some special instruction to students who need it. Certainly, the impact of these 45-minute planning sessions on the instruction the children receive must be carefully evaluated.

One must also evaluate carefully how much individualization is being achieved in each of the three reading groups. Hopefully, the teachers are not teaching one lesson to their classes under the assumption that since the students have been homogeneously grouped, they are alike in their reading needs. According to the principal the teachers are satisfied, but the question is really whether or not the students are getting the best instruction possible with the resources available.

This principal and his staff are moving rapidly toward a departmentalized school. Some questionable assumptions are being presented as the rationale for departmentalization: kids are smarter than they used to be; they will be taught content better if the school is departmentalized; middle school teachers have a subject they teach best. A careful look at the effect their projected plans may have on their students' overall development is certainly in order.

Appendix 2

Authors' Response to "Something to Think and Talk About"

We differ with the English teacher's perception that reading classes are none of his or her business. Reading is every teacher's business because of its importance in nearly all school subjects. In addition, reading is a process; and although it may be taught in reading classes, it is taught only so that it can be used for other purposes, one of which is learning content area subjects. Teachers who know what happens in the reading classes in their schools are better able to help students transport what they are learning in reading class to what they are learning in content area classes. Furthermore, they are better able to give reading teachers information about their students and suggestions for giving them the kind of help they need in reading classes. Reading classes can be a source of dissatisfaction to teachers, administrators, parents, and students when too much or too little is expected of them. The more everyone concerned knows about the contributions a reading class can make to students' growth in reading and how those contributions are made the more students can gain from the class.

The English teacher raises a substantive issue regarding the need for all upper middle grades students to take a required reading class. We will stick to the position we stated in the chapter that all but the very highest and the very lowest achievers can improve their reading skills in a reading class. And if reading classes have the kind of curriculum we described in the chapter, they can contribute greatly to students' social development and provide for individualized intellectual growth regardless of their reading skills development.

The matter of reading classes being easier than other classes and reading teachers being higher graders than content area teachers can be explained by the different mission of reading classes and the fact that greater progress has been made in individualizing reading classes than in individualizing content area classes. Reading is a skill, and many materials have been developed and can be collected to provide for the range of skill development in a reading class. Content area teachers have a body of knowledge to transmit as well as skills to teach, and providing for the range of students' abilities in a content area class is harder than in a reading class. Therefore, reading classes should be looked upon as different, rather than superior or inferior to content area classes.

Appendix 3

Authors' Response to "Something to Think and Talk About"

If the major difference between Mr. Smith's program and the present program was the greater emphasis on word indentification skills, it would probably be a waste of money to purchase the new program. Many middle grade pupils have previously mastered the majority of word identification skills. Though some children need thorough instruction in word identification, for many children such instruction could be redundant and possibly detrimental to their enthusiasm for reading.

Mr. Jones's program contains word identification exercises after *each story,* and also utilizes workbook drill. The program also boasts of "tightly sequenced" instruction. While a highly sequenced, lesson-a-day skills program may have merit in the earliest years of learning to read, it is uncalled for in the middle grades. The school would benefit more by spending some money on supplementary or individualized skills materials and on the development of assessment tests and teacher-made games and activities. Whatever funds are left over could be used to buy quantities of paperback books, magazines, and newspapers for those children who do not need practice with word identification.

Appendix 4

Authors' Response to "Something to Think and Talk About"

Obviously, the two problems the teachers chose to begin with are not easily resolved. They are related, however, and what may be suggested for one may be applied to the other; therefore, they will be treated as one and the same problem for the moment.

The essence of the problems was that students comprehended reasonably well when they were involved in guided reading activities, but not so well when they were left to their own devices. The basic question for the teachers to resolve is whether they provided a model for comprehending materials when they guided their students' reading, a model which students could apply independently. The teachers need to determine whether they are teaching for transfer. In other words, do they let the students know why they do certain things during guided reading? Moreover, do the teachers help their students realize that some of the comprehension tasks they have encountered during guided reading are similar to what they will encounter in independent reading and that the abilities they have developed to deal with such tasks during guided reading are the same ones they must use to deal with the independent tasks?

In summary, two things must be done to solve the problems brought up by the teachers. First, middle grade students need to be guided through comprehension tasks similar to those they will have to face without guidance before they are required to demonstrate such abilities independently. Too often middle grade teachers assume that their students should be able to apply certain comprehension abilities independently, even though they have never demonstrated or modeled such abilities for their students. Second, teachers must constantly teach for transfer of comprehension abilities from guided reading to independent reading situations. Students must be sensitized to this concept of transfer by being made aware of the relation between guided and independent reading activities.

Appendix 5

Authors' Response to "Something to Think and Talk About"

We find the results of the survey regarding the feelings of students and teachers in School X toward their library disappointing, and we think the staff should also find them disappointing. Unfortunately, we suspect that schools Y and Z might have similar results if they were to give the same survey to the students and staffs in their buildings. For a variety of possible reasons, school libraries and Instructional Materials Centers are not being used by a majority of teachers and students in middle schools in spite of their "good" to "excellent" collections:

1 Libraries and IMC personnel may be placing too many constraints on people (especially students) who use their resources.
2 Students are perhaps being taught how to use the resources as a unit of study which often seems boring, complicated, and irrelevant to them, thereby creating negative attitudes toward using the resources.
3 Teachers may not be setting good examples by using the resources for their own work and enjoyment.
4 Teachers may not be creating interesting assignments that require students to use the resources to find useful and interesting information.
5 Teachers, librarians, and IMC personnel may not be giving students the help in using the resources that students need while they are in search of information they want or need.

We think all middle schools should survey students and staff to discover the status of their libraries or IMC's in the eyes of the potential users. The principal in School X should indeed initiate some action by placing "the library" higher on her list of weekly concerns. The five possibilities for the disappointing survey results listed above should be considered by all staff members. The probability is that the staff of School X has not yet realized that study skills and reading efficiency are taught over a period of years by getting students involved in information searches and helping them search successfully. Units of study on how to study efficiently should be replaced by ongoing instruction and involvement in the process itself.

Appendix 6

Authors' Response to "Something to Think and Talk About"

Sally's concern is well founded. Parents, administrators and even fellow teachers may consider the allocation of valuable class time for free reading as wasteful. They may even perceive the teacher as lazy. Those who may be expected to object to this worthwhile practice should be conferred with before the practice is begun, to avoid misunderstanding. Sally should explain carefully to her principal the details of her plan and point out how important the allocation of class time for recreational reading is to the development of positive attitudes toward reading—a goal that probably appears in the list of reading curriculum objectives for the school district. Articles in professional journals and textbooks such as, and including, the present book may help Sally and teachers like her convince those who question the practice of the benefits to be derived from it. Once the practice is begun, we have no doubt that the best salespeople for continuing the practice will be the students themselves. We have personally seen this occur in many schools.

Appendix 7

Authors' Response to "Something to Think and Talk About"

The superintendent of schools addressing the teachers who are about to begin their first year of full-time teaching is rightfully concerned about not wasting tax dollars. The cost of educating a nation's children is high. And the public does have a right to demand evidence that their children are learning. However, the superintendent is ignoring the fact that certain valuable educational experiences may not be reflected in improved test scores.

Creative reading, for example, is an important dimension of the reading curriculum at all academic levels, and it is unlikely that the benefits of creative reading can be measured objectively at this time. The superintendent should be aware of the many ways other than standardized test scores that can be used to show parents that their children are becoming better readers. Written products, plays, discussions, art projects, and a number of reading-related activities look as good to most parents as higher standardized test scores. Most parents want their children to develop what creative talents they have as part of their school experience. And most teachers can achieve a good balance between teaching basic reading skills that are measured on standardized tests and teaching students to extend their thinking beyond the author's words.

We think school superintendents recognize this also. But so often creative reading is not given the attention it deserves because it cannot be measured objectively. We would urge all school administrators to challenge their teachers to teach their students how to read what is on the page and how to extend their thinking beyond the page whenever selections lend themselves to creative reading.

Appendix 8

Authors' Response to "Something to Think and Talk About"

We fear the principal's conference with the teacher was not very helpful. Again, the student and TV appear to be the culprits. Apparently neither the principal nor the teacher realizes that a textbook is not supposed to teach itself. The following are just five questions that might have been asked by the principal to give some direction to a teacher who evidently is not making good reading assignments for a science class:

1 Are your assignments too long considering the nature of the subject and the motivation of the students?

2 Do you read the selections you assign carefully before you assign them, to identify words, concepts, visual aids, sentences, and paragraphs likely to give students trouble? Then do you do something to reduce these obstacles to comprehension?

3 Do your students know what you want them to learn from a selection so they can focus upon what is important to remember?

4 Are you sure the books are at a reasonable level of difficulty for all or even most of your students?

5 Have your students learned that you will tell them what is in each reading assignment so that they don't have to read it?

Appendix 9

Authors' Response to "Something to Think and Talk About"

Some administrators, teachers, parents, and even middle grade students have a hard time accepting the idea that a school year does not equal a certain amount of work to be done correctly. The school curriculum has been developed to fit a graded organization for so long that teachers sometimes feel guilty if students are not pushed, pulled, jammed, or crammed through the material that has been purchased for use in a particular grade.

The teachers talking in the lounge are apparently very conscious of materials and time. They seem willing to turn over their opportunities to design learning activities for their students to some unknown author who they assume can do better things for their students in less time than they could. Unfortunately, they and their students are missing out on much of the fun and satisfaction that come from planning learning activities themselves. Somehow, implementing activities that grow out of the thinking of members of the class is often more stimulating than following suggestions in a manual, regardless of how good those suggestions may be.

Teachers should never resign themselves to being unimaginative or noncreative. Imagination and creativity are essential attributes of a good teacher and can be developed by reading, discussion, and by a conscious effort to notice the many different ways one can experience the world. Teachers who find themselves unable to make a story or poem exciting and meaningful to their students should get some help from reading, an evening class, or a discussion group designed to foster creative thinking and an imaginative approach to teaching.

Appendix 10

Authors' Response to "Something to Think and Talk About"

There is reason to consider seriously the alternative of "reading-free" curriculums for poor readers. In spite of our best efforts, we continue to fail in our attempts to teach all children to be functional readers. Perhaps we always shall fail, and the burden of repeated failure on the part of the school and the student is a heavy price to pay for the promise of reading.

On the other hand, many questions arise when reading-free curriculums are seriously considered for certain students. How poor a reader must a student be before becoming a candidate for a reading-free curriculum? When do we make the decision to stop trying to teach a child to read? Will the deliberate acknowledgment that some people will never be readers produce in effect a mass of citizens who will always be subservient to their reading counterparts? Will separate schools or tracks within schools be set up?

At the present time, we must take a stand against reading-free curriculums for all but a very few seriously disabled readers. Perhaps we value reading too highly and are too optimistic about improving instructional materials and methods. However, until we have tried longer and harder to design curriculums for poor readers that include repeated attempts to make them functional readers, we cannot endorse a major emphasis on the development of reading-free curriculums.

Appendix 11

Authors' Response to "Something to Think and Talk About"

The fifth-grade teacher is expressing the desire of many teachers, administrators, and reading specialists in wishing for a test that would be easy to administer and that would be valid and reliable. Unfortunately, the problem of measuring reading achievement is too complex for such a simple solution. No test that meets those requirements is likely to be developed.

The fact is that available measurement techniques do not equip us to state unequivocally that a student is reading at a particular grade level or that because of some instructional program that student has gained a certain number of months in reading ability. Obviously, this lack of precision in measuring reading growth causes difficulties for educators who must be "accountable" to people who assume that reading can be measured precisely. The pity is that reasonable explanations to the public eager for proof that tax dollars are being spent wisely often are perceived as dodging the issue or covering up program deficiencies. In this regard the best approach is probably a concentrated effort to educate the public in the realities of the limitations of standardized reading tests. The most positive way to pursue this approach would seem to be more diligent efforts to gather meaningful information from performances with instructional materials, responses to attitude scales, performances in reading-related activities, and surveys of reading habits. Certainly, we must wish for what is not, but until we get it we must use what we have. We must also expect some criticism from those who have not studied the problem thoroughly.

Teachers who excuse their neglect of program evaluation because of time pressures apparently do not realize that the best assessments of students' growth in reading and their reading needs can be made in the process of instruction. Master teachers are always teaching diagnostically and shaping their programs as abilities are exhibited and new needs emerge.

AUTHOR INDEX

SUBJECT INDEX

225

M